Industrial Psychology

DIPAK BHATTACHARYYA
Professor
Xavier Institute of Management
Bhubaneswar, India

SUTAPA BHATTACHARYA
Practicing psychologist
Kolkata, India

Universities Press

UNIVERSITIES PRESS (INDIA) PRIVATE LIMITED

Registered Office
3-6-747/1/A & 3-6-754/1, Himayatnagar, Hyderabad 500 029 (A.P.), India
info@universitiespress.com; www.universitiespress.com

Distributed by
Orient Blackswan Private Limited

Registered Office
3-6-752 Himayatnagar, Hyderabad 500 029 (A.P.) India

Other Offices
Bangalore / Bhopal / Bhubaneshwar / Chandigarh / Chennai
Ernakulam / Guwahati / Hyderabad / Jaipur / Kolkata
Lucknow / Mumbai / New Delhi / Noida / Patna

ISBN 978 81 7371 784 0

Typeset in Minion Pro Regular, 11/15 *by* Kryon Publishing Services (P) Ltd., Chennai

Printed at Sunma Graphics (P) Ltd
Chennai - 600 014

Published by

Universities Press (India) Private Limited
3-6-747/1/A & 3-6-754/1, Himayatnagar,
Hyderabad 500 029 (A.P.), India.

Industrial Psychology

Table of Contents

Dedicated to our children

PREFACE

Engineers today need to play managerial role in their workplaces, irrespective of their specific job position. The complexities of manufacturing and services have further increased the need for understanding the behavioural dynamics of people to manage their activities. To appreciate various people-related issues at workplaces, study of Industrial Engineering has become necessary. Obviously for these reasons universities across the world have included this subject along with the core engineering papers, so that students develop basic understanding of various issues pertaining to Industrial Psychology. The subject is also known as industrial and organizational psychology, and human resource management practices.

The present book is based on the syllabi of various universities in India and abroad, with specific focus on Gautam Buddh Technical University (formerly known as Uttar Pradesh Technical University) and Mahamaya Technical University (MMTU). Although we have many books available on this subject, including various customised editions for GBTU and MMTU, it is still felt necessary to bring out this book, which emphasises on the need of engineering students, to make their understanding more relevant, enjoyable and scientific. Engineering students do not require the rigours of management theories, as their time investment for this subject is much focused to build the capabilities of managing the people who carry out the activities under their supervision and control.

Keeping in view all the above aspects, this book has been developed in a student-friendly way.

Chapter 1 introduces the basic concept of industrial psychology, highlighting on its evolution, definitions, listing the areas of application and scope and significance.

Chapter 2 explains the process of development of various schools of management thought, differentiating and evaluating the perspectives, modern principles and linking its thoughts to industrial psychology.

Chapter 3 introduces work study and its use in industrial psychology, elaborates on different work measurement techniques like time study and method study, features of motion economy, human engineering and value analysis.

Chapter 4 discusses on industrial psychology and behavioural theories, listing various behavioural and human relations schools of thought, its advantages and disadvantages, McKinsey's 7S framework, theories of managerial roles and issues in the development of managers.

Chapter 5 elaborates on motivation and job satisfaction, introducing the theories and highlighting the role of industrial psychologists.

Chapter 6 introduces work environment, management of fatigue and stress and its influence on performance and productivity of employees.

Chapter 7 highlights on organizational culture and organizational development, focusing on the tools and techniques from the perspective of the industrial psychologist.

Chapter 8 discusses on leadership issues for industrial psychologists, introducing different theories and the process of developing leadership capabilities.

Chapter 9 focuses on group dynamics introducing the concept of group, listing the types of groups, understanding its effectiveness, group decision-making process, team development and the management of group conflicts.

Chapter 10 introduces job analysis and job design explaining its process and relevance for industrial psychologist. It also covers job assessment and pricing.

Chapter 11 is on recruitment and selection, and discusses its functions, process (including interview techniques and induction), and placement.

Chapter 12 focuses on psychological testing, its application, personality, intelligence quotient and emotion, NLP and ethical issues involved in psychological testing.

Chapter 13 introduces the concept of performance management, its objectives, standards, process, role, types and methods.

Chapter 14 outlines the features of training and development, policies and training needs analysis and steps in the training design process.

The special pedagogical features of this book are:

- Student-friendly approach
- Lucid language
- Coverage of applications of theories
- Illustrations
- Relevant examples
- Review questions
- Key words

We gratefully acknowledge the help and support from our family, friends and professional colleagues. We also appreciate the support of the editorial team of Universities Press, Hyderabad.

Dipak Kumar Bhattacharyya
Sutapa Bhattacharya

1 Introduction to Industrial Psychology

Learning Objectives

After reading this chapter you will be able to:

- **Understand the evolution of industrial psychology (IP)**
- **Appreciate the definitions and concepts of IP**
- **List the areas where IP could be used**
- **Understand the scope and significance of IP**

Overview

Industrial psychology (IP) has now become an important course of study for engineers, as knowledge of this subject provides basic understanding of the workplace environment. IP is also variously known as I/O psychology (industrial and organizational psychology), work psychology, personnel psychology etc. It is clear from the name that it is primarily concerned with the scientific study of workers or employees and the workplace dynamics that could affect the organization as a whole. With basic training in industrial psychology, engineers can effectively contribute to the success of the organization, by being able to address workplace issues that could have behavioural implications. With such knowledge, engineers can solve problems that relate specifically to the behaviour and attitudes of the workers so that the latter can perform better. Positive attitude and behaviour can be developed through systematic training. In a challenging work environment, knowledge of industrial psychology can help managers and engineers to change and develop the organization.

Development of Industrial Psychology

The origin of industrial psychology can be traced to the 1890s. The subject, however, came into the limelight in 1955, when Henry Landsberger re-examined the Hawthorne studies of Elton Mayo and his associates, to ascertain how change in the workplace variables can influence productivity. The Hawthorne effect, as observed by Harry Braverman, established that the workplace is a system of power and class antagonisms.

After World War I, countries felt the need for increasing industrial production for immediate restoration of their economies. Some of the early thinkers in this field were Hugo Münsterberg,

James McKeen Cattell and Walter Dill Scott (both have been President of the American Psychological Association (APA) in 1895 and 1919 respectively). However, the subject could get wide recognition and acceptance only after World War II, particularly for the influence of Hawthorne studies and the pioneering research of Kurt Lewin and Muzafer Sherif.

Research in IP began with the various studies on motivation and performance at the workplace. Walter Dill Scott published his findings on advertising executives in 1908 with his book *The Psychology of Advertising*. The German psychologist at Harvard University Hugo Münsterberg (1863–1916) published his pioneering work *The Psychology of Industrial Efficiency* in 1913 which had more practical applications. Münsterberg's book was heavily influenced by the work of Frank and Lillian Gilbreth and FW Taylor. However, the impact of IP was first observed in the work of a group of psychologists during World War I on morale, motivation and psychological impairment in soldiers. The famous study known as Army Alpha was carried out in the United States on 1,726,000 army personnel. Although the core objective of the study was to investigate into soldiers' performance, the results established the importance of the subject and extended its application to business areas. Pioneering work in this context was carried out at the Carnegie Institute of Technology in 1919 with its research on salesmen in the life insurance industry, particularly focusing on their selection and development.

The neoclassical school of management had its beginning in 1924, when Hawthorne experiments made the shift from Taylor's scientific management principles to human relations variables as being the determinants of productivity of workers. The Hawthorne study established that job performance could not be achieved by money or job design alone. In fact, human relations have a greater influence on the performance. Thus, IP became an important tool for the management in different business fields.

IP combines broad theoretical knowledge and various psychometric and research tools. For example, besides learning the basic principles of psychology as applicable to workplace problems, you will learn about survey design (surveys, experiments, quasi-experiments, and observational studies), various quantitative methods used commonly in research (correlation, multiple regression, analysis of variance, multivariate analysis of variance) as well as qualitative research tools like content analysis, focus groups, interviews, case studies etc.

Definition

Industrial psychology (IP) is defined as the science of psychology as applied to the workplace. For engineers, IP develops their problem-solving skills in handling employee behaviour at the workplace. According to the Society for Industrial and Organizational Psychology (SIOP) IP is defined as 'the scientific study of the workplace'.

Guion (1965) defines I/O psychology as 'the scientific study of the relationship between man and the world of work; ... in the process of making a living'. Blum and Naylor (1968) define it as 'simply the application or extension of psychological facts and principles to the problems concerning human beings operating within the context of business and industry'. I/O psychology has historically subsumed two broad areas of study, although this distinction is largely artificial and many topics cut across both areas. It has its roots in social psychology; organizational psychologists examine the role of the work environment in performance and other outcomes including job satisfaction and health. Industrial psychology is considered as a branch of the study of organizational behaviour and human resource management, but there is no universally accepted classification system for these related fields.

The SIOP considers that industrial and organizational psychology deals with the functioning of the workplace, focusing on the behaviour of both employees and managers. It helps in developing a productive workplace environment. Based on this definition, we can broadly relate industrial psychology to the function of employee management, which includes recruitment, training and development, performance management, motivation, leadership, improvement of productivity, organizational change and development.

Applications of Industrial Psychology

IP has wide ranging applications especially in the modern workplace that lays greater emphasis on performance of employees as being critical to the survival and growth of organizations. In this section, we will see how IP can be useful to engineers.

Motivation

Motivation is a process by which employees make their choice of the desired outcomes for their efforts at work. The behaviour of motivated employees is positive and more productive. Motivation is more individualistic, as the needs and desires of every employee are unique. Employees pursue different sets of goals and hence they behave differently. For industrial psychologists, the study of employee motivation is of the greatest priority, as they can suggest suitable motivational reinforcers and accordingly ensure that workers remain motivated and put in their best efforts to achieve organizational goals.

Leadership

In any work situation when two or more people join to work towards a goal, a structure or a group develops and the leadership emerges. Leadership can be defined as an activity which influences people to strive willingly for group objectives. It is something that goes on among people. Effective leadership makes a substantial difference to organizations. It is typically a solution for most of the organizational problems. Industrial psychologists play a crucial role in leadership studies, helping organizations to map the available leadership qualities, the gaps therein and suggest the process for filling them.

Decision-making

Decision-making is the process of selecting a course of action from a number of alternatives. Strategic decisions are often a choice from amongst competing alternatives. In order to be a successful manager, one has to necessarily develop decision-making skills. The process involves diagnosing the decision issue, gathering information, developing and evaluating alternative solutions and choosing the appropriate decision alternatives. In all these cases, the behavioural dynamics of the decision-makers play an important role. For example, managers may be risk-prone or risk-averse in evaluating the available options. The choice of the decision will necessarily vary depending upon this trait of the managers. Obviously for such reasons, industrial psychologists can also help in developing the decision-making capabilities of managers.

Organizational culture

Every organization continuously interacts with its environment. This, therefore, requires an organization to balance between the internal features and the characteristics of the external environment, which is part of the contingency theory in organization science. The theory suggests that an organization has to understand the dynamics of its environment in order to be able to adapt to the changing demands both externally and internally. Organizational culture may be defined as a set of values that are embodied in every aspect of the organization's functions. Six independent dimensions of practices have been identified as part of organizational culture: process-oriented versus result-oriented; job-oriented versus employee-oriented; professional versus parochial; open versus closed systems; tightly controlled versus loosely controlled and pragmatic versus normative. Such dimensions obviously speak out the role of industrial psychologists in managing and developing organizational culture.

Attitude

Attitude is the mental state of individuals through which they tend to act or respond to situations depending on how they perceive the consequences of their actions or desires to be directly or indirectly linked or associated. During the course of development, the person acquires tendencies to respond to objects. These learned cognitive mechanisms are called attitudes which change with changes in knowledge. Attitudes are different from knowledge as they are emotion-laden. Knowledge reinforces attitudes and reinforced attitudes in the long run reinforce individual and group behaviour. Hence, attitude is neither behaviour nor cause of behaviour but it relates to an intervening predisposition or a frame of reference which influences the behaviour of an individual. Industrial psychologists play the most pivotal role in attitude measurement using various psychometric tools.

Job analysis

Job analysis is the process of gathering information about each job and evaluating it in terms of organizational needs and relevance. A job is defined as a set of activities or tasks, performed by an individual or a group of employees. Industrial psychologists can effectively perform the task of job analysis, focusing on the technical and behavioural attributes of the job, and in the process can help the organizations come up with effective job design.

Recruitment and selection

Recruitment, selection, induction and placement are important tools for procuring and effectively using human resources in an organization. While recruitment involves employing suitably trained workforce, selection helps in choosing the right candidate for the right job. Induction and placement refers to allotting people to the right jobs. Industrial psychologists develop suitable recruitment tests, including attitude measurement tools, interviews etc for this purpose.

Performance management

Performance management is the process of deciding on organizational objectives, evaluation of employees' performance in relation to such objectives and even linking the compensation structure and quantum against such performance. For the employees, it encompasses performance improvement, career development and training. Effective performance by the employees is essential for organizations to achieve business results. Scientific performance management systems consist of various behavioural elements like feedback, counselling, coaching etc. Industrial psychologists can add value in the design and implementation of the performance management process in an organization.

Psychometric tools

Industrial psychologists make extensive use of psychometric tools, especially validated ones, in order to understand the behavioural constructs of employees. Results obtained by using psychometric tools significantly help in organizational decision-making in almost all areas where the involvement of employees is being considered. For example, using a psychometric tool to understand the propensity for team work, it is possible to scientifically form the team and get the best results.

Compensation matters

Compensation is the outcome of productivity. It is the payback for the efforts of the workers. Traditionally, the word 'compensation' was defined as all forms of financial returns and tangible services and benefits, which an employee received during the period of employment. However, in the modern context, it is viewed as a system of rewards to motivate employees, so that organizations can achieve their intended goals and objectives. Thus, it contains both extrinsic (tangible) and intrinsic (psychological) components. While the former covers both the monetary and non-monetary rewards, the latter reflects the psychological elements of accomplishment, self-worth etc. Because of this reason, industrial psychologists can play a role in designing an optimum compensation structure accurately mapped to the behavioural constructs of the employees.

Training

Training is an important activity in human resource development. Apart from the need for internal staffing, training enhances job-related skills and also facilitates acquiring new skills required for averting skill obsolescence in an organization. Training may be defined as a systematic program for developing desirable attitudes, skills and abilities in employees irrespective of their functional levels. Industrial psychologists contribute in the design of training programs by mapping the gaps in the available competencies.

Team-building

It is the most commonly used technique for organizational change with respect to task, people or relationship aspects. Task aspect defines the task or its development. Team-building emphasises on binding people together to achieve common goals of the organization, and in the process develop the shared vision to provide common direction to all. In a very simplistic term, a team consists of a group of people who work together to accomplish some common goals. People or relationship aspects focus on interaction and working together. It includes communication, mutual responses, leadership, conflict management etc. Alternatively, we can define the task aspects as those which cover content while people or relationship aspects focus on the process of working as a team. Because of underlying behavioural issues, industrial psychologists also contribute to team-building in organizations.

Ethics in management

Ethical managerial practices cascade into compliance with norms for corporate social responsibility (CSR). Today, CSR has become an important managerial responsibility; it is in-built with organizational efficiency. An ethical organization can achieve better business results. This maxim is now making more and more corporate leaders accept their social responsibilities and organizational ethics. Organizations indulging in unethical business practices or being unethical in dealing with their employees are now quickly identified in this era of technology-intensive communication systems. Organizational activities require redesigning and updating, keeping pace with public expectations and ever-rising standards. Because patterns of organizational behaviour, corporate dishonesty, exploitation and negligence can attract adverse public opinion and criticism, violation of ethics is carefully avoided. Industrial psychologists help in framing a code of ethical practices and also in setting up processes so that variances to norms may be reported.

Management of diversity

To ensure that people working in an organization pursue organizational objectives collectively, subordinating their religion, gender, ethnic background etc, managing diversity at the workplace assumes importance. It requires strict conformance to consistency. A truly diverse organization is capable of achieving efficiency and competitiveness, pooling the collective efforts of the workforce. Diversity also ensures innovation. It must be carefully and constantly nurtured. To prepare the workforce to value diversity, industrial psychologists need to educate employees. From a broader perspective, diversity issues are not only restricted to gender and race; even within the country it ranges from, according to the Society for Human Resource Management (SHRM) glossary, 'personality and work style to all the visible dimensions such as race, age, ethnicity or gender, to secondary influences such as religion, socio-economic and education, to work diversities such as management and union, functional level and classification or proximity/distance to headquarters'. Because of the extended scope of issues in the management of diversity, many organizations leverage the support of industrial psychologists.

Organizational development

Organizational development (OD) is a planned change based on the understanding of the environment, benchmarking and action research. OD can, thus, be described as a learning process. The active development of an organization towards its desired corporate identity succeeds only if this change process is undertaken holistically. From a behavioural perspective, this means the elements within a person (qualifications, motivation) as well as those that are external (organizational structure, technology) must be modified and harmonised. Industrial psychologists play a role in this aspect too. They identify the behavioural constructs of the people and recommend the appropriate approach for intervention towards organizational development.

Technology management

Technology 'is the practical application of scientific or engineering knowledge for the development or application of products or offerings, processes or operations'. Through superior technology, organizations can achieve differentiation of product or service, reduce costs, develop new business opportunities and facilitate and support strategic change. Many organizations make use of technology as a core driver for organizational change. Managing technology or technological change per se is an important area of concern for today's managers. Technology management requires imparting new skills and knowledge and addressing various behavioural issues. Obviously for such reasons industrial psychologists play the crucial role of helping the management in understanding the training requirements and the behavioural issues for effective management of technology and technological change.

Although engineers need not be professional industrial psychologists, or a specialist, an understanding of the core principles is important, for balancing the workplace environment with active interface of humans and machines.

Significance of Industrial Psychology

Industrial psychology enables scientific study of the workplace and in the process improves the working conditions to enhance the productivity of employees. Industrial psychologists collaborating with the top management reorganise the work flow, thereby bringing about positive changes in the work environment and creating a performance culture. Thus, industrial psychologists enable optimum utilisation of human capital in organizations. Further, we observe in many organizations industrial psychologists playing an active role in providing strong leadership in change management, strategic planning, surveys, job design and evaluation, restructuring and workforce planning, and even in cross-cultural understanding.

From the above discussion, it is evident that industrial and organizational psychology is primarily concerned with tackling the problems related to the employees' performance in organizations. Some of the areas of activities of industrial psychologists are: (i) Conducting studies on organizational behaviour and worker–management interactions (ii) Analysing corporate culture and individual/group interactions (iii) Developing and evaluating selection and appraisal techniques (iv) Assessing corporate leadership and employee motivation strategies (v) Identifying causes—and resolution—of internal conflicts (vi) Advising the management of the potential psychological and social impact of corporate policies. Broadly, industrial psychologists provide following services to organizations:

- Assessment of occupational requirements
- Managing workers' performance through effective and scientific assessment of workers' capabilities and their suitable placement in jobs

- Activating workers' energy for their productive use in their jobs
- Developing workers through suitable training
- Developing favourable work conditions or environment
- Balancing economic, social and organizational objectives
- Motivating workers
- Ensuring harmonious relationships
- Analysis of various human factors for effective market research management systems
- Effective job designing

However, the scope of services provided by industrial psychologists depends on specific needs of organizations.

Scope of Industrial Psychology

Industrial psychology is that part of behavioural science related to the study of behavioural dynamics in business. As behavioural issues encompass all aspects of business, the subject has far-reaching impact on different functions such as production, human resource management, marketing, finance, design etc. To elaborate on the scope of industrial psychology, we need to discuss all aspects of management activities of an organization. For engineers, some of the important areas of focus are discussed in this section.

Work behaviour: Study of work behaviour is the primary area of focus of industrial psychology. Attitudes, personalities, mental and physical abilities of employees etc are some of the important constructs of work behaviour. Industrial psychology helps us to study all these, matching with the job criteria and accordingly helps us to understand the causes. For example, nurturing positive attitude in the employees is an essential prerequisite for their effective performance. Similarly, the activities of employees may be constrained due to the absence of a work culture. Thus, organizations need to provide the basis for right work behaviour of the employees.

Management of organizations: Managerial skills can be traced to industrial psychology. Managers, in addition to their respective functional expertise, need to develop the skills for supervision by identifying training needs, resolving conflicts, motivating employees and providing opportunities for leadership. All these require inputs from industrial psychology.

Designing the work environment: Design of the work environment is another area of industrial psychology. Properly designed workplaces positively influence performance and productivity. Knowledge of industrial psychology can help in designing a proper layout and physical arrangements of the workplace incorporating ergonomic features, providing the right balance between comfort and efficiency.

Product design: Effective product design is essential for the success of any business. Engineers play a crucial role in this regard. With the knowledge of industrial psychology, they can carry out detailed study to design more customer-friendly, competitively priced and better quality products. These can substantially benefit the organization.

Organizational studies: Finally, engineers with the knowledge of industrial psychology can also undertake organizational studies, for proper job description, design of organizational structure and so on.

Branches of psychology

Psychology is broadly defined as the science of the mind and its impact on behaviour. We are concerned with the configuration of thoughts, emotions, memories, perceptions, cognition, moods etc. Psychologists study the functioning of the human mind based on patterns of behaviour. The study of psychology consists of various interdisciplinary subjects like biology, anthropology and sociology. Psychology, as a subject, deals with human behaviour over a broad spectrum. Research and practice are the two cornerstones of the subject. Since human behaviour is complex and has wide variations, there are different branches of psychology. Some of these are briefly explained here.

Cognitive psychology: It refers to the investigation into our mental processes like, decision making, problem-solving, memory, learning and language recognition. For organizations, principles of cognitive psychology can be applied to analyse how employees acquire and use knowledge. It can also be applied to the study of intelligence.

Biopsychology: Behavioural neuroscience, psychobiology and neuropsychology are the major areas of study. The thrust is on the study of relationships between the brain and behaviour. Our brain exerts impact on our thoughts, feelings and moods, which flow as our behaviour. Biopsychology combines core psychology with neuroscience.

Clinical psychology: It applies the core principles of psychology to investigate and diagnose mental and emotional illness. It is a major area of specialisation in psychology. With a medical background, clinical psychology practice becomes more effective.

Developmental psychology: Developmental psychologists study the process of physical and cognitive development over the lifespan of a human being beginning from infancy and upto old age. Many developmental psychologists specialise in a specific stage of the human life cycle, viz., child psychologists, adolescent psychologists and so on.

Forensic psychology: Forensic psychologists command medico-legal power. They study criminal behaviour and its treatment. These psychologists are largely employed by the police and other investigating agencies.

Industrial–organizational psychology: This sub-field of psychology is widely used in business, as it primarily deals with the workplace-related issues that exert an impact on the behavioural issues pertaining to productivity and performance of workers. In this book, you will study this subject in much detail.

Occupational psychology: This is a branch of industrial and organizational psychology, and it studies performance, training and development issues, group behaviour and so on.

Personality psychology: Human thoughts, feelings and behaviour largely get influenced by the personality construct of an individual. Personality psychologists study such characteristic patterns, and help bring about changes in personality leading to development on a case-to-case basis.

Social psychology: These psychologists study the social behaviour of individuals that are influenced by social interactions.

Educational psychology: These psychologists work on issues in education in relation to the emotional and social needs of the students.

Evolutionary psychology: It looks at human behaviour that emerges out of psychological adjustments through the process of evolution. The thrust of this branch of psychology is that our psychological constructs are the outcome of our processes of adaptation for survival.

Health psychology: It refers to the study of illness and health in the context of our behaviour, biology and social influence. Health psychologists, while studying illness and health relate the same not only to the physiological causes but also to the socio-economic status of the patients.

Pillars of industrial psychology

The term pillar denotes an object that provides structural support. Here, we use the word metaphorically to describe the core elements of IP. From our discussion so far, we understand that IP is the scientific application of the principles of psychology to solve organizational problems. It is for this reason the subject is now known as industrial and organizational psychology. From the operational perspective, IP helps find the optimum approach to build the human resources and address their behavioural needs. Obviously, we observe two main pillars of industrial psychology: personnel psychology and organizational psychology. Personnel psychology looks into the recruitment, training and issues in personnel management. It has greater focus on the individual. On the other hand, organizational psychology deals with collective behaviour in organizations, and focuses more on organizational change and development. Extended application of industrial psychology is also observed in consumer research and advertising, as well as engineering. This textbook is intended for engineers and hence we shall focus on the latter too.

Influence of management theories in IP

After the Industrial Revolution (which started in Europe in mid-1700s), organised production activities took the form of factory-centred production system. It was at this time people started working in groups to accomplish goals of the organizations. Management then became an inevitable task coordinating the individual efforts within and between groups. Industrial psychology as a subject is highly influenced by thoughts of different management thinkers such as FW Taylor, Henri Fayol, Mary Parker Follet and Max Weber. In Chapter 2, we have discussed their contributions and their impact on IP.

There are many schools of management thought such as the operational school, the human behaviour school, the systems school and the decision theory school. Management is often defined as a dynamic process concerned with getting things done through and with the efforts of others by harnessing human and other resources of the institution—business or otherwise—and creating an environment favourable for performance by people for the accomplishment of desired objectives with minimum of unsought consequences.

Although the term management has been defined by different authorities differently, the process of management is essentially the same in all organised activities and at all levels in an organization. FW Taylor (1911), the father of scientific management, defined 'Management is the art of knowing what you want to do ......in the best and cheapest way'. Davis (1951) defined 'Management is the function of executive leadership anywhere'. Brech (1953) on the other hand defined 'Management is concerned with seeing that the job gets done; its tasks all centred on planning and guiding the operations that are going on in the enterprise'. Peter Drucker (1954) in an attempt to narrow the debate defined 'It is a multipurpose organ that manages a business and manages managers and manages worker and work'.

Reinforcing all these thoughts further, Lawrence A Appley (1956) also defined 'Management is the development of people and not the direction of things ....Management is personnel administration'. Stanley Vance (1959) defined 'Management is simply the process of decision-making and control over action of human beings for the express purpose of attaining pre-determined goals'. Harold Koontz (1961) defined 'Management is the art of getting things done through and with people in formally organized groups. It is the art of creating the environment in which people can perform and individuals could cooperate towards attaining of group goals. It is the art of removing blocks to such performance, a way of optimising efficiency in reaching goals'. A Dasgupta (1969), the father of Indian management education defined 'Management is the creation and control of technological and human environment of an organization in which human skill and capacities of individuals and groups find full scope for their effective use in order to accomplish the objectives for which an enterprise has been set up. It is involved in the relationships of the individual, group, the organization and the environment'.

The second series of definitions of management converges on the core issue of management, i.e., accomplishment of goals and objectives through the efforts of people. Reviewing the definitions we observe various dimensions of management as under:

- Productivity orientation, which is concerned with increasing productivity
- Human relations orientation that emphasises primarily on people
- Decision-making orientation that focuses on problem-solving as the primary function of management
- Leadership orientation, that considers leadership as the essence of management
- Process orientation that considers management as a process

Considering all these areas of focus of management, we can understand the active human interface. Hence, industrial psychologists play an important role in management both in terms of coordinating with the behavioural inputs and also as potential managers in troubleshooting various issues pertaining to the management of an organization.

Key Points

- ☛ Industrial psychology has assumed importance for engineers as they also need the skills to manage people in their organizations.
- ☛ Industrial psychology is concerned with the understanding of the work environment by focusing on the behavioural dynamics. Because of its application, it is also known as organizational psychology, work psychology, personnel psychology and so on.
- ☛ The main applications of IP are in the areas of motivation, leadership, performance management, job analysis, recruitment, decision-making, use of psychometric tools, compensation management, training, attitude, team-building, organizational culture, managerial ethics, managing diversity, organizational development and technology management.
- ☛ The two main pillars of IP are personnel psychology and organizational psychology.
- ☛ Management theory has had a great influence on the development of IP.

Important Terms

Attitude: Attitude is the mental state of individuals through which they tend to act or respond to situations depending on how they perceive the consequences of their actions, or desires to be directly or indirectly linked or associated.

Cognitive psychology: This branch of psychology investigates into our mental processes like decision-making, problem-solving, memory, learning and language. For organizations, the application of cognitive psychology investigates into the process of acquiring and storing information. It is also related to the study of intelligence.

Diversity: Managing diversity means harmonising the various elements in a consistent manner. A truly diverse organization is capable of achieving efficiency and competitiveness by pooling the collective efforts of the workforce. Diversity also ensures innovation. It must be carefully and constantly nurtured.

Occupational psychology: This is a branch of industrial and organizational psychology and it studies employee performance, training and development issues, group behaviour etc.

Personality psychology: Human thoughts, feelings and behaviour largely get influenced by the personality construct of the person. Personality psychologists study such characteristic patterns, and help in bringing about personality changes or development on a case-to-case basis.

Product design: Effective product design consists of packaging, safety and ergonomic features. Psychological attributes of product design requires satisfaction of elements like customer friendliness, competitive pricing and quality.

Psychometric tools: These tools are validated and help in understanding the behavioural constructs of the employees.

Team-building: It is the most commonly used technique for organizational change and for relating tasks to people and their relationships.

Work behaviour: It indicates behaviour of the workers at the workplace. Attitudes, personalities, mental and physical abilities of employees etc are some of the important constructs of work behaviour. Industrial psychology helps us to study these factors matched to the job criteria, and accordingly helps us to understand the causes.

Self-assessment Questions

1. Define the term Industrial Psychology (IP). Explain why the study of IP is important for engineers?
2. Explain briefly the history and process of development of industrial psychology.
3. What are the pillars of industrial psychology?
4. List the branches of psychology and explain how they have influenced IP.
5. Explain how the various schools of management thought have influenced IP.
6. Discuss atleast four areas of application of industrial psychology that are directly related to the job of an engineer.
7. As a student of engineering, explain why do you need to study industrial psychology.
8. Explain the role of FW Taylor in industrial psychology.
9. 'Without industrial psychologists, organizations cannot function!' Do you agree with this statement? Explain.
10. Write short notes on the following:
    i. Organizational culture
    ii. Ethics in management
    iii. Organizational development
    iv. Technology management
    v. Design of work environment
    vi. Biopsychology
    vii. Clinical psychology
    viii. Developmental psychology
    ix. Forensic psychology
    x. Social psychology
    xi. Educational psychology

Select Bibliography

1. Aamodt MG (1999). *Applied Industrial/Organizational Psychology*. 3rd edition. Pacific Grove: Brooks/Cole.
2. Bhattacharyya DK (2009). *Organizational Behaviour: Concepts and Applications*. New Delhi: Oxford University Press.
3. Bhattacharyya DK (2010). *Cross-cultural Management*. New Delhi: PHI Learning.
4. Bhattacharyya DK (2011). *Organizational Change and Development*. New Delhi: Oxford University Press.
5. Dale E (1965). *Management Theory and Practice*. New York: McGraw-Hill.
6. Drucker P (1986). *The Practice of Management*. New York: Harper and Brothers.

7. Dunnette MD (ed.) (1976). *Handbook of Industrial and Organizational Psychology*. Chicago: Rand McNally.
8. Jex SM and TW Britt (2008). *Organizational Psychology*. New Jersey: John Wiley and Sons.
9. Koontz H (1961). The management theory jungle, *Acad Man J*, 4 (3), 174–88.
10. Massie JL (1987). *Essentials of Management*. New Delhi: Prentice Hall.
11. Muchinsky PM (1999). *Psychology Applied to Work*. 6th edition. Belmont: Wadsworth.
12. Stone P and M Cannon (1997). *Organizational Psychology*. Brookfield: Ashgate Publishing.

2 Scientific Management and Industrial Psychology

Learning Objectives

After reading this chapter you will be able to:

- **Explain the process of development of various schools of management thought**
- **Differentiate between and evaluate the different perspectives in management thinking**
- **Discuss the modern principles in management**
- **Link management thoughts to industrial psychology**

Overview

Management is as old as civilisation. We find evidence to prove this in events that happened centuries ago. It would not have been possible to build the pyramids in Egypt or construct the Great Wall of China or the eternal Taj Mahal without managing the activities successfully. We may not have any documentary evidence for existence of management principles during those days but certainly management was practised to get things done. The earliest reference to management as we understand today can be found in the philosophy of division of labour in the work of Adam Smith.

History of Development of Management Thought

Throughout history, we find that organised activities and efficient management of such activities existed even in the ancient civilisations. However, management has undergone changes over the years and has now matured into a common body of knowledge. From Adam Smith's *Wealth of Nations* (1776), we observe that he had mentioned about the economic advantages of division of labour, and the need for breaking down jobs into narrow and repetitive tasks. In his work, we observe that division of labour can increase productivity by enhancing the skill of the workers. With the advent of the Industrial Revolution, machines began to replace human effort. Therefore, the pace of production activities increased and formal management practices emerged.

The classical approach to management emerged with the scientific management theories and general administrative theories. The former emphasised on the mechanism to improve the productivity of workers. General administrative theories, on the other hand, were concerned with the overall effectiveness of organizations. Frederick Winslow Taylor (1911) is acknowledged as the father of scientific management. Taylor could observe that employees use different techniques to do the same job. In order to improve productivity of workers, he developed the scientific method for the jobs. Applying this method, organizations could improve the productivity of their workers.

Frank and Lillian Gilbreth were followers of Taylor. This couple experimented on the wasteful hand and body motion, and designed appropriate tools to optimise the performance of workers. They also classified 17 basic hand motions, which they named as **'therbligs'**, i.e., the transposed version of their name.

Another associate of Taylor, Henry L Gantt, devised the incentive system, i.e., payment of bonus to workers for completing their jobs in less than the standard time. Also he devised the bar chart, which is used till date as a scheduling tool for planning and controlling work.

General administrative theory was pioneered by Henry Fayol and Max Weber. Fayol considered management as an activity and advocated 14 principles as universal truths. Max Weber developed the theory of authority structures to describe the activities of the organization on the basis of authority relations. This is what he had called the bureaucracy which contains division of labour, hierarchy of authority, formal selection, rules and regulations, impersonality and career orientation.

Impact on Industrial Psychology

Management is influenced by various disciplines like sociology, economics, political science, anthropology, psychology and even literature. Because of such multidisciplinary approaches, we even find authors like Harold Koontz refer to it as 'jungle'. In fact, there are also differences in the classification of various approaches. Broadly, the history of management thinking consists of the following categories: (i) Classical approach (ii) Neo-classical approach and (iii) Modern approach. However, we start our discussion from the pre-classical approach, as the system of managing the work of people existed from time immemorial, and the concept of industrial psychology existed even before the classical approach.

Pre-classical approach

Even though most of the discussions on the evolution of management thought start with the classical approach, here we have acknowledged the contribution of some of the authors

Table 2.1 Early contributors and their pioneering ideas

Thinker	Principles outlined
Robert Owen (1771–1858)	He is considered as the pioneer in the processes of Human Resource Management (HRM). He had advocated the necessity for a concern about the welfare of workers.
Charles Babbage (1792– 1871)	As an inventor and management scientist, he had built the practical mechanical calculator, which we consider as the basis of modern computers. Further, he had also advocated the idea of specialisation of intellectual work and suggested the necessity of profit-sharing.
Andrew Ure and Charles Duplin (1778–1857)	They had emphasised the necessity of management education, which paved the way for making management functions as a distinct profession.
Henry Robinson Towne (1844–1924)	Emphasised the significance of business skills in running a business

briefly to appreciate their role in the process of development of management principles (Table 2.1).

Reviewing the contributions of pre-classical theorists, it is clear that their emphasis was more on developing specific techniques to solve some identified problems. Because of their obvious technical background, they could not think of management as a separate field. By and large they had integrated management with their respective areas of specialisation. It was Ure, Duplin and Towne, who had laid the foundation for the other management theorists, which ultimately shaped the management principles as we see today. The behavioural aspects of work were recognised even in the pre-classical era.

Classical School of Thought

This school of thought is actually divided into two different approaches—scientific approach and administrative approach. Thinkers of this era laid the foundations for managing an organization following certain principles. In Table 2.2, the thinkers and their core principles are listed.

Table 2.2 Thinkers of the classical school of management

Thinker	Associated theory
Scientific Management	
Frederick W Taylor (1856–1915)	Theory of scientific management
Frank B Gilbreth and Lillian M Gilbreth (1868–1972)	Time and motion studies
Henry L Gantt (1861–1919)	The Gantt chart
Administrative Theory	
Henri Fayol (1841–1925)	General theory of management
Max Weber (1864–1920)	rules

Scientific management

It is considered the pioneering approach, which emphasised on the scientific study of work methods to improve efficiency of the workers. Among all the contributors to this school of thought, we consider the contribution of FW Taylor as the most important. Taylor developed specific principles of scientific management in 1911 and is called the father of scientific management. He had started his experiments in 1878 at Midvale Steel Co in the USA. During his days at Midvale, he had seen that employees were 'soldiering', that is, deliberately working at a pace slower than their capabilities. He had identified that workers indulged in 'soldiering' primarily for three reasons: (a) Fear of losing jobs if they increase their output (b) Faulty wage systems and (c) Outdated methods of working.

For eliminating this problem, Taylor developed the principles of scientific management, emphasising mainly on five important issues as under:

- Emphasis on organised knowledge rather than relying on rule of thumb
- Obtain harmony in group action
- Achieve cooperation
- Work for maximum output rather than restricted output
- Develop all workers both for their self-improvement as well as organizational prosperity

Therefore, Taylor emphasised on the following points to achieve organizational efficiency: (i) Develop scientific method of completing the jobs (ii) Train and develop the workers and (iii) Establish harmonious relations between management and workers. Figure 2.1 illustrates the scientific management process.

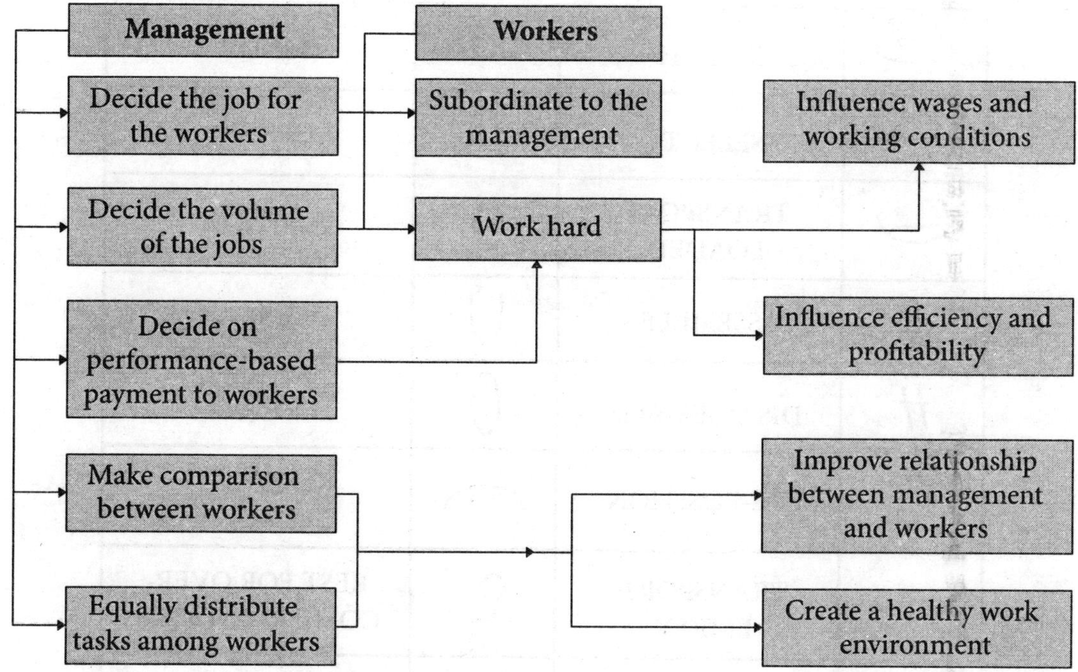

Fig. 2.1 The scientific management process

In order to ensure that the objectives are achieved, Taylor suggested two important managerial practices, namely, piece-rate incentive system and time and motion study.

- The piece-rate incentive system rewards the worker who produces the maximum output. Such an incentive system can motivate workers to maximise their earnings. This system requires workers to perform at some pre-decided standard rate to earn their base wages. Standards are decided using time and motion Study. If workers are able to produce more, then in addition to their base rate, they get incentives on the number of excess units produced over and above the standard units. This serves the interests of the workers and the management, as the former feel motivated to maximise their earnings, while the latter get the benefit of increased productivity and thus higher profits.
- Time and motion study, as already pointed out, facilitates determination of the standard time for performing a job. Time study helps in the determination of time required, duly defining the art of recording, analysing and synthesising the time elements of each operation. Motion study, on the other hand, involves study of movements in doing a job, in parts, and eliminating wasteful movements while retaining only the necessary ones.

Symbol	Motion	Symbol	Motion
	SEARCH		FIND
	SELECT		GRASP
	TRANSPORT LOADED	9	POSITION
#	ASSEMBLE		USE
#	DISASSEMBLE		INSPECT
	PRE-POSITION		RELEASE LOAD
	TRANSPORT EMPTY		REST FOR OVER-COMING FATIGUE
	UNAVOIDABLE DELAY		AVOIDABLE DELAY
	PLAN		HOLD

Fig. 2.2 Various hand movements identified by Frank and Lillian Gilbreth

In fact, time and motion study concepts were developed by Taylor in association with Frank and Lillian Gilbreth. The latter explored ways of reducing fatigue. They classified 17 basic hand motions, like search, select, position, hold etc, which they called **therbligs.** Their approach led to the analysis of the exact elements of a worker's hand movements. A simple modification of the brick laying process, following the Gilbreths' approach, helped to increase hourly output from 120 to 350 bricks. Figure 2.2 lists the various movements identified by the Gilbreths (therbligs).

Henry Gantt also worked as a close associate of Taylor at Midvale and subsequently at Bethlehem Steel. His contributions to the scientific management school of thought are the introduction of task and bonus system and a chart commonly known as the **Gantt chart.** As per his incentive plan, workers receive their day wages even when they do not perform their complete job. But they get bonus, when they complete the work in better than the normal standard time. He also recommended payment of bonus to foremen, based on the incremental performance of workers.

The Gantt chart, on the other hand, is used for production planning to compare the actual and planned performances. It is a visual device for production control, indicating progress of production in terms of time rather than quantity. In fact, Programme Evaluation and Review Technique (PERT) concept was developed later based on the Gantt chart. With computer support, Gantt charts can be generated with more detailed information. A typical Gantt chart is shown in Fig. 2.3.

The horizontal bar graph on the chart represents the time requirement for the activity. This is an example of the occupancy style Gantt chart. A PERT chart based on the Gantt chart is shown in Fig. 2.4.

Advantages: Taylor's scientific management principles provide some advantages and benefits to organizations, encompassing various technological, human and organizational issues. Some of these benefits are: scope for specialisation, scientific planning, on-time delivery, standardisation of methods of doing the work, improved quality, minimisation of costs, reduction in wastage of materials, time and energy, and last but not the least maintaining harmonious relations between the supervisors and workers.

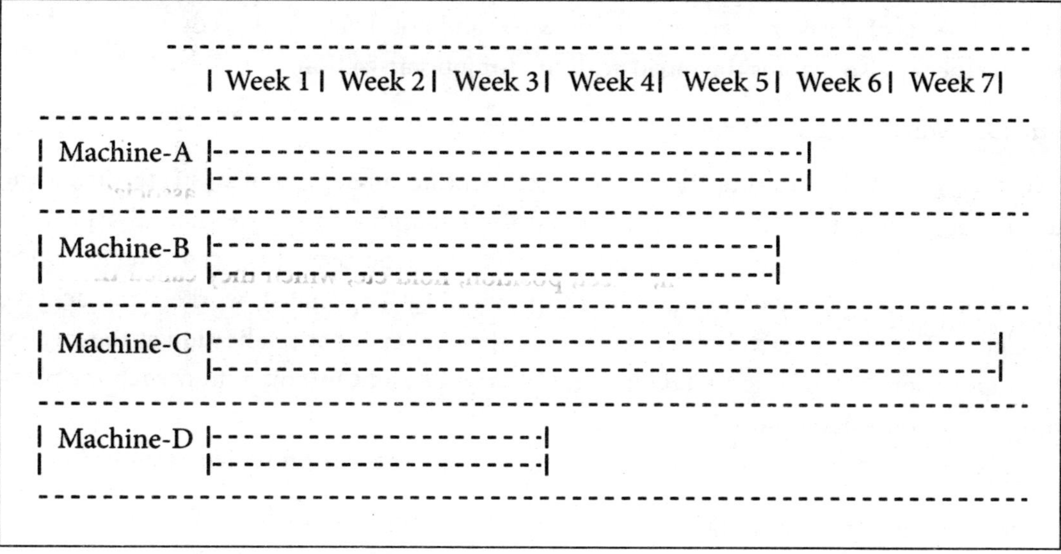

Fig. 2.3 Model Gantt chart; it shows that Machine A has been loaded till week 5 for a given job, and Machine B has been loaded till the first half of week 5 and so on.

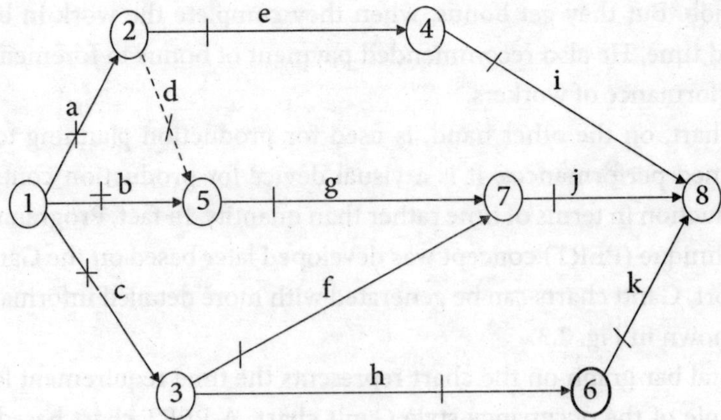

Fig. 2.4 A PERT pathway for a job with eight nodes and 11 tasks

Drawbacks: This school of management thought has the following disadvantages.

- The basic principles of scientific management revolve around operation-level problems and do not focus on managerial issues, essential for managing an organization. Hence, it is often said that it relates more to engineering than to management.
- While framing the principles, assumptions about people only consider that they are rational and primarily driven for their desire to fulfill material gains. Therefore, economic and physical needs of the people are only emphasized and not their social needs.
- The theory also ignores the intrinsic desire for job satisfaction.

Functional foremanship

FW Taylor while advocating the concept of scientific management has introduced the term functional foremanship. He developed the technique to ensure that all aspects of work are entrusted to a single supervisor, who has the expertise. This, according to Taylor, can improve the quality of work. When supervised by a specialist, workers can achieve efficiency. The idea, in fact, is the extension of the concept of specialisation at the level of the supervisors. According to Taylor, there should be eight foremen: four each for planning and implementation.

Briefly we can list the names and functions of these specialist foremen as under:

- Instruction card clerk to tag down job instructions for workers
- Time and cost clerk to set the time table for doing the job and specifying job-specific material and labour costs

- Route clerk to design the route map for flow of materials
- Shop disciplinarians to make rules and regulations for enforcing discipline in the workplace
- Gang boss to arrange for machines, tools, materials and workers
- Speed boss to maintain the speed and to remove delays in the production process
- Repair boss to ensure maintenance of machines, tools and equipment
- Inspector to maintain quality of products

Administrative theory

Administrative theory, another part of classical school of thought, focuses on principles to coordinate the internal activities of the organization. Henri Fayol, the French industrialist, through his pioneering work on general and industrial management explained that satisfactory results can be achieved with scientific forecasting and proper methods of management. Fayol at the outset, classified business operations of an organization into six activities and then outlined 14 principles of management. Six activities are as under:

Technical—Concerned with production and manufacturing

Commercial—Activities related to buying, selling and exchange

Financial—Ensures optimal use of capital

Security—Protect employees and property

Accounting—Concerned with costs, profits and liabilities, maintaining balance sheets and compiling statistics

Managerial—The functional approach to management concerned with planning, organising, commanding, coordinating and controlling

After detailing all these activities, Fayol focused mainly on the managerial activities and outlined 14 principles to achieve efficiency in managerial activities. Those principles are given below:

Division of labour: If workers become specialised, they can perform their tasks better. It recommends grouping of people as per their area of specialisation. The modern concept of assembly line is an outcome of division of labour.

Authority: Managers must have the authority to get things done. But formal authority alone may not help to compel obedience from the subordinates; managers must have the expertise to exert personal authority.

Discipline: People working in an organization need to comply with rules and agreements that govern the organization. Without discipline, results cannot be achieved. Good discipline translates to good leadership and together this can create an environment of good work culture.

Unity of command: Members in an organization must receive instructions from only one person. Conflict will arise when one receives orders and instructions from multiple bosses. Therefore, ideally the reporting relationship of one subordinate should be with one superior.

Unity of direction: All operations of an organization need to be directed towards the overall objectives.

Subordination of individual interest to the common good: Interest of an individual employee should not take precedence over the interests of the organization as a whole.

Remuneration: It should be fair to both employees and employers.

Centralisation: It reduces the role of the subordinates in decision-making while decentralisation enhances it. Managers should retain responsibility by adequate centralisation while giving their subordinates enough authority to do their jobs properly.

Hierarchy: There should be a line of authority, in the form of an organization chart, showing clearly the reporting hierarchy from the top management to the shop floor.

Order: People and materials should be in the right place at the right time. Job should be allocated to people according to their suitability for the respective job.

Equity: Managers should be fair to their subordinates.

Stability of staff: Employee turnover should be less to ensure efficiency.

Initiative: Subordinates should have the freedom to conceive and do their task, even though they may commit mistakes.

Esprit de corps: Team spirit should be promoted to develop a culture of unity in the organization. Use of verbal communication instead of formal written communication wherever possible may help in developing team spirit.

Bureaucratic theory

This theory was pioneered by Max Weber who emphasised on the authority structures and description of an organization based on the authority relations. According to Weber 'a bureaucracy is highly structured, formalised, and impersonal organization'. In fact, he has advocated the necessity of a formal organisational structure with set rules and regulations. Characteristics of a bureaucratic organization described by Weber are shown in Table 2.3.

Table 2.3 Features of a bureaucratic organization

Characteristics	Description
Specialisation of labour	Jobs are broken down into routine, well-defined tasks so that members of the organization know what is expected of them and can become competent enough to do a particular subset of tasks.
Formal rules and procedures	Written rules and procedures should specify the desired behaviours from members of the organization and facilitate coordination and ensure uniformity.
Impersonality	Rules, procedures and sanctions should be applied uniformly regardless of individuals.
Well-defined hierarchy	Multiple levels of positions must be designed carefully keeping in mind the reporting relationships among the levels. This should provide for supervision, handling of situation of exceptions and ability to establish accountability of actions.
Career advancement based on merit	Selection and promotions should be based on the qualifications and performance of the members.

Bureaucracy is often misunderstood as 'red tape' or having too many rules. However, Weber's concept is intended to remove ambiguity, inefficiencies and patronage.

Criticisms of the classical approach

Behavioural theorists criticised the classical approach for the following reasons.

- The management principles are not universally applicable in today's complex business situation. Some principles of Fayol are also contradictory, viz., the principle of specialisation versus principle of unity of command.
- Similarly, Weber's bureaucracy takes away the individual's creativity and flexibility, which reduces his ability to respond to a complex situation in a global environment.

- Classical theorists also ignored the important aspects of organizational behaviour. These theories do not deal with the problems of leadership, motivation, power or informal relations.
- These theories fail to consider the influence internal and external environmental forces have on an organization. They only stress upon the necessity of achieving productivity, more than anything else.

Modern Approaches to Management

Modern approaches to management basically centre on the quantitative school, the systems theory and contingency theory. We call it modern because all these approaches have emerged over the years, primarily based on industry practices. For example, the quantitative school of management thought had emerged during World War II, when the team of managers, the government, and the scientists worked together to help the army with models for effective utilisation of resources. This interdisciplinary team integrated the existing mathematical approaches with the concepts of Taylor and Gantt. This school of thought has now expanded into many branches like management science, operations management and management information systems.

Management science approach visualizes management as a logical entity, expressing management in terms of mathematical symbols, relationships and measurement data. It is also known as operations research approach, and it extends to various functions of management. For example in finance, it is used in capital budgeting and cash flow management. In production and operations, it helps in scheduling and framing of product strategies. In human resource management, it helps in resource planning. In materials function, it is used in inventory management. Using this approach, managers can reduce their errors significantly. More extended approach of management science is known as operations management. Although initial focus was on issues in production and operations management, now it is used in all functional areas of management.

Management Information Systems (MIS) approach depends on computer-based information systems for use by the management. It converts raw data into information inputs, which are subsequently used by the management in decision-making. Now, of course, MIS helps in building organization-wide Decision Support Systems (DSS), like various Enterprise Resource Planning (ERP) modules, Human Resource Information Systems (HRIS) etc.

More advanced form of computer-based information systems is the systems theory approach which considers the organization as a system, and its various units as subsystems. With this approach, managers can effectively coordinate the efforts of related subsystems.

Contingency theory approach discards the concept of universality in management principles and determines managerial decisions considering situational factors. The task of a manager, as per this theory, is to identify which techniques will, in a particular situation, under particular circumstances, at a particular point of time, best contribute to achieving organizational goals. With the integration of contingency and systems theory, we get the integrative school of management thought, which we consider to be the best in a given situation.

Key Points

- Various theories of management evolved with the growth of the Industrial Revolution.
- All these theories were developed in various phases and have their importance in specific areas, keeping pace with the times.
- We cannot really discard the importance of any of these theories; rather we should consider these as contributing forces for subsequent development.
- The foundation of management principles lies in these theories. However, in the modern context, we find more relevance of systems approach and contingency approach to management.
- All these theoretical management inputs strengthen our base to understand IP. Therefore, IP is viewed as a configuration of various practices and theories on management, with specific focus on structure- and people-related issues.

Important Terms

Classical approach: It represents the traditionally accepted views on management.

Contingency theory: It emphasises on the manager's competence in responding to the various situations that may arise during the course of his work.

Gantt chart: It is a chart used to compare the actual and planned performance in production planning.

Modern approach: This approach is a combination of the previous two schools of management thinking.

Neo-classical approach: It emphasises on the human relations aspect of management.

Project Evaluation and Review Technique (PERT): It is used in scheduling and managing complex projects.

Scientific management: It laid stress on organised knowledge rather than the rule of thumb.

Self-assessment Questions

1. Briefly discuss the various schools of management thought.
2. What are the important features of a bureaucratic organization? Point out the merits and demerits of such an organization.
3. Explain briefly the contributions of FW Taylor to the evolution of management thought.
4. What are the principles of management put forth by Henri Fayol? Do you think all these principles are relevant in today's organizations?
5. Distinguish between neo-classical and classical approaches to management. What are their advantages and disadvantages?
6. What are the important characteristics of modern management thought? How they are different from earlier approaches?
7. Discuss the principle of scientific management and show how it relates to the psychology of the employees?
8. Define therbligs. Why are they important in workplaces?
9. Write short notes on the following:
   i. Gantt chart
   ii. Situational approach
   iii. Esprit de corps
   iv. Bureaucratic organization

Select Bibliography

1. Argyris C (1964). *Integrating the Individual and the Organization*. New York: Wiley.
2. Bhattacharyya DK (2009). *Organizational Behaviour: Concept and Applications*. New Delhi: Oxford University Press.
3. Dale E (1965). *Management Theory and Practice*. New York: McGraw-Hill.
4. Drucker P (1954). *The Practice of Management*. New York: Harper and Brothers.

5. Koontz H (1961). The management theory jungle, *Acad of Man J*, 4 (3): 174–88.
6. Massie JL (1987). *Essentials of Management.* New Delhi: Prentice Hall.
7. Ouchi WG and AM Jaeger (1978). Type Z organization: Stability in the midst of mobility, *Acad Man Rev* (April): 305–14.
8. Peters IJ and RH Waterman (1982). *In search of Excellence: Lessons from America's Best Run Companies.* New York: Harper and Row.

3 Work Study

Learning Objectives

After reading this chapter you will be able to:

- Understand the concept of work study and its use in IP
- Appreciate the human context of work study—response from trade unions
- Understand work measurement, time study and method study
- List the features of motion economy, human engineering and value analysis

Overview

In Chapter 1, we have seen that engineering psychology is concerned with the sensors at the workplace and the issues in work design. Therefore, work study has much importance in industrial psychology. Literally, the term work study means the study of human work. As per the British Standards 3138:1969 Work Study is defined as, 'a management service based on those techniques, particularly Method Study and Work Measurement, which are used in the examination of human work in all its contexts, and which lead to the systematic investigation of all the resources and factors which affect the efficiency and economy of the situation being reviewed, in order to effect improvement'.

Therefore, it is a generic term for two interdependent techniques, i.e., Method Study and Work Measurement. The British Standard defines Method Study as '.... the systematic recording and critical examination of the factors and resources involved in existing and proposed ways of doing work, as a means of developing and applying easier and more effective methods and reducing costs'. Method study, hence, is concerned with the way in which work is done. The British Standards defines Work Measurement as '... the application of techniques designed to establish the time for a qualified worker to carry out a specified job at a defined level of performance'.

Analysing these definitions of Work Study given by the British Standards Institute, we conclude that it is a procedure for understanding and determining the work done by the people. It also helps us to identify the factors that affect efficiency and help in achieving economy through optimum utilisation of resources. Most productivity improvement techniques involve major capital expenditure in plant or equipment, whereas work study, being a management technique, ensures greater productivity by using existing resources. The human element is emphasised and importance is given to operation as opposed to the technical process. It, therefore, helps the management to achieve its primary objectives in the following manner: (i) Effective use of plant and equipment (ii) Effective use of human effort (iii) Evaluation of human work.

Work study and response from trade unions

If work study techniques are applied properly, the manager can avoid resistance to change that will be encountered at different levels. It is, therefore, important to estimate the response from individuals in order to design the program for investigation and implementation suitably. Most unions are aware that work study provides benefits to the workers by eliminating drudgery, frustration and an unhealthy working environment. It also gives an opportunity to the workers to increase their earnings (by achieving increased rate of output). However, to satisfy the unions, the following points need to be considered:

- Consult the workers before introducing any scheme. This is likely to affect their interest and morale one way or the other.
- Define a policy for those workers who become redundant on the implementation of the recommendations of the work study team.
- Procedure to deal with the changes in the method of work and for measurement of work should be laid down and communicated to the workers.

The International Labour Organization (ILO) has emphasised the importance of such sharing of information with the workers in a resolution concerning Consultation and Cooperation between Employers and Workers at the level of the Undertaking in the 35th session at Geneva in the 1952.

Method Study

As a step to improve productivity, method study helps to achieve the same output using fewer resources or produce more with proportionately lesser inputs. It reduces, if not eliminating, waste. Method study fosters creativity, innovation, optimal decision-making power, good organizational practices and better communication. Any method study program has the following elements: (i) Economic considerations (ii) Technical issues and (iii) Human factors.

Thus, it is clear that method study has the following important roles for the organization:

- To appraise the purpose and objectives of the organization
- To assess the tasks of the organization
- To evaluate the communication and control structure of the organization
- To optimise the use of resources of the organization
- To improve procedures, methods and processes of the organization
- To ensure individual and group effectiveness and work satisfaction in the organization

Importance and Objectives of Method Study

The primary objective of method study is to find better ways of doing things, so as to improve efficiency by eliminating unnecessary work, avoidable delays and other forms of waste. Method study achieves this by systematic recording, analysis and critical examination of methods and movements during the performance of the existing or proposed ways of doing the different tasks at work. The main objectives of method study are based on its role in the organization:

- Reorientation of corporate objectives and mission
- Review of plans and programs
- Evaluation of tasks, targets and available resources
- Balancing the structure of the organization
- Introduction of a good communication system in the organization
- Quality control by standardisation of products and procedures
- Improvement of workflow by simplified process through better design
- Planning and control of work
- Cost control through optimum use of resources
- Improving the layout of the shop floor
- Better working conditions through higher standards of safety and health at work
- Satisfaction at work

Process of Method Study

The method study technique is flexible enough so that it can be applied to different situations. A simple framework to be used is shown in Table 3.1.

Table 3.1 Elements of work study program

Step of the program	Coverage
Select	Identify the work or task to be studied
Record	Collect the relevant facts of the present or proposed method
Examine	Analyse the findings in sequence
Develop	Find the most effective method taking into account contingencies and cost considerations
Install	Establish the method as standard practice
Maintain	Monitor the standard practice with regular feedback mechanism

Though we have indicated five basic steps for an actual study, it is not necessary to follow the same sequence or pattern. The selection of the subject of study may be preceded by the study of possibility of data collection. Identification of the task or work area to be studied is the first and most important step. In fact, preliminary critical examination (pilot study) may be needed in order to identify the problem area. There may be a need for more detailed data gathering during a pilot study. It may also be revealed during preliminary critical examination that the real problem is something other than the one selected.

There should be total transparency during method study. Discussions, exchanges of views and efforts at mutual understanding are the very basis of method study. There are also several undefined stages in this study. The final plan has to be discussed with all concerned before implementation. In the same way, prior to installing the new system, all concerned need to be familiarised through reorientation programs. Once installed, the system has to be maintained to ensure that it becomes an accepted standard. Each step of method study is explained in the following section.

Selection of the job: In the first step, the main objectives are determined. The problem must be defined. Some common problems that require the expertise of the method study investigator are:

- Bottlenecks that disrupt the smooth flow of materials or processes
- Scope for cost control to produce economically
- Economic utilisation of factory space, including land and buildings
- Economic utilisation of labour, material and machinery
- Elimination of idle time caused by problems of flow, queues and congestion

While selecting the issues for the study, it is essential to remember that the ultimate objective of method study is to improve achievement by raising the level of productivity and increasing satisfaction at work. Further, the term 'select' does not merely refer to making a choice from amongst many. It must include a preliminary survey, which enables the investigator to decide on the progress of the study. Moreover, in this step, the appropriate techniques required to be applied are also selected.

Collecting relevant data: Adequate data about the existing system must be collected. This ensures that an objective record of the way the job is being presently carried out is created. To eliminate the chance of bias, this record is based on direct observation by the concerned investigator. It is not compiled from second-hand accounts—the manager's version on how he thinks the job is done, or an operator's description of how the job is done.

Critical examination: The collected information is scrutinised and each part of the job is critically examined to determine whether it can be (i) eliminated (ii) combined with another part of the job (iii) placed in a different sequence or (iv) simplified. Some of the questions generally asked during the examination phase are as follows:

a) What is done and why?
b) Who does it and why that person?
c) Where is it done and why there?
d) When is it done and why then?
e) How is it done and why this way?

Rearranging, simplifying and combining the existing records provides the base for designing an improved method.

Developing the new method: The alternatives selected are used to reshape and develop the new method, layout or procedure. These may require test runs to determine their feasibility. It is preferable that tests of this nature are carried out at a place away from the work site, if possible. It is good to involve the departmental officers to ease the problems of acceptance for the new method in the department. The result of the study must be an improved method. It must be acceptable to the departmental staff and workers. It must meet all their practical requirements and technical specifications.

Installing the new method: Prior to installing the new method, the following decisions must be taken:

- Ordering for new plant/machinery or additional inventory (if any)
- Changes in the production process
- Deciding the extent of redeployment and training

- Introducing new documentation procedures
- Setting new standards for quality and procedures for testing
- A detailed timetable for effecting these changes

After the installation stage, the new method is in operation at the work site. Line managers can take control as all members of their department become fully conversant with the new method.

Maintaining the new method: When a new method has been installed, it undergoes some changes as a result of minor alterations made by the operators or supervisors. To detect any such alterations, a reference standard (job instruction sheet) is needed to compare the actual performance on the job. Likewise, a corresponding document for an incentive scheme, which could contain details such as the standard time for each job, is prepared. With this data, changes in the method can be detected. If changes are considered to be useful, the instruction sheet can be amended to incorporate them. If they are thought undesirable, they can be removed through the line managers.

Work Measurement

The ILO defines Work Measurement as '... the application of techniques designed to establish the work content of a specified task by determining the time required for carrying it out at a defined standard of performance by a qualified worker'. This is conventionally known as time study and is primarily carried out to determine the standard time to perform a specific task. This standard time is used for planning and scheduling work, estimating costs, labour cost control or may serve as the base for its most popular application—a wage incentive plan.

Techniques of Work Measurement

The principal techniques of work measurement are listed below:

- Time study
- Ratio-delay study (statistical sampling technique)
- Synthesis from standard data
- Predetermined motion–time standard
- Analytic estimation

Out of the above, time study is the most widely used. We shall discuss this technique in detail in this section.

Time Study

The ILO defined Time Study as 'a technique for determining as accurately as possible from a limited number of observations, the time necessary to carry out a given activity at a defined standard of performance'. The equipment required to carry out a time study are: stopwatch, study board, pencils, slide rule etc. Stopwatches are of different types:

- A stopwatch that records one minute per revolution by intervals of 1/5th of a second, with a small hand recording 30 minutes
- One that records one minute per revolution, calibrated in 1/100th of a minute, with a small hand recording 30 minutes
- A decimal-hour stopwatch recording 1/100th of an hour per revolution graduated in 1/1,000th of an hour and a small hand that records up to one hour in 100 divisions

Steps in time study

Time study for measurement of work consists of the following steps:

1. Collect and complete all available information about the job. This should include conditions at work and the attitude of the operators, which is likely to affect the work.
2. Record the details of the method and also break down different operations into elements
3. Record the time taken by operators to complete the task (element-wise), measuring preferably with a stopwatch
4. Assess the efficiency of the operators, comparing the same with a predetermined standard speed
5. Convert the observed time to normal time
6. Estimate the rate of overtime wages
7. Determine the allowed time for operation

Some other techniques of work measurement

As conducting a time study for each job is a time-consuming task, statistical techniques like ratio-delay study, are often done. **Ratio-delay** is a statistical technique based on sampling of readings taken at random intervals Like in all other sampling techniques, under this method also there are bound to be some errors. However, since the cost of such studies is much lesser, many organizations that have the expertise may prefer this method. Another advantage in this method is that rating is not done and hence, recording the time directly using a stopwatch encounters no resistance from the workers.

Under the method of **synthesis from standard data**, synthesised times are time standards that are built up or synthesised from element times previously obtained from direct time study. Organizations that have an independent work study department usually build up synthetic tables covering the common elements. Some units also use such time records of other organizations as standard data. For obvious non-uniformity of technology, skill, process and working environments, this type of synthesis may not always be correct.

Based on elementary movement, predetermined **motion–time standards** have been developed for different job elements. For time measurement, work factor and basic motion times are usually recorded in any predetermined time standard. These time standards are used by work study analysts as the basis for comparing the observed time of the present workers. This enables them to quickly estimate the efficiency of the workers.

A compromise between straight rate fixing and time study, **analytical estimation** is normally used in maintenance and repair roles. Since these jobs call for creativity and the right attitude, it is difficult to fix or enforce straight rates, as the skill element would then be ignored.

Analytical estimating is difficult and not always foolproof for inexperienced investigators. A time study table is shown in Fig. 3.1.

Ergonomics

Derived from two Greek words, *ergon* meaning work and *enomos* meaning laws, ergonomics refers to the study of the effects of the work parameters on the workers. The objective of this science is to fit the work to the men doing the job, with a view to enhancing comfort thereby increasing their efficiency. According to the ILO, ergonomics is defined as, 'the application of human biological sciences, in conjunction with engineering and sciences, to the worker and his working environment, so as to obtain maximum satisfaction for the work which, at the same time, enhances productivity'.

An analysis of the above definition shows that an ergonomist tries to integrate the work system (which includes the tasks, equipment, working conditions and workspace) with the capabilities and requirements of the job. In this process, he tries to ensure job satisfaction for the workers, to increase their productivity.

Ergonomics can be applied to all types of workspace, namely, offices, factories, shops, ships, aircraft and even a spacecraft. Some areas where ergonomics has been successfully applied are:

- Design of equipment, power and hand tools
- Design of displays and warning systems
- Design of furniture, seats, rests and steps for operators
- Design of tools, jigs and fixtures
- Layout of the plant

Dept: Flavour room Week commencing: Name: Job title:

Non-conformance elements	Mon	Tue	Wed	Thur	Fri	Sat	Sun	Total
1. Find pallet truck								
2. Availability of pallet								
3. Tool availability (e.g., spanner)								
4. Equipment breakdown (e.g., mixer)								
5. Re-cleaning (e.g., hose, transit tank)								
6. Find stacker driver								
7. Wrong information (e.g., packing instruction)								
8. Raw material availability								
9. Waiting for quality assurance check								
10. Internal enquiries (e.g., QCM)								
11. Label problems								
12. Disruptions in production schedules (e.g., change over)								
13. Remix/Re-sample/Re-filter/Re-homogenising								
14. Remake								
15. Removing/disposing of rejected product								
Total								

Comment: ....
....
....

Fig. 3.1 A model time study table

- Improvement in working conditions and environments
- Computation of allowances for relaxation for workers
- Selection, training and placement of personnel
- Motivation of workers

Impact of Ergonomics on Work Study

Work study refers to the scientific analysis of a work system to increase productivity and satisfaction at work. It is dependent on ergonomics for research data on the many facets of human response to a given work situation. This information makes the task of a work study practitioner more scientific and result-oriented. Such inputs/data cover the following areas:

- Limits of sustained physical endurance, normal speeds of movement and optimum method of handling controls
- Receptivity to sensory inputs and time required for perception of deviations
- Time required for evaluation and decision-making and response time for motion output
- Anthropometric data to guide the design and layout of equipment, workplace and furniture
- Effects of different environmental conditions and features that can be improved
- Effects of working conditions so as to raise the standards of comfort, safety and health
- Qualitative and quantitative analysis of factors contributing to industrial fatigue for computation of 'relaxation allowances'

Features of ergonomic investigation

The areas studied by an ergonomic analysis are discussed below.

Human characteristics: Features such as health, physique, anthropometric data, personal background, education, training, experience, age, sex, intelligence, aptitude, response time, interests, personality characteristics, temperament, attitude towards work and level of motivation are studied. This is necessary to relate the response of the workers in the context of physiological and psychological factors that impact their response at the workplace.

Work: Physical loads, mental stress or anxiety, displays and warning systems, controls, compatibility of inputs and outputs are features related to the tasks comprising the job. These help in designing appropriate procedures in tune with the human characteristics mentioned earlier.

Working conditions: Layout of the workplace, postures, motion and movements, fatigue, monotony and relaxation allowances, comfort, safety and health, working hours and shift work conditions determine the productivity of the workers. Hence, these features are also studied.

Work environment: This refers to the features of the physical environment such as illumination, ventilation, temperature and humidity, colour dynamics, fumes, dust, odour and smoke, landscape, gardens, cleanliness and sanitation.

Ergonomics is also known as human engineering, human factors in engineering, engineering psychology, applied experimental psychology, applied and human engineering research, man–machine system analysis etc. This subject was developed during the second World War due to the joint efforts of physiologists, psychologists and design engineers. Its earliest application could be traced to Frederick Winslow Taylor (1856–1915). His experiments were aimed at developing optimum design of equipment for specific types of work and also to train the workers to suit each kind of task. Frank Bunker Gilbreth (1869–1924) and his wife Lillian elaborated the principles of motion economy and introduced rest pauses and spacing out in the work environment, to reduce fatigue and eliminate stress. Since then, with the advances in experimental physiology, psychology and method study, it has been possible to obtain a better and more scientific understanding of the effects of working conditions and environment on the human body and mind.

Ergonomics and Management

Ergonomics has great use to the management right from the planning and design of a work system. To organise, direct and control human effort towards a specific end, management needs to have an appreciation of the human factors involved in a work system.

The results of ergonomic research on perception and mental stress have a special impact on the work conditions that can be challenging for effective managerial performance in an organization. The aim of such analysis is to eliminate all perceptual and mental loading that could arise from the examination and evaluation of reports on the normal activities of the organization, highlighting only the deviations from the standard state. This allows application of management time and talent to really important problems. Thus, ergonomics helps in increasing the productivity of the managers. This on its own, without any change in the methods on the shop floor, can lead to spectacular increase in the overall productivity of the organizations.

Work areas

The work area of an operator can be categorised into three groups: normal, immediate and maximum working areas. The normal working area is one that can be reached by the operator using any movement up to, and inclusive of, class 3 (Table 3.2) movements and is the area bound by two arcs made by the fingers using the elbow as the pivot.

Table 3.2 Classes of movements

Class	Pivot	Body-member movement
1	Knuckle (Finger joint)	Finger(s)
2	Wrist	Hands and fingers
3	Elbow	Forearm, hands and fingers
4	Shoulder	Upper arm, forearm, hands and fingers
5	Trunk (body apart from limbs)	Torso, upper arm, forearm, hands and fingers

The immediate working area is the surface immediately in front of the operator where the two arcs of the normal working area overlap. The maximum working area is one that can be reached by the operator using any movement up to and inclusive of class 4 (Table 3.2) movements and is the area bound by two arcs made by the fingers with the shoulders as the pivot. The space between the normal area and maximum working area is accessible through a class 4 movement. Anything beyond the maximum working area may be reached only through a class 5 movement, including body bending or stretching. The immediate working area is most suitable for bimanual operations. If the various equipment, materials and tools are replaced within the normal working area, they can be reached without using the upper arm and shoulder muscles. It is not desirable to place anything outside the maximum working area.

While considering working areas, the field of vision should also be taken into account. The normal cone of vision without head movement is restricted. Covering the whole perimeter of the normal working area would impose undue strain on the eye and sometimes involve excessive head movements. Therefore, due care must be taken to place all the materials—well within the cone of vision. During inspection, as much of the work as possible must take place right in front of the operator. Table 3.2 shows the classes of movement based on the pivots around which the body-members move.

A similar classification is available for movements corresponding to the leg. For economy of motion, the movement should be of the lowest classification possible, compatible with the normal capacity of the body-member affected.

Motion economy

Motion economy can be defined as the process of minimising the physical and perceptual loads imposed on people engaged in any type of work. It could be in the office, shop floor, kitchen, or at the driving wheel. It leads to better design of equipment, jigs and fixtures, hand tools, furniture and labour-saving devices. It also facilitates better layout of offices, warehouses, plants and operating areas like the office desk, work bench, aircraft, cockpit and crew compartments of armoured vehicles etc. The application of the principles of motion economy eliminates or minimises wasteful and tiring movements and increases productivity of the workers. It deliberates on minimising movements with respect to: (i) number, complexity and extent of movements (ii) classification of movements (iii) number of body parts used (iv) need for control and the muscular force required (v) distance and time required for eye fixation. Specialists have suggested the following principles for achieving motion economy:

- Principle of minimum movement
- Principle of natural movement
- Principle of simultaneous movement
- Principle of rhythmic movement
- Principle of habitual movement
- Principle of continuous movement

Greater fatigue is caused when only one hand is working while the other is idle. Simultaneous movements reduce fatigue and increase the rate of output. These include movements of the feet, while both the hands are operating, e.g., driving a car. The application of this principle, enabling both hands to work similar tasks simultaneously, leads to better design of jigs, fixtures, and duplication of tools.

It is advisable that the principle of symmetrical movements be applied in conjunction with simultaneous movements. Proper balance is achieved only when the movements of one hand are like the mirror image of those of the other, that is, they collaborate together. Symmetry in movements eliminates mishandling and promotes ease and speed. When movements of the hands are asymmetrical, operators tend to throw in additional non-productive movements in order to achieve balance.

Rhythm is the regular repetition of a pattern of movement. It often includes the emphasis of a specific part of a cycle. Rhythm plays an important role in increasing speed, eliminating fumbling and reducing fatigue. Examples of rhythmic movements are rowing a boat, hammering at the blacksmith, and drawing water from a well using a seesaw lift.

The pattern of movements should be designed so as to facilitate habit formation. When a cycle of activities becomes a habit, movements are executed almost as a reflex action. Habitual movements eliminate hesitation and increase the speed of performance. Rhythm helps to speed up habit formation. Tools, materials, displays and controls must always be located in the same position. The pattern must be standardised for similar types of panels, work places and equipment. Continuous movements that are smooth and curved are superior to jerky straight-line movements, which involve sudden changes of direction and loss of momentum. Materials, tools and jigs must be so positioned to eliminate undue changes of direction and to incorporate smooth, curved and continuous movements.

These principles should not be treated as inflexible rules, but as guidelines. For optimisation, a proper evaluation of all the principles, is required. This is because conditions differ between jobs. At times, it may be necessary to compromise the principle of minimum movements in order to equitably distribute the physical load over the various muscles. At other times, it may be necessary to give due weightage to the principle of continuous movement. Hence, it is essential that the principles be applied flexibly.

Human Engineering

Method study seeks to determine the most efficient combination of workers, machines and the working environment. It is necessary to distinguish the functions according to suitability by human effort or mechanical efficiency since each is superior in certain aspects. It is economy which influences the right combination of men and machines. The term Human Engineering is more appropriately used to solve these problems in design, operation and maintenance of plants and machineries. In fact, it is not appropriate to treat this science as an independent discipline as it comes broadly under the purview of ergonomics. Ernest McCormick gave the most widely accepted definition of Human Engineering as, 'the adaptation of human tasks and working environment to the sensory, perceptual, mental, physical, and other attributes of people. This adaptation for human use applies to such functions as the design of equipment, instruments, man–machine systems and consumer products, and to the development of optimum work methods and work environment'.

Impact on Design of Machines

While designing a machine, one should know how the human body functions, its dimensions, physical limitations and so also the conditions under which a person performs perfectly. For performing a task, a person normally does the following three things:

- Receives information through different sense organs
- Makes decisions by acting on the perceived information
- Takes action on the basis of the decision

Thus, the basic control cycle for a human being is sense, decide and act. The power to reason inductively, exercise judgement, develop concepts and create methods is unique to human beings. On the other hand, performing repetitive routine tasks quickly, rapid computation of a large volume of data, applying great force, multitasking etc are characteristic features of machines. A designer should, therefore, consider all the above details in designing better machines for productive use. Most Computer Numerically Controlled (CNC) machining centres developed by large industrial organizations in India are not performing well because they have been designed without considering the human factor. A point to note is that sophisticated machining centres, whenever introduced, have become instrumental in giving rise to problems in industrial relations, as these adversely affect the wages of the workers.

Since a badly designed machine may be responsible for poor performance of workers, the application of ergonomics/human engineering techniques is necessary. Modern machines are ergonomically designed to prevent stress and fatigue in workers. They not only facilitate ease of work, but also provide gain in terms of increased rate of production. The application of human engineering/ergonomic techniques has been found useful even in designing consumer products, kitchen gadgets, furniture etc. Recently, Blow Plast Ltd, under technical collaboration with Klober of Germany, has been offering ergonomically designed office chairs.

Value Analysis

In 1947, drawing lessons from World War II, Henry Erlicher of General Electric Company, USA, observed that substitution of materials (as manufacturers were then compelled to go for substitution to encounter shortages of original materials) often led to cost reduction and better functionality. This prompted further research in alternative materials and processes. In fact, LD Miles, another top executive of the company, was directed by him to go into the details of this substitution, which was later called Value Analysis. By 1949, this approach was used in a more institutionalised form at General Electric and gradually in the US Department of Defence. By 1970, the concept of Value Engineering gradually received international attention.

Value Engineering is the organised creative technique to analyse functions of a product, service or a system to achieve the required functions at the lowest cost ensuring its performance, reliability and maintainability. This is also known as Value Analysis or Value Management.

Value is literally the worth of an article/product/service. It is determined in terms of cost and function. The value of a product can be improved by (i) improving function (keeping cost constant) (ii) reducing cost (keeping function constant) (iii) by improving function as well as by reducing cost. There are different types of value for an industrial product. They are classified as:

Use value: It refers to the properties and qualities which are useful and which enable the accomplishment of the given work. Use value may be either for primary use, secondary use or for auxiliary use.

Esteem value: It refers to the aesthetic features or properties which attract a customer to own it.
Cost value: It refers to the cost required to produce the item.
Exchange value: It refers to the properties which enable the owner to exchange it for anything else, if he so desires, in future.

However, for all practical purposes, industrial situations are primarily concerned with the first two features only.

From the above discussion, value analysis can be defined as a 'method of search, a systematic procedure resulting in the orderly utilisation of alternative materials and processes. It focuses engineering, manufacturing and purchasing with attention on one objective—that of obtaining equivalent or even better performance for lower cost'.

Steps in value analysis

Following are the steps to be followed in value analysis:

1. Collection of full facts and information about the product
2. Get the details of the cost break-up
3. Determine the function
4. Think creatively
5. Compare and evaluate the alternatives

To succeed in each step, it is necessary to take the following line of action:

- Eliminate the redundant parts
- Initiate action of cheaper substitutes without impairing the use value
- Standardise the parts
- Develop alternative methods
- Re-design, if necessary

Advantages

Value analysis has the following benefits:

- Lowering of cost through increased efficiency
- Optimum resource utilisation
- Improved methods of production
- Better quality of product leading to greater customer satisfaction
- Increased job satisfaction and motivation in workers as well as high level of morale and team spirit

Value analysis has now been replaced by the term Value Engineering in corporate circles, and most organizations follow these practices by forming a Value Engineering team of workers (a small group like Quality Circles). This provides opportunity to workers to derive creative satisfaction and also to fulfil their intrinsic needs. At the same time, organizations also get active services from the workers.

Problem on Time Study

Time study is a work measurement technique that is widely used in industry to decide standard time and then to compare the time taken by the workmen. Though it basically helps in pricing a job, it is also used for other purposes like deciding on training requirements, payment of incentives and rewards etc.

Set the standard time for manufacturing ball point pens based on the following activity details. You have observed the ongoing job for 100 hours and have seen that within this period 1,000 pens have been manufactured. Assume that during work, workmen get personal time allowance @ 10%. Compute the standard time for manufacturing a pen.

Activity	Rate (%)	Number of times jobs observed (hours)
A	120	200
B	90	300
C	80	500
D	70	100
	Idle time	200
	Total observed time	1,300

Solution

To solve this problem, at the outset, it is necessary to compute the average cycle time, dividing the observed period by the number of pens produced, i.e., 100 hours/1,000 pens = 1/10th of an hour, i.e., 6 minutes.

Thus, on an average 6 minutes is the time taken for manufacturing a pen.

Now, we have to compute activity-wise distribution of time using this formula:

Average cycle time × (Observed time/Total time) × Rating

Average cycle time is 6 minutes.

Observed time is the activity-specific time available from the table.

Total time is the total observed time. Rating is the perceived rate of efficiency of the observer given in the problem.

i. Time taken for activity A
   6 × (200/1,300) × (120/10) = 1.1 hours
ii. Time taken for activity B
   6 × (300/1,300) × (90/100) = 1.2 hours
iii. Time Taken for activity C
   6 × (500/1,300) × (80/100) = 1.8 hours
iv. Time Taken for activity D
   6 × (100/1,300) × (70/100) = 0.3 hours

Total normal time 4.4 hours

Now, we have to compute standard time using the formula:

Total Activity-wise time or Normal time/ (1 – Personal fraction time)

4.4/(1 – 0.1) = 4.89 hours approximately

Key Points

- Work study is defined as the procedure for understanding and determining the work done by the people and its relationship with plant and machinery.
- Work study helps us to identify the factors that affect efficiency and in achieving economy through optimum utilisation.
- Most techniques for improving productivity involve major capital expenditure in plant or equipment, whereas work study, being a management technique, ensures greater productivity by using the existing resources.
- The human element is emphasised in work study and importance is given to operation rather than the technical process.
- Like work study, method study also helps in enhancing productivity.

Important Terms

Human engineering: It is a part of method study that seeks to determine the most efficient combination of workers, machines and the working environment. It aims to solve the man–machine problems in design, operation and maintenance of plant and machinery.

Method study: It helps to improve productivity. Method study helps to produce the same output using fewer resources or produce more with proportionately lesser inputs.

Motion economy: It refers to the process of minimising the physical and perceptual loads imposed on people engaged in any type of work. The application of the principles of motion economy eliminates or minimises wasteful and tiring movements and increases the productivity of workers.

Value engineering: It is the organised creative technique to analyse functions of a product, service or a system to achieve the required functions at the lowest cost ensuring its performance, reliability and maintainability. It is also known as value analysis or value management.

Self-assessment Questions

1. Define work study. What are its important objectives?
2. Why do trade unions react to work study programs? How can you combat such adverse reactions?
3. List the important objectives achieved by method study. Identify and discuss at least five areas of contribution in detail.
4. Discuss in detail the steps involved in a method study program.
5. Define work measurement. What are the different techniques included in work measurement? Elaborate on at least three of them.
6. What are the steps involved in a time study program? How does it help the work measurement program in an industrial unit?
7. What is ergonomics? How does it help in increasing productivity? Discuss with examples.
8. What are the basic principles of motion economy? Discuss these principles in relation to a work area with which you are familiar.

9. Explain how human engineering techniques influence the design of machines. Select an advertisement of a furniture item and discuss its ergonomic features.
10. What are the steps involved in value analysis? Suggest the steps in a study of value analysis and discuss each step in detail.
11. Write a critical note on time and motion study.
12. Write short notes on the following:
    i. Ergonomics and machine design
    ii. Esteem value
    iii. Human engineering
    iv. Classes of movements
    v. Working areas

Select Bibliography

1. Bhattacharyya DK (2012). *Production and Operations Management*, Hyderabad: Universities Press.
2. Chase RB, RF Jacobs, NJ Aquilano and NK Agarwal (2009). *Operations Management for Competitive Advantage*, 11th edition. New Delhi: Tata McGraw-Hill.
3. Cohen MA (1997). *Manufacturing Automation*. Chicago: Irwin.
4. Konz S (1983). *Work Design: Industrial Ergonomics*, 2nd edition. New York: John Wiley and Sons.
5. Schmenner RW (1995). *Service Operations Management*. Englewood Cliffs NJ: Prentice Hall.

4 Behavioural Theories and Industrial Psychology

Learning Objectives

After reading this chapter you will be able to:

- **Appreciate how human relations relate to IP**
- **List the various behavioural and human relations schools of thought**
- **State the advantages and disadvantages of the behavioural school**
- **Outline Mckinsey's 7S framework**
- **Understand the various theories of managerial roles**
- **List the issues involved in the development of managerial skills**

Overview

Industrial psychology has been influenced by the different approaches starting from the classical school to the modern human relations perspective. We have discussed the scientific and administrative management theories in Chapter. In this chapter, we shall focus on human relations (neo-classical) and behavioural science approaches.

It was Hugo Münsterberg (1913) who first institutionalised the concept of industrial psychology through the analysis of the jobs in terms of workers' mental and emotional requirements. He developed various testing devices for the scientific process of selection, placement, testing and training and research. He had emphasised the use of psychology in the field of personnel testing, interview, attitude measurement, learning theory, training, monotony study, safety, job analysis and human engineering. He had introduced job analysis, based on the mental and emotional requirements of the job. His observations were subsequently confirmed by the Hawthorne study of Elton Mayo and his associates, which could establish that workers' productivity could be increased by the psychological stimulus, more specifically the feeling of importance. Although Hawthorne study was initially intended to examine the impact of the physical environment, such as brightness of lights, humidity etc, subsequently it moved to the study of various psychological constructs and their impact on the workers' productivity or performance. Such psychological constructs are breaks, group pressure, working hours, managerial leadership etc. Some of the findings of the Hawthorne experiments that vindicated the importance of psychological variables are: less relevance of workers' aptitude to work, influence of informal organization and work-group norms on productivity and the prevalence of social system in workplaces.

Many organizations reported benefits of the application of industrial and organizational psychology in the form of improved morale of the workers, improved industrial relations, reduced rate of absenteeism, employees' turnover etc. However, application of industrial psychology in workplaces often encounters problems like resistance to change and bottlenecks in communication.

Human Relations and Behavioural Theories

This school of management emphasises on the human element in an organization, duly recognising its importance. It stresses on individual attitudes and behaviours and on group processes. Major contributors to this school of thought are given in Table 4.1.

Mary Parker Follet: She is considered the pioneer of the behavioural approach to management. She recognised the significance of the human element and attributed greater importance to the functioning of the groups at workplaces. According to Follet, the critical role of managers should be to bring constructive change in the organization, following the principle of 'power with' rather than 'power over'. She stated that power should not be based on hierarchical level but should be collectively developed, fostering a cooperative concept, involving superiors and subordinates and finally working together as a team. Hence, there is a greater need for power sharing. Organizations need to become democratic to accommodate employees and managers. People work harder when the organization recognises individual's motivating desires.

Table 4.1 Contributors to the human relations school of management principles

Mary Parker Follet (1868–1933)	Group influences
Elton Mayo (1880–1949)	Effect of human motivation on productivity and output
Abraham Maslow (1808–1970)	Relationship between motivation and hierarchy of needs
Douglas McGregor (1906–1964)	Emphasis on human characteristics namely, Theory X and Theory Y and the corresponding style of leadership
Chris Argyris(1923–)	Human and Organizational development Model I and Model II (maturity and immaturity continuum)

Elton Mayo: He is considered as the father of the human relations approach. Mayo and his associates conducted the study at Western Electric's Hawthorne plant between 1927 and 1932 to evaluate the attitudes and psychological responses of workers 'on-the-job'. Their experiments were carried out in the following four phases: (i) Illumination experiments (ii) Relay assembly test room experiments (iii) Interview phase (iv) Bank wiring observation room experiment.

We shall look at these experiments in further detail.

Illumination experiments

These experiments were conducted between 1924 and 1927, at the Hawthorne plant of the Western Electric Company in the USA, involving the company's industrial engineers. The experiments involved manipulation of illumination for one group of workers (test group) and comparing their performance and productivity with another group, for whom illumination was not manipulated (control group). In the first spell of experiment, for the test group, performance and productivity improved. However, it did not last very long. In fact, the control group's performance also rose with the alteration of lighting conditions of the test group. With such contradictory results, researchers concluded that the productivity of workers is not related to the intensity of illumination. There must have been something else besides illumination that could have influenced the performance of the workers of Western Electric Company. Elton Mayo and his associates from Harvard University, therefore, decided to move to the next phase of experiments.

Relay assembly test room experiments

These experiments were conducted under the guidance of Elton Mayo between 1927 and 1933. At this stage also the researchers were concerned about other working conditions like working hours, refreshments, ambient temperature etc. To start with, the researchers selected six women employees of the relay assembly test room. Their jobs were to assemble relays (a small electrical device) using 35 spare parts. Selected women employees (sample group) were put in a separate room and briefed about the experiments. In the test room, a number of variables were altered, like increased wages and rest period, shortened workday and workweek etc. In addition, the sample workers were also give the freedom to leave their workstation without permission and were also given special attention. Productivity increased over the study period. Such results, therefore, led the researchers to believe that better treatment of subordinates made them more productive. They highlighted the significance of social relations. Finally, researchers were convinced that workers would perform better if the management looked after their welfare and supervisors paid special attention to them. This finding was later labelled as the **Hawthorne effect**.

Interview phase

In this phase of experiments, about 21,000 people were interviewed over the three years between 1928 and 1930. The purpose of the interview was to explore in depth attitudes of the workers. Results of the interview were as under:

- A complaint may not necessarily have an objective recital of facts. It could also reflect personal disturbance, which may be traced to some deep-rooted cause.
- All objects, persons and events carry some social meaning. They relate to employees' satisfaction or dissatisfaction.
- The personal conditions of the workers can be configured to their relationships, involving sentiments, desires and interests. Such relational variables when related to workers' own past and present interpersonal relations result in their personal situation.
- Workers assign meaning to their status in the organization and give value to the events, objects, their specific feature of environment (like hours of work, wages etc).
- Workers derive satisfaction or dissatisfaction from the social status of an organization. It means they also look for social rewards by associating with an organization.
- Social demands of workers are influenced by experiences in groups, both inside and outside the workplace.

Bank wiring observation room experiment

This part of the Hawthorne experiment was conducted to test some of the ideas developed during the interview phase. It was conducted in 1931–32. In this experiment, there were 14 participants (samples), including wiremen, solder men and inspectors. At this phase of the experiment there was no change in the physical working conditions. Sample workers were paid based on an incentive pay plan, relating their pay to their output. Sample workers had the opportunity to earn more by increasing the output. However, researchers observed that the output was constant at a certain level. Analysis of the results showed that the group encouraged neither too much nor too little work. Workers, on their own, enforce 'a fair day's work'. Group norms, therefore, are more important to workers than money. The study, thus, provided some insights into informal social relations within groups.

The Hawthorne experiments, therefore, focused on the importance of human relations and thus contributed immensely to management theory.

Criticisms of the experiments

Despite the brilliant contributions to the theories of management, it was criticised on the following grounds:

- It was felt that procedures and analysis of the findings and conclusions drawn thereon have little relevance. In fact, conclusions were not supported by adequate evidence.

- The relationship between satisfaction and happiness of workers with productivity were established with simplistic assumptions, while in reality, the situation is more complex due to behavioural phenomena.
- Further all these studies failed to focus on the attitudes of workers, as attitudes play a crucial role in influencing performance and productivity of workers.

In the behavioural school, other contributors like Abraham Maslow, Douglas McGregor and Chris Argyris have also made significant contributions. Maslow and McGregor's contributions are covered in Chapter 5. While Maslow focused on the importance of human needs, which are the major driving force for human motivation, McGregor had made certain assumptions about people, categorising them under theory X and theory Y. Theory X essentially represents a negative view about people, i.e., people are lazy by nature, have little ambition, dislike work, avoid responsibility and require direction to work. Theory Y, on the contrary, assumes people are more positive, capable of self-control, innovative and creative and do not inherently dislike work.

Chris Argyris' contributions to the behavioural school include maturity–immaturity theory, integration of individual and organizational goals and Model I and Model II patterns. According to maturity–immaturity theory, people progress from a stage of immaturity and dependence to a state of maturity and independence. If organizations keep their employees in a dependent state, they allow them to remain immature and thereby prevent them from achieving their potential. Further, he had also contended that a formal organization develops a rigid structure, compelling people to behave in an immature way. This leads to incongruence between the individual and organizational goals, hinders organizational development, results in failure and fosters frustration and conflict. People, therefore, show their aggression, regression and suppression. Model I and Model II patterns are two different assumptions. Workers in Model I type of organization are motivated by the desire to manipulate others and protect themselves from others. Workers in Model II type of organization are less manipulative and more willing to learn and take risks. Argyris, therefore, suggested that managers should always try to create a Model II type of organization.

Rensis Likert (1903–1972) and Peter F Drucker have also contributed significantly to this school of thought. Likert attributed low productivity and poor morale of employees to typical job-centred supervision techniques. He has suggested some typical leadership styles to ensure better productivity and improved morale of workers (see Chapter 8). Peter F Drucker, on the other hand, pioneered several modern management concepts in the fields of innovation, creativity, problem-solving, organization design, MBO etc.

Modern Approaches to Management Theory

Some modern approaches also played a significant role in the evolution of management theories, and have influenced the development of the principles of industrial psychology. Such approaches are: the quantitative method, the systems and contingency theories.

Quantitative approach

It emerged during World War II. During the war, managers, government officials and scientists were brought together to help the army to effectively utilise its resources. These experts used mathematical approaches to the concepts advocated by Taylor and Gantt to solve many logistical problems in the war. Such techniques, subsequent to the war were applied by many organizations to solve their business problems. This school of thought extensively relies on statistics, optimisation models, information models and computer simulations for decision-making in business. The different branches of this approach are: (i) Management science, (ii) Operations management and (iii) Management Information Systems (MIS). Modern industrial psychology makes extensive use of various quantitative techniques for proper interpretation of behavioural attributes of people and its impact at the workplaces.

Management science approach: It visualises management as a logical entity, expressing it in terms of mathematical symbols, relationships and data. This approach is also known as operations research approach. In areas like capital budgeting and cash flow management, production scheduling, development of product strategies, human resource planning, inventory management etc, such approach is used. Various mathematical tools like, queuing theory, linear programming, program evaluation and review technique (PERT), critical path method (CPM), decision theory, simulation, replacement, probability theory and sampling, time series analysis, index numbers etc are used to minimise the error in management decisions. In modern management education programs, all these techniques are taught to develop managerial skills. Obviously, it also helps extensively to solve issues in industrial psychology.

Operations management approach: It is primarily concerned with production management and its related areas. In fact, it is difficult to draw a line between management science and operations management. In operations management also, we use most of the mathematical tools mentioned earlier. Moreover, such an approach also helps in decision-making in other functional areas like finance, marketing, human resource management and so on.

Management information systems approach: It focuses on designing and implementing computer-based information systems for use by the management. It converts raw data into information inputs, which are subsequently used by management for decision-making. Now-a-days, Management Information Systems help in enterprise-wide decision-making, integrating all the functions of management. Enterprise-wide Decision Support Systems like Human Resource Information Systems is an important example, which is used for any critical or strategically important decisions, as it provides valuable information inputs.

Systems theory approach

This approach considers the organization as a whole because of the interdependent nature of activities and the interaction with the external environmental factors. In this competitive scenario, any organization cannot function in isolation. It has to operate in open systems, interacting with the environment. Whether it is development of a new product or employee selection, the organization's decisions are interrelated and interdependent on the external environmental circumstances. Synergy is the phenomenon of open systems of management by which the total system is more than a simple sum of its parts. It means, if a manager effectively coordinates the efforts of related subsystems, the result would be greater than the sum of such independent efforts, i.e., two plus two would be greater than four. Entropy is a syndrome, by which systems and processes eventually decay. The systems approach to management is also important because it helps in avoiding entropy. By relating the organization to its environment, by following a systems approach, such a situation can be averted.

Contingency theory approach

This approach has also contributed significantly to the evolution of management thought. It discards the concept of universality in management principles and determines managerial decisions considering the situational factors. The task of a manager, as per this theory, is to identify which techniques will, in a given situation, under particular circumstances, at a specific point of time, best contribute to achieving organizational goals. The theory contends that organizational phenomena exist in a logical pattern, which managers can understand by gradually interpreting various situations. They can thereby frame their managerial styles, which vary from situation to situation.

Contingency theory and Systems theory together are classified as **Integrative school of management thought,** because these two theories integrate the classical, behavioural and quantitative theories into a framework that uses only the best of each approach in a given situation.

Contemporary Approaches in Management Thought

This school provides a framework of management practices, based on more recent trends like globalisation, theory Z concept, McKinsey's 7S approach, excellence models, productivity and quality issues and so on.

With the World Trade Organization (WTO) and the European Economic Community (EEC), we are now operating in a global economy. Our managers now require thinking globally even to operate in the domestic market. We are losing market share even in our

Table 4.2 Management styles under theory Z concept

Type A (American)	Type J (Japanese)	Type Z (Modified American)
Short-term employment	Lifetime employment	Long-term employment
Individual decision-making	Consensual decision-making	Consensual decision-making
Individual responsibility	Collective responsibility	Individual responsibility
Rapid evaluation and promotion	Slow evaluation and promotion	Slow evaluation and promotion
Explicit, formalised control	Implicit, informal control	Implicit, informal control with explicit, formalised measures
Specialised career path	Non-specialised career path	Moderately specialised career path
Segmented concern	Holistic concern	Holistic concern, including family

domestic market because of competition from foreign companies. Hence, understanding management with a global perspective has now become important.

Theory Z concept

This theory was pioneered by Ouchi and Jaeger (1978). It incorporates Japanese and American management culture and emphasises on the need to study and adopt appropriate management practices from other countries. Table 4.2 sets out the concept.

McKinsey's 7S framework

McKinsey identified seven independent organizational factors that need to be managed. These are as follows.

- **Strategy**—to determine allocation of scarce resources and commit the organization to a specific course of action
- **Structure**—to determine the number of levels (in hierarchy) and authority centres
- **Systems**— to determine organizational processes, procedures, reports and routines
- **Staff**—to determine key human resource groups in the organization and describe them demographically
- **Style**—to determine the manner in which managers should behave in achieving organisational goals

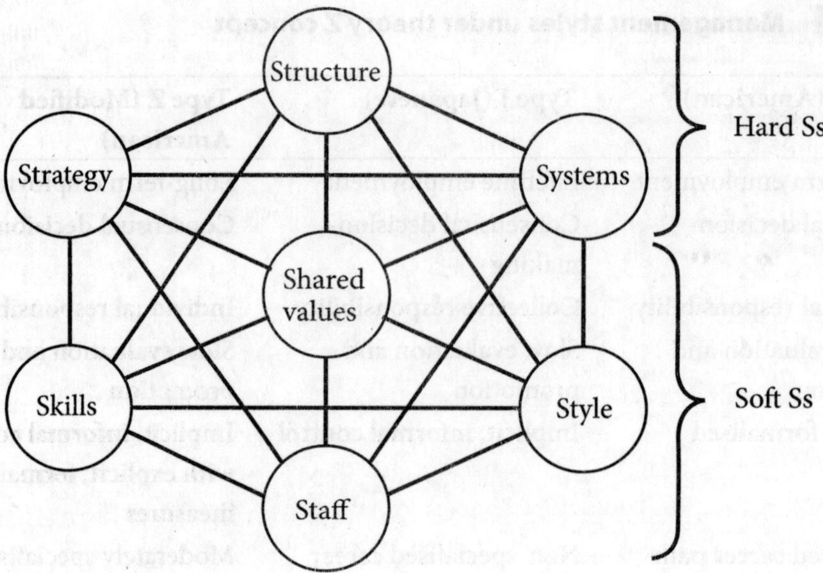

Fig. 4.1 Mckinsey's 7S framework

- **Superordinate goals**— also called shared vision, to determine the guiding principles that an organization has to instil in its members
- **Skill**—to determine the abilities of the people in the organization

The 7S framework suggests that any change in any S factor may result in an adjustment of other S factors. Now, however, the concept of 8S has been introduced, which adds one more S to McKinsey's 7S framework, i.e., **Streaming**. It includes those areas, which either indirectly or directly influence or shape the other Ss. them. Figure 4.1 illustrates the 7S framework.

Peters and Waterman (1982) in their pioneering work, *In search of Excellence* identified some common characteristics of excellent organizations. Such characteristics have now become important management principles.

- Bias for action—Excellent firms make things happen.
- Closeness to the customer—These firms know their customers and their needs.
- Autonomy and entrepreneurship—They value these in each employee.
- Productivity—They achieve this through people based on trust.
- Hands-on, value-driven management—They make it mandatory.
- Stick to the knitting—They always deal from strength.
- Simple form lean staff—They develop cost-effective work teams.
- Simultaneous loose–tight properties—They decentralise many decisions, while retaining tight control over certain others.

Global competition has also accentuated the need for enhancing quality and productivity. These two are the basic requirements to retain competitive advantage for any organization. Hence, management practices should focus on these by developing the human resources to sustain their competitive advantage.

Managerial Roles

A managerial role is a position-specific behavioural pattern of managers. Henry Mintzberg (1973), based on his study of five organizations, identified ten different roles of managers broadly classifying them into (i) interpersonal (ii) informational and (iii) decisional.

Interpersonal roles are classified into figurehead, leader and liaison roles. Informational roles are classified into monitor, disseminator and spokesperson roles. Decisional roles are classified into entrepreneur, disturbance handler, resource allocator and negotiator roles. In Table 4.3 these managerial roles are explained.

Table 4.3 Mintzberg's managerial roles

Role category	Role type	Nature of the role
Interpersonal	Figurehead	Representing the organization to perform ceremonial duties
	Leader	Influencing subordinates to achieve their goals and objectives
	Liaison	Maintaining horizontal chain of communication
Informational	Monitor	Collecting information concerning the organization and shortlisting relevant information
	Disseminator	Sharing relevant information with subordinates
	Spokesperson	Maintaining protocol to share information with outsiders
Decisional	Entrepreneur	Focusing on innovation and change within the organization
	Disturbance handler	Managing conflict situation by taking corrective action
	Resource allocator	Optimising resource allocation to different competing needs within the organization
	Negotiator	Representing the organization in all major negotiations

Managerial Skills and Competencies

Skills of the managers have now become an important factor at the organizational level to achieve global competitiveness. Obviously, imparting skills through training and development is yet not recognised as an important initiative due to the inability to quantify the benefits. Skill is defined as a coordinated series of actions that serves to attain some goal or accomplish a particular task. Operationally, skills are defined widely as overt responses and controlled stimulation. Overt responses may be verbal, motor or perceptual. Verbal response consists of speaking; motor response consists of movements of limbs and body parts while perceptual responses stress on understanding of sensory stimuli. Controlled stimulation, on the other hand, are energy inputs to the workers, which we express in units of frequency, length, time and weight. Technological change and skill requirements have been made a subject of investigation in a number of studies around the world. There is a general consensus that technological change alters the job but the observations differ in its nature and form.

The neo-classical economic theory advocated that technological changes require broader range and higher average level of skills in the workers. New forms of skill and responsibility along with technological change have been studied in continuous process industry and chemical manufacturing units, petroleum refining, metal working industries, banking operations and in many other industries, which used advanced mechanisation. Another school of thought advocates technology as being instrumental in fractionating and de-skilling of jobs. Redesigning of jobs subsequent to technological change separates the planning and holistic view of the job from its implementation or execution aspects. De-skilling and skill downgrading also occur due to differential growth of higher versus low skill occupations and industries.

The focal point of this hypothesis is that technology induces differential point of growth for different sectors of the economy and produces skill polarisation by eventual occupational shift to skilled jobs in some industries and unskilled jobs in many others. These phenomena are especially evident in India. From the 1981 census reports onward we find a major occupational shift of workers from primary to the secondary sectors and from secondary to tertiary sectors. Simultaneous structural change in occupational pattern is also evident, as the number of blue-collar workers has been drastically reduced while the number of white-collar workers has significantly increased. Another school of thought argues de-skilling is a secondary consequence of de-industrialisation, which again is prompted by technological change. The other approach, i.e., the mixed change or conditional position, is more a characterisation of the empirical evidence than a well-developed theory.

Transformations in skills due to technological change occur along two tracks.

- **Compositional shift**, involves structural change in the occupational pattern due to creation or elimination of jobs of a given skill level and the distribution of persons to different jobs in the economy.
- **Changes in work content** involve variations in the technical nature of work and the role relations surrounding work performance.

Internationally, careers of the future will require greater education (more in the form of institutionalised knowledge) at the entry level and will also demand continuing education to keep pace with technological dynamism. Greater level of technological literacy even for lower skill and low-paying occupations will be the trend in the coming years.

Tracing our own history, we find that the Indian social system had a definite orientation towards developing and maintaining different social groups. The quality elements in a particular craft and the necessary skill were the deciding factors for the purpose of ranking that craft in the order of importance. There was a time when carpenters, goldsmiths and weavers were the craftsman-groups in India that enjoyed the highest status. However, it is pertinent to mention that in the Indian system greater importance was attached to values than to formal occupational skills.

From the above perspective, we can therefore, categorise skills either as generic or technical, entry level or advanced. Conventionally, skill can be defined as the knowledge or attributes deemed vital to organizational success. There are four general types of skills:

- **Technical**—relates to concepts, methods and tools specific to an organization
- **Supervisory**—enables one to effectively supervise
- **Interpersonal**—enables people to communicate and interact effectively
- **General business**—indicates lines of business and support infrastructure

Technical skills are demonstrable and testable. Others are 'soft' skill types, more subjective and difficult to quantify. Any organization seeking skill renewal or skill-change, needs to undertake the following tasks :

(i) Profile the skills required by jobs
(ii) Assess the skill levels acquired by individuals and
(iii) Conduct a gap analysis between the required and acquired skill.

Training should ideally occur before the skill is needed so that daily work can reinforce training.

Skills inventory

A skills inventory is a device for pinpointing information about individuals and their suitability for different jobs. Such an inventory includes the name of the employee and a listing (or 'inventory') of job-related skills, training, and/or experience which could prove useful in future assignments. The purpose of skills inventories is to provide the organization with quick, accurate information on all employees in order that management can choose the best qualified person for promotion or transfer. For example, a skills inventory may consist of the following information: age, address, health, education, willingness to travel, experience in past and present jobs and foreign languages spoken. If an assignment requiring knowledge of German is available or if the assigned person is not able to take it up, the skills inventory could quickly identify those candidates who possess the needed qualifications to be the replacement.

Multiskilling

Multiskilling is defined as the process to train employees in specific skills that cross the traditional trade-specific or craft-specific skill sets. Thus, to develop multiple skills, employees require additional training to enable them to perform more jobs within the same job family or to do the entire jobs from a holistic point of view. Multiskilling is often misconstrued to succeed downsizing. But downsizing occurs for skill obsolescence, among other reasons, while multiskilling is for holistic development of human potential to effectively address the requirements of changing production process (more flexible and customised), organizational systems (decentralised control) and state-of-the-art technology (Numeric Control, Computer Numeric Control, Direct Numeric Control etc).

Competencies

Competencies consist of behaviours, which encompass skills, knowledge, abilities and attributes. Competencies need to be assessed both at the organizational and individual levels. Individual competencies together reinforce organizational competencies. However, there always exists a possibility of major incongruence between the two. Manpower planning exercise helps us to analyse such gaps and develop a competency model. Such a model is a map to display a set of competencies. It is future-oriented and helps to describe an ideal workforce. Such a model developed and documented helps in managerial decision-making as it is well aligned with the vision, mission, objectives, goals and strategies of an organization. It also helps employees of an organization to understand the functional requirements and initiate the enrichment of their skills, knowledge, abilities and attributes. This would be independent of the organization-wide competency enrichment exercise.

Competency mapping: This is always done in the defined job context following a set of approaches as listed below:

- Workforce Skills Analysis
- Job Analysis
- Supply and Demand Analysis
- Gap Analysis
- Situation Analysis

Skill analysis: It helps to describe skills required to carry out a given function. However, this is a dynamic approach, as it also considers the nature of changes in the work processes in an organization.

Job analysis: It focuses on tasks, responsibilities, knowledge and skill requirements, which are required for successful job performance. Both the above analyses are done from inputs collected from survey (through questionnaire), interviews with managers and employees and benchmarking information with successful organizations. For technology-intensive and machine-enabled jobs, skill sets required and cycle-time for jobs (as printed in the literature) also contribute as critical input information.

Supply analysis: This is done considering the demographic features of the workforce (in terms of occupations, grades, structure, race, origin, gender, age, service experience, education, training, health status, retirement time and so on), trends and competencies of the current workforce. It, therefore, helps to understand the level of the existing workforce.

Demand analysis: It helps to identify the workforce of the future in line with the vision, mission, objectives, goals and strategies of an organization. Critical inputs from demand analysis contribute to the development of the competency model for workforce of the future.

Gap analysis: With the above input reinforcers, the organization undertakes gap analysis to understand the differences between the workforce of today and the workforce of the future. After such identification of differences, it needs to plan to address those.

Solution analysis: It helps to address the gaps taking into account both ongoing and planned changes in the workforce. It also weighs different options to get the work done, either through recruitment or contracting. New recruitment, restructuring, training and retraining, redeployment and rightsizing are done, in the light of the new competency model, in this phase.

After suitable competency mapping, the next course of action for an organization, however, is to decide whether to downsize/rightsize or to go for training, retraining and redeployment.

Management by Objectives (MBO)

Peter F Drucker (1954) emphasised on the organizational need for setting objectives to make performance more measurable. When objectives are set in a systematic manner, consciously directed towards effective and efficient achievement of organizational and individual targets, we call it MBO. It was General Electric Company, which used the elements of MBO during reorganisation, introducing decentralised decision-making. For most of the organizations, MBO is required for performance appraisal, as it calls for active involvement of subordinates in setting the objective standards, which require a heightened degree of commitment from them to achieve the results. Likewise, MBO also acts as a motivating factor for the employees, because they can understand their specific objectives and can assess on their own the degree of their achievement. Thus, MBO helps in managing an organization with clarity, encourages personal commitment and develops effective controls. It, in fact paved the way for participative management, involving people in framing objectives, aligning their individual goals with the organizational goals, or vice versa.

Key Points

- Following the Industrial Revolution, various theories of management evolved. These were developed in phases and have their importance in specific areas, keeping pace with the times. For industrial psychology, the theories are considered as contributing forces for subsequent development.
- While the earlier theories gave a foundation for the principles, the current business scenario demands the use of the systems approach and contingency approach to management.
- Theoretical principles are necessary to strengthen our understanding of industrial psychology, as they provide the framework to design the various practices and theories, with specific focus on structure- and people-related issues.
- Competency mapping requires identification of the gaps between available and required set of competencies of employees due to changing technology and the work or business process. To meet this gap, we develop competencies.

Important Terms

Management science: It views management as a logical entity, expressing relationships and data for measurement through mathematical symbols.
Modern approach: It is a combination of the classical and neo-classical approaches and suggests quantitative method, systems and contingency theories for solving management problems.
Multiskilling: It is defined as the process to train employees in specific skills that cross the traditional trade-specific or craft-specific skill sets.
Neo-classical approach: This approach emphasises behavioural aspects. Hence, it is called the human relations approach.
Theory Z: It combines the Japanese and American approaches to develop a modification in management practices.

Self-assessment Questions

1. Briefly discuss the various behavioural schools of management thought.
2. Discuss the major findings of the human relations theory and examine how this theory contributes to industrial psychology.
3. Distinguish between neo-classical and classical approaches to management. What are their advantages and disadvantages?
4. What are the important characteristics of modern management thought? How are they different from earlier approaches?
5. Examine the importance of contingency approach and systems approach to management.
6. Explain the different types of experiments carried out by Elton Mayo.
7. Discuss the contributions of McKinsey and Peter and Waterman in the development of modern management thought.
8. Explain the concept of neo-classical theory of organization.
9. Distinguish between the human relations and scientific management schools of thought.

10. Critically evaluate the human relations approach to management.
11. Write short notes on the following:
    i. Hawthorne experiments
    ii. Situational approach
    iii. Contemporary school of management thought
    iv. McKinsey's 7S framework
    v. Theory Z

Select Bibliography

1. Argyris C (1964). *Integrating the Individual and the Organization*. New York:Wiley.
2. Beehr TA (1996). *Basic Organizational Psychology*. Massachusetts: Allyn and Bacon.
3. Dale E (1965). *Management Theory and Practice*. New York: McGraw-Hill.
4. Drucker P (1954). *The Practice of Management*. New York: Harper and Brothers.
5. Koontz H (1961). The management theory jungle, *Acad of Man J*, 4 (3): 174–88.
6. Landy FJ and DA Trumbo (1976). *Psychology of Work Behaviour*. Homewood, IL: The Dorsey Press.
7. Locke EA (1976). The nature and causes of job satisfaction, *In* MD Dunnette (ed), *Handbook of Industrial and Organizational Psychology*. Chicago: Rand McNally.
8. Massie JL (1987). *Essentials of Management*. New Delhi: Prentice Hall.
9. McClelland DC (1973). Testing for competence rather than intelligence, *American Psychologist*, 28 (1): 1–14.
10. Ouchi WG and AM Jaeger (1978). Type Z organization: Stability in the midst of mobility, *Acad of Man Rev* (April): 305–14.
11. Peters IJ and RH Waterman (1982). *In Search of Excellence: Lessons from America's Best Run Companies*. New York: Harper and Row.

5 Motivation and Job Satisfaction

Learning Objectives

After reading this chapter, you will be able to:

- **Understand and define motivation**
- **Appreciate the theories of motivation**
- **Discuss the role of industrial psychologists in improving motivation**
- **Link motivation with morale and Job satisfaction**

Overview

Industrial psychologists can enable the efforts in creating a motivating and satisfying work environment. Applying psychometric tools, they can assess the motivating factors for the employees, and accordingly suggest appropriate motivational tools for the organizations. Similarly, they can help in identifying the factors for job satisfaction. In this chapter, we shall first outline the different theories of motivation and then discuss the link between the job satisfaction.

Motivation means the desire or willingness to work; by motivating workers managers can get work done in the desirable manner. It can also be considered as a force that gives rise to or influences behaviour to achieve favourable results. It is a feeling or urge to do or not to do a thing to fulfill certain needs. It is distinctly different from the capacity to work. Various management gurus like Taylor, Mayo, Follet, Fayol, Maslow, McGregor, Herzberg, Argyris, McClelland and others have contributed to the theories of motivation. Here, however, our principal concern is to consider psychological and behavioural aspects of motivation, as industrial psychologists play a crucial role in these areas.

Motivation

Motivation is a force because of which a person shows a certain type of activity to reach the desired goals. Employees chose their preferred outcomes, and accordingly direct their behaviour to achieve the same through their work. Motivation is different from motives. Motives are learned influences on our behaviour, which guide our behaviour to pursue the particular goals. Motivation, on the other hand, is the degree of our wants that drives us to engage in certain behaviours. Therefore, individual behaviour is at the heart of human motivation. Individual behaviour being the reflection of motivation at the workplace, we can understand the underlying motivation of employees by analysing their behaviour.

For individuals: Analysis of motivation based on individual behaviour is important for the following reasons:

- Individual employees pursue certain set of needs and goals.
- Individual employees behave in a way to satisfy their needs and fulfill their goals.
- The behaviour of individual employees can be vastly different.
- Organizations can meet such needs of individual employees through work that fulfills their needs and goals.
- Individual employees feel motivated to satisfy such needs.

For organizations: Motivation is important for organizations for the following reasons:

- Motivated employees perform better and help organizations to increase productivity.
- Motivated employees perform better quality work, reducing wastage and optimising the resources.
- Motivated employees are more agile; hence, they perform the task quickly.
- Motivated employees provide more feedback and suggestions, which can improve the way the organization functions.
- Motivated employees show a sense of ownership, attend to customer problems, resolve the same quickly and in the process contribute to customers' satisfaction.
- Motivated employees work to the highest level of their abilities.

Objectives of Motivation

We have already mentioned that motivation enhances performance and improves productivity. An organization achieves success because of its motivated workforce. Some of the objectives of motivation may be listed as under:

- Productive use of physical, financial and human resources
- Increased efficiency of employees
- Increased quality consciousness among employees
- Promotes goal-directed behaviour of employees
- Promotes a friendly work culture
- Ensures organizational stability

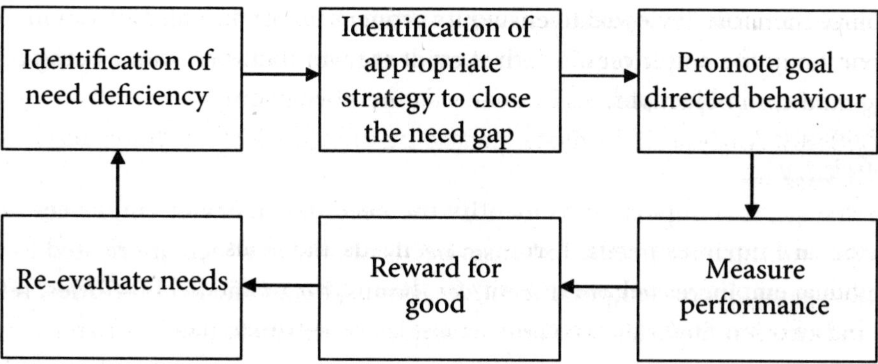

Fig. 5.1 A simple model of motivation

Elements of motivation

Perceptions of employees around the world with respect to motivation are changing in response to a number of key variables. The conventional motivational reinforcers, either extrinsic or intrinsic are gradually losing importance. What exactly can motivate an individual varies with time and space. In India also, it is not at all possible to identify and indicate one single motivational tool commonly applicable to a cross-section of employees. But we can estimate the relative importance of one or the other tool for a particular segment of employees belonging to some homogeneous organizations. Figure 5.1 shows a model of motivation.

Let us discuss some motivational elements in detail, supported by leading theoretical and empirical works.

Process of Motivation

Motivational factors are the perceived needs of the employees, which when satisfied contribute to performance and productivity. But motivation, per se, can be better defined as a process of making choices. According to Robbins and Judge, this process may be 'internal or external to the individual that can arouse enthusiasm and persistence to pursue a certain course of action'. The motivation process 'starts with a physiological or psychological deficiency or need that activates behaviour or a drive that is aimed at a goal or incentive'. All the definitions, therefore, authenticate that motivation is a behavioural mechanism, which develops when there is a perceived incongruence between the needs and expectations of the employees. With a widening of such a perceived gap, employees feel demotivated and reduce their level of performance and productivity. On the contrary, if the gap is reduced, employees feel motivated and contribute their best for achieving organizational objectives. The process of motivation follows certain defined steps, which need to be periodically reviewed to ensure its proper operation. This helps in maintaining the motivation of the employees, which is evident from their behaviour being congruent with organizational objectives.

Need deficiency

In the first stage, it is important to identify the need deficiency of employees. It centres on extrinsic and intrinsic needs. Extrinsic needs are those which are related to material and tangible gains. Increased pay, incentives, bonus, better medical facilities, retirement benefits and canteen facilities are some examples of extrinsic needs. Intrinsic needs, on the other hand, are abstract in nature and are related to contentment and satisfaction. Increased status, challenge, sense of belonging, scope for growth and creativity, recognition, sense of achievement etc, are examples of such needs. Identification of need deficiency is possible through direct observation of employees' behaviour and through a survey using structured questionnaire. But, employees by and large hesitate to answer a survey questionnaire, obviously fearing they will get identified for giving any response that criticises organizational policy. Confidentiality in survey responses can be ensured through a secret opinion poll without revealing the identity of the respondent-employees. However, for better results, it is always desirable to integrate survey findings with personal interview, which can be in the form of an open discussion with employees by their respective seniors. Some organizations try to document such information from 360° performance appraisal, incorporating certain items in the appraisal form itself. Presence of need deficiency can also be understood from the trend of employees' performance through a performance index or productivity index.

Closure of need deficiency

In the second phase of the motivational process, organizations try to identify the appropriate strategy to close the perceived need gap of employees. There are many innovative ways to close such a need gap without impairing the budget too much. For example, the need for 'increased pay' can be ensured by reducing the deferred benefits or non-wage labour costs (NWLC) and including such reduced amount to the current pay of the employees. NWLC represents those costs which an organization incurs to meet future expenses for the employees. This is particularly important for those organizations that employ mostly young people in the exploratory age group (less than 35 years). Similarly, linking the pay to performance also facilitates creation of a proper compensation structure to reward and motivate good performers. Further, the gap in the intrinsic needs can be reduced, by adopting an enabling structure for the organization, which among others, fosters creativity and growth.

Theories of Motivation

The evolution of the theories of motivation closely parallels the movement from work motivation of the scientific management school to the behavioural approach of the contemporary thinkers. Work motivation, Maslow's need hierarchy model and Herzberg's theory are some of the important developments in the study of motivation. Figure 5.2 summarises the important theories of motivation.

Work motivation

Taylor believed that workers are inherently capable of doing hard work, but they can only exhibit the same when they get adequate pay and rewards (incentives), matching with their efforts.

Mayo and his associates, through a series of experiments, could establish that the link between work satisfaction and performance is not essentially economic. In fact, it also

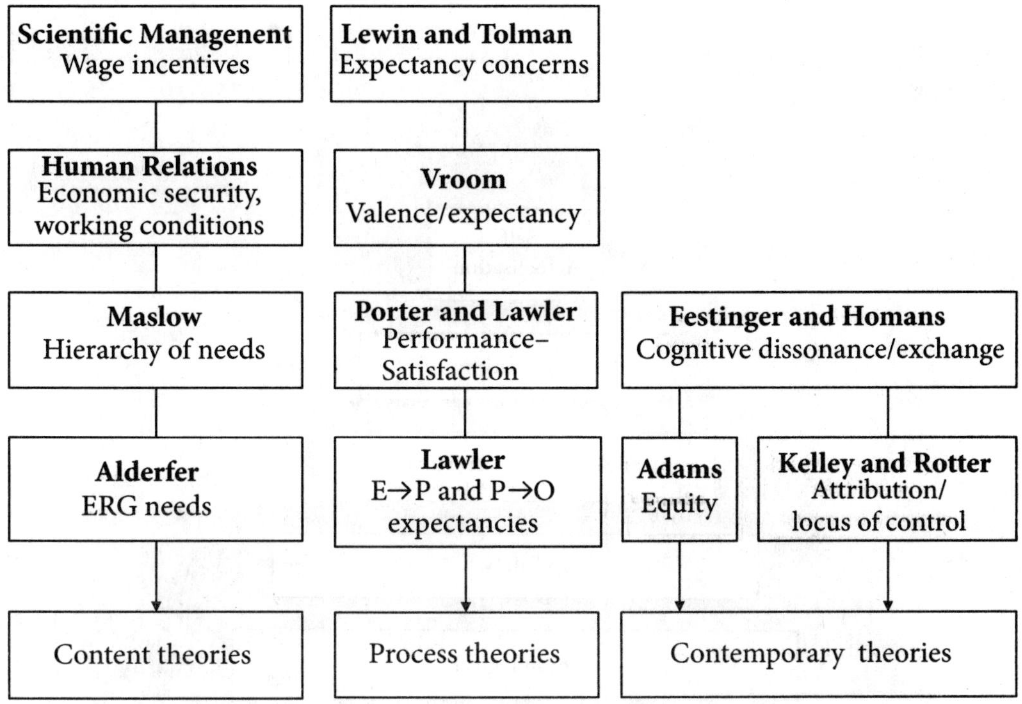

Fig. 5.2 Classification of theories of motivation

(***Source***: Luthans F (1998). *Organizational Behaviour*, 8th edition. Irving: McGraw-Hill.)

depends more on working conditions and attitudes, communication, positive management response and encouragement, working environment etc.

Abraham Maslow (1908–1970) put forth his need hierarchy theory to establish that our motivation arises from the levels of our hierarchy of needs. Maslow's theory has the following features:

- Our wants and desires influence our behaviour.
- We prioritise our needs. Hence, the perceived need factors differ from person to person.
- Only after the preceding need factors are satisfied, do we move forward to the next level of need hierarchy.
- We feel more motivated to work as we progress through the higher-order needs.

Maslow's need hierarchy theory considers needs belonging to five levels or orders as shown in Fig. 5.3.

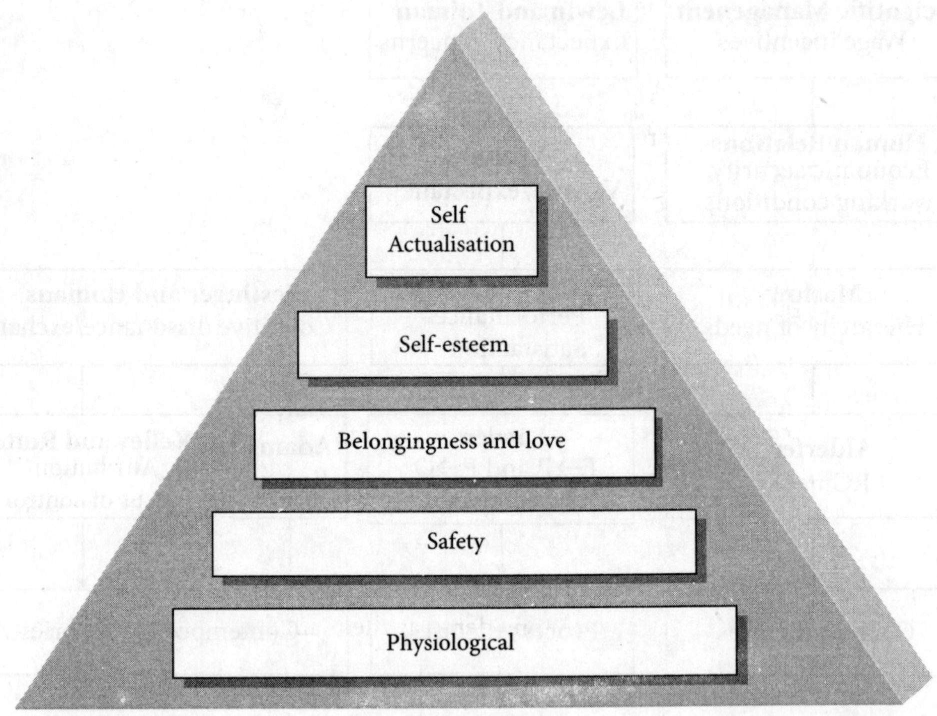

Fig. 5.3 Maslow's pyramid of need hierarchy

Maslow's need hierarchy theory

Physiological needs are our basic needs, which are essential for our survival. Such needs are food, water, air, clothing and shelter. From the organizational point of view, such needs are met through salary and basic working conditions.

Safety needs are those which ensure protection from economic and physical environment. Basically, they reduce our perceived uncertainty in the work environment. Job security, degree of continuity, order, structure and predictability are the nature of such needs.

With the satisfaction of physiological and safety needs, there arises the need for belongingness and love. These can be met by developing an appropriate work culture. When these needs are satisfied, they ensure a strong sense of affiliation amongst employees.

At the next level, employees look for satisfaction of their craving for self-esteem or the ego. Esteem needs indicate both self-respect and recognition by others. While we achieve self-respect by developing our competence, confidence and personal strength, respect from others emanates from prestige, recognition, status etc. Organizations need to carry out the following to fulfill such needs of employees:

- Provide challenging work assignments
- Feedback on performance
- Recognition of performance
- Participative work culture
- Empowerment
- Participation in decision-making

At the stage of self-actualisation needs, employees desire to become what they realise they are capable of. They would like to achieve their ambitions by using their talent, innovativeness and creativity. Organizations try to fulfill such needs of employees by nurturing an environment that fosters creativity and growth.

Evaluation of need hierarchy theory

The concept of needs helps managers to understand human behaviour at work. It also accounts for interpersonal variances in results at work. Another important aspect of this theory is its orientation towards motivation as a constantly changing force.

Criticisms: The following points are considered as the main drawbacks of the theory:

- The theory has no empirical support. Maslow did not even intend to relate his theory to work motivation. His theory was, in fact, popularised by others (like Douglas McGregor) as work motivation theory.

- Needs cannot be split into strictly defined levels. In fact, the hierarchy of needs is actually a misnomer. Employees who are motivated by self-actualisation need may still have lower-order needs like food and shelter.
- The theory is not universal in the sense of being adaptable to different cultures. It is more laden with western values. To illustrate, perception of work is different across cultures. Hence, motivation to work also varies between countries and sometimes between work groups in the same country. Therefore, the theory cannot hold good for heterogeneous workgroups.
- Maslow's existential philosophy is questioned, as people may reach a content plateau with the satisfaction of their lower-order needs. They may not like to move further up in the hierarchy.
- Diagnosing need deficiency for employees, following Maslow's approach is time-consuming. Even after such diagnosis, it may not help an organization to develop a tailor-made model for motivating the employees.

Herzberg's motivation hygiene theory

Frederick Herzberg (1959), extending the work of Maslow, developed the content theory of motivation. He drew responses of 200 accountants and engineers, drawn from 11 industries in the Pittsburgh area in USA. Using critical incident methods, he had asked the samples to respond to two aspects as given below:

- When did they feel particularly good about their job?
- When did they feel exceptionally bad about their job?

Herzberg found that the samples described different types of conditions for good and bad feelings. Factors responsible for promoting job satisfaction or otherwise were quite different. Their reported good feelings were found to be associated with job experiences and job content. The reported bad feelings were found to be associated with the peripheral aspects of the job, i.e., job context. Since his study was based on a two-factor hypothesis, we call his theory two-factor theory. As his study established that opposite of satisfaction is not dissatisfaction and removing dissatisfying elements from a job does not necessarily make the job satisfying, he has classified the factors into two categories: (i) Motivation factors (ii) Hygiene or maintenance factors. When these factors are present in a job, a motivating environment develops, but their absence does not necessarily cause dissatisfaction. According to Herzberg, there are six motivation factors as given below.

- Recognition
- Advancement
- Responsibility

- Achievement
- Possibility of growth
- Job content

According to Herzberg, there are ten hygiene or maintenance factors as listed below:

- Company policy and administration
- Technical supervision
- Interpersonal relations with subordinates
- Salary
- Job security
- Personal or family life
- Working conditions
- Status
- Interpersonal relations with supervisors
- Interpersonal relations with peers

These are the context factors. Their existence just creates an environment for doing work. But factors on their own cannot motivate people to work. In Herzberg words, their absence can dissatisfy people but their presence, per se, cannot bring satisfaction.

The crux of the two-factor theory of motivation, therefore, is that managers should cater to both satisfiers and dissatisfiers. Mere improvement of hygiene factors cannot guarantee a motivating environment.

Evaluation of Herzberg's theory

Herzberg's theory was the first of its kind based on field research. While Maslow's work was based on clinical observations (laboratory-based findings), he did his study in the work environment. Secondly, his study recommends actions for managers to improve motivation in the work environment. His emphasis on content factors shifted our focus from traditional money motivators concept, which were earlier viewed as the most potent factors for work motivation. He has also contributed to an alternative approach to motivation by job enrichment. Finally, he introduced depth or the second dimension to the needs, instead of the linear approach of Maslow.

Criticisms: Despite all the above listed merits, Herzberg's theory has also been subjected to following criticisms:

- The theory seems to suggest that as long as things go well people tend to take credit for themselves while they attribute failures to the external environment. This is a rather simplistic argument and may not be true in all cases.

- Herzberg's theory is bound by method. Using other methods, we do not get similar results. Critical incidents method, by nature, may cause people only to recall the recent incidents or experiences. But, experiences are always subject to change. More-over, while narrating a critical incident, respondents get wide flexibility to give vent to their opinions rather than the realities. Thus, survey findings could become laden with opinion.
- His model talks more about job satisfaction than on-the-job motivation.
- The theory ignores situational variables, as it is not backed by adequate research in different work environment.
- Even though the theory assumes a relationship between job satisfaction and productivity, the methodology applied by Herzberg limits its focus only on job satisfaction and not on productivity.

Comparison of Maslow and Herzberg models

Herzberg's framework is compatible with Maslow's hierarchy of needs. Maslow referred to the needs or motives, while Herzberg dealt with goals or incentives which tend to satisfy those needs. To illustrate, hygiene or maintenance factors of Herzberg are compatible with the physiological, safety and belongingness needs, while motivation factors tend to correspond to self-esteem and self-actualization needs. It is for this we often call Herzberg's theory as an extension of Maslow's. Despite similarities, we find some major differences between the two theories. Maslow's need hierarchy is a sequential arrangement of needs while Herzberg's model is not so. Maslow believed that any unsatisfied need, irrespective of its level of hierarchy could be a potential motivation. But, Herzberg believed that only higher-order needs served as motivators.

Richard Hackman and Greg Oldham (1975) developed a job characteristic model based on Herzberg's two-factor theory, showing how a good job design can lead to internal motivation of the employees and contribute to better job performance. The theory postulates that five job characteristics lead to three psychological states, which affect the motivation and satisfaction of the employees. Those five job characteristics are (i) Skill variety (ii) Task identity (iii) Task significance (iv) Autonomy and (v) Feedback.

Skill variety: It denotes the range or extent of skills, abilities and talents of the employees. The more they are able to utilise their skills in the job, the greater their level of satisfaction. Hence, jobs should be designed in such a way to ensure utilisation of the wide variety of skills of individuals.

Task identity: It signifies the extent of involvement of the employees in the total job. This enables an individual to identify himself in the total creation, which gives him a sense of pride and satisfaction.

Task significance: It denotes significance of a job on the life of others—both within and outside the organization. A positive significance of a job gives psychological satisfaction to the person who does it.
Autonomy: It is the extent of freedom given for a job. The degree of autonomy depends on the extent of independence given to an employee in deciding about job scheduling, formulating the procedures and decision-making without interference from others. With more job autonomy, job satisfaction increases and so also motivation.
Feedback: It refers to the opportunity to assess performance on the job and rectify the errors.

The three psychological states, which an individual can experience are as follows.

- Skill variety, task identity and task significance provide 'experienced meaningfulness'.
- Autonomy provides 'experienced responsibility'.
- Feedback ensures 'experienced knowledge of results'.

Once an employee experiences arousal of these three psychological states, they feel intrinsically rewarded, which leads to intrinsic motivation.

Hackman and Oldham developed a Motivating Potential Score (MPS), based on their study, which measures the motivation propensity of a job. The formula is presented below:

$$\text{MPS} = \left(\frac{\text{skills variety} + \text{task identity} + \text{task significance}}{3}\right) \times \text{autonomy} \times \text{feedback}$$

Existence, Relatedness and Growth (ERG) theory

Clayton Alderfer (1972) of Yale University developed the ERG theory based on empirical research. He modified Maslow's five levels of needs into three levels and labelled them as needs for existence, relatedness and growth. It differs from Maslow's theory in the following ways:

- It considers only three need hierarchies.
- While need hierarchy theory postulates rigid progression from one level of needs to another, ERG theory assumes that more than one need may be operative simultaneously. This means an employee working on growth need, may even remain dissatisfied in relatedness and existence needs.
- Basic postulates of ERG theory are that it works on the Frustration–Regression model. If for any reason, employees continually become frustrated to satisfy their needs at one level, they intensify their desire to satisfy needs at a lower level. It is like a failure to get recognition is compensated by the desire to make more money. But Maslow suggests that people will stay at a certain need level until it is satisfied.

Evaluation of ERG theory

It is pragmatic in its approach, as it considers individual differences among people. Individual differences in terms of education, family background and culture can alter the motive strength vis-à-vis perceived need factors. The theory is more appealing, intuitive and logical than Maslow's theory. Despite such advantages, the theory does not offer any clear-cut guidelines. It just indicates people will be motivated to behave in a particular way to satisfy one of the three sets of needs, i.e., need for existence, need for relatedness and need for growth. Moreover, the theory is yet to be backed by adequate research.

McClelland's achievement motivation theory

David C McClelland (1976), through his 20 years study at Harvard University, documented differences in the needs of people in three important areas as under:

Achievement need (nAch): People in this need category drive to excel and achieve in relation to a set of standards. They like challenge and wish to succeed in a competitive environment. They willingly work hard and volunteer for work which stretches their ability fully. This category of people does not get motivated by money. They feel more motivated with a sense of accomplishment and achievement.

Affiliation Need (nAff): This need emerges from the desire for friendly and close interpersonal relationships. Obviously, they try to fulfill such needs with satisfying relationships with the organization, peer groups, work teams etc. Since people belonging to this need group try to identify themselves with the organization, they always prefer to foster a friendly work culture and try to meet their needs through friendly relations.

Power Need (nPow): People in this need group always try to get satisfaction by controlling others. This need emerges from the drive for superiority and obviously people in this need category look for leadership positions in the organization.

Evaluation of the theory

McClelland highlighted the importance of matching the individual to the job. People with high achievement need always prefer challenging assignments while people with low achievement need, prefer a job situation that ensures stability, security and predictability. Organizations by manipulating the achievement need can get the complex jobs accomplished by high achievers. However, McClelland's contention that a sense of achievement or associated motivation can, in fact, be taught to an adult is criticised by many thinkers. It has been rejected in the psychology literature. Further, his postulate that needs can be changed through education and training is contrary to the opinion of many psychologists that needs are permanently acquired. The Thematic Appreciation Test (TAT) used by McClelland is also subject to criticism as interpretation of responses using TAT could suffer from the researcher's bias.

McGregor's theory X and theory Y

Douglas McGregor (1990) of MIT defined organizations as psychological entities, and therefore can be characterized by their assumptions about what motivates people. The basic hypothesis is that managerial decisions and actions are based on certain assumptions about human nature and behaviour. McGregor proposed two distinct views and assumptions about human behaviour. People of the negative behaviour group were categorised by him under theory X and positive behaviour group people were categorised under theory Y. Theory X considered that, in general, employees disliked work, were lazy, avoided responsibility and should be coerced to get work done. Theory Y stated that employees liked work, used their creativity, accepted responsibility and could exercise self-direction. Motivational implications of McGregor's analysis, therefore, can be best analysed in the context of Maslow's need hierarchy theory. Theory X people could be motivated by satisfaction of lower-order needs while theory Y types could be motivated by satisfaction of higher-order needs. Differences in the attributes of theory X and theory Y individuals as observed by McGregor are presented in Table 5.1.

Table 5.1 Differences in theory X and theory Y attributes

Theory X	Theory Y
The average human being inherently dislikes work and will always try to avoid work.	People exercise self-direction and self-control in achieving objectives to which they have committed.
With such inherent human characteristics, people must be coerced, controlled, directed and threatened with punishment to get them to do the work.	Commitment to objectives is a function of reward associated with their achievement.
The average human being prefers to be directed, avoids responsibility, is less ambitious and likes security above all.	The average human being learns (under proper conditions) not only to accept but also seek responsibility.
For motivating this group of people, the organization has to enforce strict control and limit the motivational reinforcements only to those areas that fulfil their lower-order needs.	They have the capacity for imagination, intensity and creativity in the solution of organizational problems. These people can be motivated with the satisfaction of their higher-order needs.
The organization does not believe that the employees have sufficient potential.	Organizations are able to only partially utilise their potential.

Process Theory

Content theories of motivation emphasised on the importance of inner needs in motivation. On the contrary, cognitive models or process theories of motivation state that people take conscious decisions about their job behaviour. Therefore, to motivate, process theory suggests that organizations must understand how an individual takes decisions and the efforts he puts in the job. Expectancy theory, equity theory and performance satisfaction model are the important approaches to understand the cognitive or process theories of motivation.

Expectancy theory

This theory states that people feel increasingly motivated if they perceive that: (i) their effort will result in successful performance and (ii) successful performance leads to the desired results. It is also known as instrumentality theory, path–goal theory and Valence–Instrumentality–Expectancy (VIE) theory. It has its roots in the cognitive concepts of Kurt Lewin and Edward Tolman and in the choice behaviour and utility concepts from classical economic theory. However, it was Victor H Vroom (1964), who formulated an expectancy theory, as an alternative to content models, for work motivation. The theory identified relationships among variables, which affected individual behaviour in a dynamic environment. It was an attempt to capture how people determined their extent of effort for a job and how their perceived expectation influenced such effort. Strength of a tendency to act in a certain way depended on the strength of an expectation of outcome, which is likely to accrue upon accomplishment of the job. So, motivation is the product of the strength of one's desire (valence) and perceived probability of getting something good (expectancy). We can show such relationship as under:

(Valence – Strength of one's desire for something)		(Expectancy – Probability of getting it with a certain action)		(Motivation – Strength of drive towards an action)
V	$\times$	E	$=$	M

Valence is the degree of desirability of a certain outcome. It is, therefore, the strength of an individual's preference for a particular outcome, which may be a promotion, pay rise, recognition, etc, after he successfully accomplishes the job. Since people may have positive or negative preference for an outcome, valence may be negative or positive. Therefore, valence varies from −1 to +1.

Expectancy is the perceived possibility of a particular outcome that would follow an action. It is, therefore, the strength of the belief that an act will be followed by a certain outcome. The strength of expectations is based on past experience. People expect happenings in the future on what has occurred in the past. As expectancy is an association of action to outcome, it may range from zero to one. If employees perceive no possibility of an outcome from certain acts, their expectancy would be zero, while the value of expectancy would be one, when they feel (from their experience of action–outcome relationship) that they are likely to achieve something with certainty.

Vroom has used one more term besides expectancy and valence, which is usefulness or instrumentality. It is defined as the belief that the first-level outcome would lead to the second-level outcome. For example, one may be motivated to perform at a superior level due to his desire to get promoted. Here, the first-level outcome (superior level performance) is seen as being instrumental for second-level outcome (promotion).

Therefore, the strength of motivation to perform a certain act will depend on the sum of the products of the valences (including instrumentality) and the expectancies, which can be represented as under:

$$\text{Motivation Strength} = \sum V \times I \times E$$

Evaluation of the theory

It is believed that content theories oversimplified the process of work motivation. But Vroom's model highlighted the importance of organizational behaviour, clarifying the relationship between employees and organizations. His model has generated research interests among the corporate and academic circles. The theory also has a cognitive dimension, as individuals are viewed as thinking and reasoning beings and not just as those who simply act for satisfaction of their unfulfilled needs.

Criticisms: Despite such unique features in Vroom's approach, his theory was also criticised for the following reasons:

- It was not adequately tested in different work environments.
- Employees may not always take a conscious decision. It was observed they were also prone to take reckless decisions and later try to rationalise the action with their own logic.
- Linkages between efforts, performance and performance-rewards may not be linear. Organizational policies may further complicate the process. For example, promotion may be based on seniority, educational background etc, and not just performance.
- The theory is complex. In real life situations, managers may face time and resource constraints to implement it.

Equity theory

This theory owes its origin to several contributors like Festinger, Heider, Homans, Jacques, Patchen and Weick. However, James Stacy Adams' (1965) contribution is discussed much widely in the literature on motivation. The theory proposes that in any work environment, motivation is influenced by one's perception of how equitably he or she is treated compared to others. The theory is also known as social comparison theory or inequity theory. Employees perceive and try to reduce their inequity through such comparison or by establishing a hypothetical exchange relationship. An individual accounts for the amount of work he or she puts in and the corresponding rewards received and then compares the efforts and rewards of a similarly placed person in the organization. If equity exists, the individual feels alright. In case any inequity is perceived, the employee propels into action to create conditions for equity. Since inequity propels action, it is the motivator. The greater the perceived inequity, the greater the motivation to reduce it. While doing so, individuals can make any of the following choices:

- Change or alter inputs
- Change or alter outcomes
- Distort inputs and outcomes
- Distort inputs and outcomes of others (whom they compare with)
- Select a different referent (to compare)
- Withdraw from the field

Evaluation of the theory

It is a promising theory of work motivation as well as job satisfaction. For this reason, it has generated extensive research. Since the basic theory works on perception in a social comparison process, it is by default dynamic as the perceived inequity motivates employees to restore equity.

Criticisms: However, the theory is criticised on the following counts :

- It is complex and difficult in application.
- Perceptions are difficult to measure or assess.
- Choice of the person for comparison may not always be always appropriate.
- A given factor may be an input as well as an outcome.
- The study is based on laboratory experiments rather than real-life situations in organizations.

Performance satisfaction theory

Layman W Porter and Edward W Lawler (1968), based on Vroom's expectancy model, observed that performance led to satisfaction and not vice versa. Other interesting observations made by them were that motivation (efforts), performance (accomplishment) and satisfaction were separate variables. This is in contrast to the common belief that motivation led to performance, which in turn led to satisfaction. Efforts (force or motivation) did not directly lead to performance. It was mediated by abilities, traits and role perceptions. After performance, rewards that followed and the way they were perceived, determined satisfaction. The theory is illustrated in Fig. 5.4.

Whether an individual will make an effort depends on interaction between the value of reward (1) and perceived effort–reward probability (2). Effort (3) is the motivation.

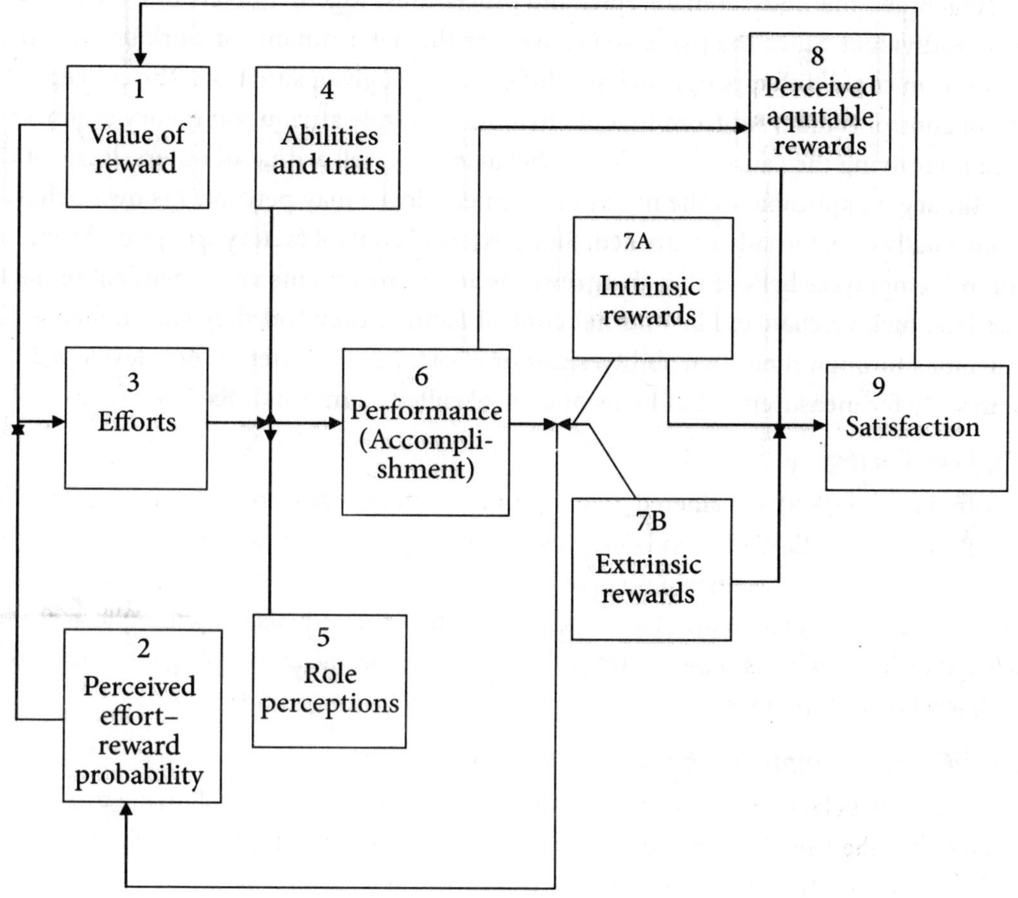

Fig. 5.4 Performance satisfaction model

Performance or accomplishment (6) is not the direct consequence of effort. It is the product of effort (3), abilities and traits (4) and role perceptions (5). Performance leads to certain outcomes in the form of intrinsic rewards (7A) and extrinsic rewards (7B). Both provide satisfaction (9). However, such reward–satisfaction relationship is moderated by the perceived equity of rewards (8).

Attribution theory and locus of control

Harold Kelley advocated this theory which is mainly concerned with the cognitive process by which an individual interprets behaviour that can be attributed to certain parts of the relevant environment. Such causal relationships or attributes are interpreted by an individual for his own behaviour or for that of others. Fritz Heider contended that both perceived internal forces (ability, efforts and fatigue) and external forces (supervision by others, machines, methods, climate, rules and procedures) together determine the behaviour of an individual. Since the perceived causes are the determinants of work behaviour and perception could differ, people behave differently in a given situation. The concept of locus of control is different from that of attribution. While attribution theory is concerned with identifying the causes of one's own behaviour as well as that of others, locus of control theory is applicable to the individual. An employee may perceive his own behaviour as internally or externally controlled. Since external control factors are beyond their own control, employees believe that their rewards and punishments are dependent on factors like fate, luck or chance. For internal control factors, they feel they can influence their outcomes through their own ability, skills or effort. Julian Rotter (1966) developed a 23-item scale for measurement of locus of control called as Internal–External (I–E) scale.

Goal-setting theory

Edwin Locke (1968) considered two cognitive determinants of behaviour: values and intentions (goals). Emotions and desires represent the form of values and value judgements. Intentions are goals to satisfy desires or emotions (values) for which the consequences are feedback and reinforcement. The study suggests that individuals are willing to work hard when they know what is required from them. Setting specific attainable goals is related to a high level of performance.

Classification of motivation theories

Megginson has classified the leading theories of motivation into the following three groups.

Perspective theories: This group consists of Taylor's approach, the human relations theories and McGregor's theory X and theory Y which guide the management in motivating employees.

Content theories: These consist of Maslow's hierarchy of needs theory, Herzberg's two-factor theory and McClelland's achievement need theory, which try to identify the causes of behaviour.

Process theories: Various behavioural theories based on stimulus–response relationship vis-à-vis motivation (Skinner's behaviour modification theory) and cognitive theories (Vroom's expectancy theory and Porter–Lawler's future-oriented expectancy theory) deal with the genesis of behaviour.

Motivation and Morale

Edwin Flippo (1961) defined, 'Morale is a mental condition or attitude of individuals and groups which determines their willingness to cooperate'. Yoder Dale (1972), on the other hand, explained morale as 'the overall tone, climate or atmosphere of work perhaps regularly sensed by the members. If workers appear to feel enthusiastic and optimistic about group activities, if they have a sense of mission about their job, if they are friendly with each other, they are described as having a good or high morale. If they seem to be dissatisfied, irritated, cranky, critical, restless and pessimistic, they are described as having poor or low morale'. Elton Mayo defined it as "the maintenance of cooperative living", which means a sense of belongingness. On the other hand, many authors defined morale as a pursuit of a common purpose, attitude, individual and group job satisfaction, participative attitudes, team spirit and so on. From the above definitions it is evident that morale is a cognitive concept, encompassing feelings, attitudes and sentiments, which together contribute to a general feeling of satisfaction at the workplace.

Like morale, motivation is also a cognitive concept but is different in certain important aspects. Motivation stimulates individuals into action to achieve desired goals. It is, therefore, a function of needs and drives. It mobilises energy, which enhances the potential for morale. Morale, on the other hand, is the individual or group attitude towards a particular subject. It contributes to a general feeling of satisfaction at the workplace. It is, therefore, a function of freedom or restraint towards some goal. It mobilises sentiments, which form an important part of the organizational climate. Attitudes and sentiments, i.e., morale, per se, affect productivity. High morale is an index of good human relations, which, inter alia, reduces labour turnover, absenteeism, indiscipline, grievances etc.

Factors which affect morale are primarily attitude and job satisfaction level of individual employees. We have discussed about attitude and its measurement in Chapter 11. From the organizational point of view, such factors can be grouped into, organizational goals, leadership style, attitude of coworkers, nature of work, the work environment as well as the employee himself.

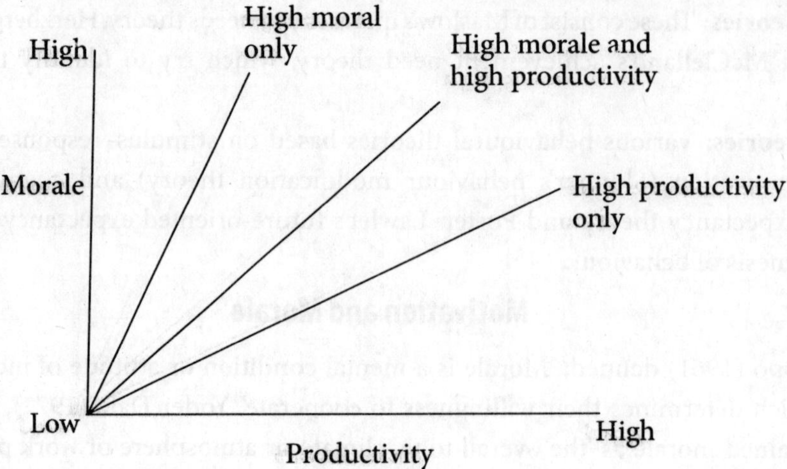

Fig. 5.5 Relationship between motivation and morale

High morale is conventionally considered as a contributor to high productivity, but such correlation may not be always true. This is because high productivity may be the outcome of many other organizational initiatives, which may be independent of employee morale. Hence, even with low employee morale, high productivity is achievable. This can be illustrated using the model by Keith Davis as shown in Fig. 5.5.

Job Satisfaction

Quality performance largely depends on the zeal of the employees or workers. Zeal at work is in proportion to motivation. The more we feel motivated, the more we are satisfied in our job. Hence, through work, organizations need to ensure material and psychological rewards, for positive change of values, attitude and motivation. It is for this reason, attitude, motivation and job satisfaction are considered as integrated, as positive change in all these ultimately led to increased performance and productivity. Attitude to work is the general approach for acceptance or rejection of certain values. Motivation is the process of incitement of employees to perform well. Job satisfaction is the matching of employees' expectations and the actual job experience.

Job satisfaction is the positive attitude of the workers. With satisfaction in jobs, employees nurture positive attitudes and values that modify their behaviour, leading to higher performance levels. Locke (1976) defined job satisfaction as a 'pleasurable state resulting from the appraisal of one's job and experience.' Using various psychometric tools, industrial psychologists can measure the job satisfaction score of employees. Measurement of job satisfaction may be holistic, i.e., global, or specific on a particular aspect, i.e., measurement of some facet.

Determinants of job satisfaction

Job satisfaction is influenced by a variety of factors, and depends on the individual employees and their organizations. However, there are some common factors, like quality of interpersonal relationships, especially between employees and their superiors, physical work environment, prevalence of motivating factors such as achievement, recognition for good work, opportunity for promotion, satisfaction of core physiological needs etc. Such factors being highly specific to individuals and organizations, it is difficult to suggest a tentative list of such factors. However, from the general organizational perspectives, we can list these as follows.

Psychological rewards: Through psychological rewards employees derive positive inner balance through favourable work experiences. Such positive inner balance is created by good salaries, high job status, adequate opportunities for improvement, high sense of job security etc.

Opportunities for socialisation: Employees also derive job satisfaction when they enjoy the opportunity to learn and acquire new skill sets that could enhance their scope for promotion in the job.

Workplace facilities: The workplace should also be designed in such a manner that it can fulfill the need for physical comfort of employees. Among others, it includes provision for drinking water, lunch room, canteen, rest room etc. This is especially required to prevent employees from getting fatigued and create a humane environment allowing relaxation.

Security needs: When employees enjoy security at the workplace, and also feel availability of adequate provision for their future comfort in terms of provident fund, pension, health insurance etc, they feel satisfied.

Good interpersonal relationships: With good interpersonal relationships at the workplace, employees feel more relaxed and satisfied. Positive interpersonal relationship creates friendly and relaxed work environment, as employees can freely interact with each other, and enjoy a sense of togetherness.

Self-esteem: This is ensured by offering recognition to the employees. By doing so, organizations can improve the self-confidence of employees which significantly increases job satisfaction.

Self-actualisation: This is ensured by creating an opportunity to grow in the job. It inculcates a sense of pride, as employees derive personal satisfaction through personal and professional fulfillment.

The criteria discussed above are quite generic. They vary between individuals and across organizations.

Benefits of job satisfaction

When employees are satisfied in their jobs, it benefits the organization in the following ways.

Increased work performance: Satisfied employees perform efficiently; as a result, overall performance improves.

Reduced absenteeism and employee turnover: Satisfied employees find their workplace a compelling place to work; they remain less absent, and also prefer to continue with the same organization.

High sense of commitment to jobs: Satisfied employees become loyal and committed to work.

Key Points

- Motivation is dynamic behaviour of the employees. At workplaces, the behaviour of employees largely stems from their unmet needs. By identifying those, organizations try to select appropriate motivational tools which satisfy the needs of the employees and also fit into organizational purposes.
- Since needs of the people vary widely, there cannot be a single motivational tool that can be applied to all types of organizations.
- The content and process theories on motivation suggested various methods for enhancing employee motivation.
- Many empirical studies carried out in India and abroad, validated such tools, wholly or partially.
- Motivation through both intrinsic or extrinsic reinforcers, contributes to employee satisfaction and enhances performance and productivity.
- For effective management of an organization, managers align objectives, purpose and values between the employee and the organization and in the process can better nurture a motivating work environment.
- Organizations with a high level of employee motivation typically enjoy high-level performance from the employees. Sustained motivational reinforcement is considered as the important strategic intervention for organizational competitiveness.

- Since motivation depends on human needs that do not remain constant, it is a complex area of study for managers. However, it is clear that employees can get motivated the most towards something, which they can relate to and believe in.
- Strategic alignment of people's needs and values with the organizational purpose can be best achieved, if employees can trace them as partners in the process.
- Employees' morale and job satisfaction are also dependent on motivation.

Important Terms

Attribution theory and locus of control: This theory is mainly concerned with the cognitive process by which an individual interprets behaviour attributing to certain parts of the relevant environment. An individual for his own behaviour or for others' behaviour interprets such causal relationships or attributes.

Esteem needs: It pertains to self-respect and respect or esteem from others. Self-respect is groomed by achieving competence, confidence, personal strength, adequacy, achievement, independence and freedom. But respect from others comes from prestige, recognition, acceptance, attention, status, reputation and appreciation.

Equity theory: The theory proposes that in a work environment, motivation is influenced by one's perception of how equitably he or she is treated compared to others. The theory is also known as social comparison theory or inequity theory.

Goal-setting theory: It considers two cognitive determinants of behaviour: values and intentions (goals). Emotions and desires represent the form of values and value judgements. Intentions are goals to satisfy desires or emotions (values). This results in consequences like feedback and reinforcement. The study suggests that individuals are willing to work hard when they know what is required of them. Setting specific attainable goals is related to a high level of performance.

Job characteristic model: Based on the studies by Hackman and Oldham (1975) on Herzberg's two-factor theory, the model shows how a good job design can lead to internal motivation of the employees and contribute to better job performance. Five job characteristics, which lead to employee motivation are skill variety, task identity, task significance, autonomy and feedback.

Performance satisfaction theory: The theory postulates that performance leads to satisfaction and not vice versa.

Self-assessment Questions

1. Define the term motivation. Why is it important to managers?
2. What is the motivational tool that should be used for knowledge workers? Would your approach be different for operators in a shop floor?
3. Critically review the contribution of Maslow and Herzberg to theories of motivation. Do you think they have any relevance for the new generation of workers?
4. How do you distinguish process theories and content theories of motivation?
5. Distinguish between motivation and morale. Discuss how morale can influence productivity.
6. Can motivation be defined as perception? What are the circumstances when perception can influence motive strength of a worker?
7. Write short notes on the following:
   i. Job satisfaction
   ii. Performance satisfaction theory
   iii. Motivation and morale
   iv. Theory of expectancy
   v. Motivation and productivity

Selected Bibliography

1. Atkinson JW (1966). *An Introduction to Motivation*. New Delhi: Affiliated East-West Press.
2. Bhattacharyya DK (2006). *Human Resource Management*. 2nd edition. New Delhi: Excel Books.
3. Bhattacharyya DK (2007). *Human Resource Research Methods*. New Delhi: Oxford University Press.
4. Herzberg F, B Manser and Synderman (1967). *The Motivation to Work*. New York: John Wiley and Sons.
5. Robbins SP and TA Judge (2007). *Organizational Behaviour*. New Jersey: Prentice Hall.
6. Spector PE (1967). *Job Satisfaction: Application, Assessment, Causes and Consequences*. Thousand Oaks: Sage Publications.
7. Vroom VH (1964). *Work and Motivation*. New York: Wiley.
8. Whyte WF (1955). *Money and Motivation*. New York: Harper and Row.

6 Work Environment: Management of Fatigue and Stress

Learning Objectives

After reading this chapter, you will be able to:

- **Understand the meaning and elements of work environment**
- **List the issues in the internal and external work environment, which influence performance and productivity of employees**
- **Understand the dynamics of fatigue**
- **List the effective measures to manage fatigue**
- **Define monotony and boredom and its effect on employees**
- **Appreciate the issues relating to safety at workplace**
- **Define stress and outline its management**

Overview

Industrial psychologists play a crucial role in creating the right work environment, managing hazards at the workplace, and eliminating fatigue, boredom and stress. Since these have far-reaching implications on the behavioural dynamics of workers, industrial psychologists need to understand negative behavioural impact of all these factors, and suggest corrections to the environmental issues at the workplace, so that productivity and performance of the workers remain satisfactory.

The term work environment has two dimensions: task and mega environment. Task environment is internal to an organization, while the latter is exogenous to organizations and yet influences the task or internal environment. We can clarify this using an example. Change of work process through organizational re-engineering, is a construct of task or internal work environment. On the other hand, increase in global competition is a component of mega environmental issues. Both have a strong influence in changing the organizational work environment.

Globally, the work environment is undergoing constant changes. In factories, manufacturing units and production houses, the work scenario and working conditions are changing. Some of the changes like prolonged working hours, specialization of job profiles, technical complexities, increase in work pressure etc are globally visible. Industrial psychologists need to extend support to the organizations to manage all these changes and survive in a competitive business environment. Achieving increased production, maintaining quality requirements by ensuring long working hours, managing safety and welfare of the employees, reducing fatigue and workplace stress, have now become almost essential business imperatives to stay ahead of the competition. Certain aspects of the work environment can exert positive or negative effect on the working capacity of the employees. A better working environment, for example, may exert positive influence. But unhygienic physical environment may have an adverse influence on the employees.

Internal Task Environment

The internal task environment has the following issues.

Hours of Work and Its Effect on Production

It is our general belief that by increasing the working hours, organizations can achieve increased production. But this may not be always true. Even by analysing the ratio of total working hours and the total production, either in value or volume terms, we cannot establish the relationship conclusively. This is because of the difference between the real working hours and nominal working hours. Working capacity of employees is limited to the real working hours. Stretching the working hours (nominal), may require employees to contribute more, but with reduced work energy, the change in the value and volume of production may not match proportionately. Therefore, increasing the working hours may not always be the right choice. During the extended working hour period, it is observed that the unproductive working time of the employees, rest pauses and work pace change significantly. Hence, it creates the difference between actual hours of work and the nominal hours. For industrial workers, payment of overtime is a statutory obligation. Many organizations, to keep pace with their increased production plan, often feel compelled to retain such workers on overtime. However, globally it has been established that in overtime period production actually reduces.

Various psychological studies conducted in industrial organizations suggest that breaks or work pauses during working time enhance the working capacity of employees and assist in increasing production. Hence, HR managers need to study the implications of the length and frequency of the breaks, particularly its impact on performance of the employees. For example, in call centres, telecallers cannot leave their workstations. . Thus, the system of giving one break in between eight working hours may not be the right approach. Rather they may be given staggered breaks, batch-wise, to ensure manning of workstations, namely, after every two hours or so, limiting the time of the total breaks as per organizational policies. This renews the work energy of employees and reduces their work-related fatigue. Thus, regular rest pauses to employees decreases fatigue or monotony, enhances production and productivity and also develops good corporate image. The type and nature of work determines the duration and frequency of the rest pauses. Organizations should ensure that during the rest period, employees are allowed to relax a bit. For example, change their posture if the work requires sitting. Employees should be allowed to stand and walk around. This would decrease the level of fatigue.

Prolonged working hours also increases absenteeism and increased absenteeism affects the level of production. Although there are many other reasons for absenteeism, but work-related fatigue due to prolonged working hours can be construed as one of the important causes.

There are many other factors related to the physical work environment that affect productivity. These are illumination and ventilation, amount of noise and temperature of the work environment etc. When we make the work environment employee-friendly, we can achieve success in making the workplace a compelling one. Employees volunteer to come regularly and due to the enhanced quality of work life, become more productive. Use of various colour schemes on walls, ergonomically designed machines, chairs, benches and rest rooms, music at the workplace all exert positive influence in the minds of the workers, which by default increase the total output or production.

Music at Work

Music at work is the most popular change in the work environment. However, a decision on its intensity and variety is crucial. Instrumental, classical, jazz, pop etc. are the examples of variety, while the volume of playing is an example of intensity. During lunch breaks in industrial production units, playing of pop songs with increased intensity is a normal practice. Jazz and instrumental music with low intensity during working hours, on the other hand, is a popular practice both in offices and factories. Industrial psychologists must ensure that music should not interfere with the efficiency of the employees, diverting their attention. Some organizations instead of playing music uniformly throughout the working time, may play it at synchronized intervals, may be for 10 minutes after every hour, to use it as a fatigue buster. In jobs that are of a complex nature, use of music may often be counterproductive. Hence, the decision on exerting positive work environment changes through music at work should be taken very carefully. Psychological research on music at work suggests use of music as a rhythm, keeping pace with the work rhythm as it eases out the work.

Noise Level at Work

Any sound that is unpleasant to the ears is considered as noise. It is generally an annoying sound, which distracts our attention, and interferes with our work. In some workplaces, there are steady noises from machine operations. It may even exceed the required 65-decibels limit. A good example is a jute mill. In such cases, workers adapt themselves to the noise level. Since they become used to it, barring their impaired hearing, it may not interfere with their work efficiency. But intermittent noise may be distracting and interfere with work efficiency. In a steady noisy work environment, a sudden silence may be a distraction. In such an environment, if the noise level exceeds the permissible limit, employees should be protected with ear plugs or mufflers, to protect their hearing capacity.

Illumination

Illumination is maintaining daylight or equivalent brightness at the workplace. Natural light is the best source of illumination for work. However, this may not be available or practicable in all workplaces. There may be reasons like nature of work (which may require to be done in closed environment), night shifts or even the particular layout of the office or the production unit. Wherever artificial lighting is required, the organization should ensure that it is more proximate to daylight both in colour and composition. While installing the lighting system in the workplace, it is important to emphasise on factors like distribution, location and glare of the lights, so that it properly illuminates the workplace. To the extent possible, illumination should combine daylight and from the artificial source. Artificial light should be free from colours. However, where it is difficult to avoid colourful lights, Mazda or yellow light should be the best choice. Unbalanced or unmatched colour causes hindrances. Further, artificial lighting should have adequate diffusion, i.e., it should have minimum glare. Excessive brightness leads to visual discomfort. To avoid this, proper lighting accessories like translucent bowls, should be used, so that light is directed to the ceiling and then reflected to the work areas. It ensures better transmission of light downward and serves the purpose of both direct and indirect lighting.

Miscellaneous Factors

To make the work environment free from dullness and monotony and free from physical discomfort, some other measures are also adopted. One such is building cafeterias, which provides the opportunity to employees not only to feel relaxed but also to further their thought process either in discussion with other team members or in solitude over a cup of tea or coffee. The cafeteria concept was more common in IT or software development organizations, but now even manufacturing organizations have their own. A cafeteria is different from a conventional canteen which only serves food and functions during lunch breaks, by being open throughout and offering tea, coffee, soft drinks or snacks. However, the management has to guard against this facility becoming the centre of criticism as is often observed. To avoid administrative hassles, often organizations may not directly provide food or snacks; they may outsource this either by installing self-service vending machines or to some professional canteen service providers. Even in some organizations (depending on their area of location), there is the system of giving food coupons to employees. In such cases, employees use their coupons to buy food or snacks from nearby restaurants.

Another important aspect of work environment is the availability of proper rest rooms. Hygienic sanitation, appropriate temperature and humidity level, ventilation etc significantly contribute to inculcating positive attitude in workers and improves their overall productivity and efficiency. Therefore, organizations should not limit their focus on those workplace environment aspects, which are statutorily required, but provide more, to develop the workplace into a compelling one for the employees.

Fatigue at the Workplace

Fatigue is physical and/or mental exhaustion that can be triggered by stress, medication, overwork, or mental and physical illness or disease. Everyone experiences fatigue occasionally. It is the body's way of signalling its need for rest and sleep. But when fatigue becomes a persistent feeling of tiredness or exhaustion that goes beyond normal sleepiness, it is usually a sign of a more serious syndrome.

Physically, fatigue is characterised by a profound lack of energy, feelings of muscle weakness and slowed movements or responses of the central nervous system. Fatigue can also trigger serious mental exhaustion. Persistent fatigue can cause a lack of mental clarity (or feeling of mental 'fuzziness'), difficulty in concentrating, and in some cases, memory loss.

Causes of Fatigue

Fatigue may be the result of one or more environmental causes such as inadequate rest, improper diet, work and home stressors, poor physical condition or symptom of chronic medical condition or disease. Heart disease, low blood pressure, diabetes, end-stage renal disease, iron deficiency anemia, narcolepsy, and cancer can cause long-term, ongoing fatigue symptoms. Acute illnesses such as viral and bacterial infections can also trigger temporary feelings of exhaustion. In addition, mental disorders such as depression can also cause fatigue.

A number of medications, including antihistamines, antibiotics and antihypertensive drugs, may cause drowsiness as a side effect. Individuals suffering from fatigue who are prescribed one of these may wish to check with their healthcare provider about alternative treatments.

Extreme fatigue which persists, unabated for at least six months, which is not the result of a diagnosed disease or illness and is characterised by flu-like symptoms, such as, swollen lymph nodes, sore throat, and muscle weakness and/or pain is suggestive of a diagnosis of chronic fatigue syndrome (CFS). Also called chronic fatigue immune deficiency syndrome, it is a debilitating illness that causes overwhelming exhaustion and a myriad of neurological and immunological symptoms. About 1.5 to 2 million Americans are estimated to suffer from the disorder.

Work-related fatigue may have a variety of causes. Conventional wisdom has attributed it to work-related stress or ergonomic concerns such as working at a computer/computer terminal for extended periods of time. There is no doubt that the strain of working at a computer for 4–8 hours a day can result in headache and fatigue, which is particularly noticeable late in the day. Work-related stress may also be expected to cause late afternoon fatigue and headache. It is not unusual for office workers to experience fatigue as early as 10 o'clock in the morning. Such fatigue is not likely to be work-induced. There must be some other causes. In most cases, such symptoms appear to be related to ventilation deficiencies. Buildings need to be ventilated to remove contaminants that we produce. These contaminants are referred to as bioeffluents. They include carbon dioxide (CO_2), acetone, ammonia, methane, a large number of volatile fatty acids, solvents previously inhaled etc. These bioeffluents are not believed to be individually harmful. However, as bioeffluent levels increase (as determined from CO_2 concentrations), building occupants increasingly begin to complain of unpleasant human odour, stale, unpleasant air, lack of air movement and, yes, fatigue and headache.

Symptoms of Fatigue

Fatigue is a symptom, rather than a specific disease or disorder. People who are fatigued feel tired all the time—in both body and mind. An employee with fatigue suffers from reduced reflexes and functions at less than the level of desired efficiency. Fatigue can cause a vast range of other physical, mental and emotional symptoms including:

- Chronic tiredness or sleepiness
- Headache and dizziness
- Weak and/or aching musles
- Slowed reflexes and responses
- Loss of appetite
- Reduced immune function
- Blurry vision
- Impaired decision-making and judgement
- Irritability or short-temperedness, hallucinations
- Poor concentration and impaired hand–eye coordination
- Short-term memory problems, low motivation

The Range of Causes

The wide range of causes that can trigger fatigue include:

- Undiagnosed medical conditions
- Unhealthy lifestyle choices
- Workplace issues
- Emotional concerns and stress
- Combination of any of the above factors

Medical causes

Many diseases and disorders can trigger fatigue. From the HR managers' point of view, such medical causes of fatigue are difficult to measure. However, by keeping track of the medical status of individual employees, HR managers can ascertain possible link of employee fatigue with medical reasons. Some of the diseases, which are known to create an effect on employee fatigue, are listed in Table 6.1. However, the list is not exhaustive.

Diagnosis: Since fatigue can present a vast range of symptoms and be caused by different factors working in combination, diagnosis can be difficult. Doctors may diagnose fatigue from the following:

Medical history: Recent events such as childbirth, medication, surgery or bereavement may contribute to fatigue.

Physical examination: Signs of illness or disease can be identified and the doctor may also ask detailed questions about diet, lifestyle and life events.

Tests: This may include blood tests, urine tests, x-rays and other investigations. The idea is to rule out any physical causes, such as anemia, infection or hormonal problems.

Table 6.1 Common medical conditions causing fatigue

Flu	Tuberculosis
Glandular fever	Chronic pain
Anemia	Gluten intolerance
Sleep disorders, such as sleep apnea or restless leg syndrome	Addison's disease
	Parkinson's disease
CFS/ME (formerly known as chronic fatigue syndrome or myalgic encephalopathy)	Cardiac disease
	HIV
Hypothyroidism	Cancer
Hepatitis	

Workplace-related causes

Common workplace issues that can cause fatigue are as follows.

Working in shifts : The human body is designed to sleep during the night. This pattern set by a small part of the brain is known as the circadian clock. For a shift worker the circadian clock is thrown out of gear by working when the body is programmed to be asleep. Sleeping during the day is usually difficult, because brain chemicals (neurotransmitters) are naturally set to the 'wakefulness' mode.

Poor workplace practices: These include long work hours, hard physical labour, irregular working hours (such as rotating shifts), stressful work environment (such as excessive noise or temperature extremes), boredom, working alone with little or no interaction with others, or repetitive tasks.

Workplace stress: This is caused by a wide range of factors including job dissatisfaction, heavy workload, conflicts with bosses or colleagues, bullying, constant change, or threats to job security.

Burnout: It refers to long-term exhaustion and diminished interest in any activity. It can be described as striving too hard in one area of life while neglecting everything else. 'Workaholics', for example, put all their energies into their career, which puts their family life, social life and personal interests out of balance.

Unemployment: Financial pressures, feelings of failure or guilt, and the emotional exhaustion of prolonged job hunting can lead to stress, anxiety, depression and fatigue.

Psychological causes

Studies suggest that psychological factors are present in at least 50% of fatigue cases. Some of these are given below.

Depression: This illness is characterised by severe and prolonged feelings of sadness, dejection and hopelessness. People who are depressed commonly experience chronic tiredness.

Anxiety and stress: A person who is chronically anxious or stressed keeps the body in overdrive. The constant flooding of adrenaline is exhausting and fatigue sets in.

Grief: Losing a loved one causes a wide range of emotions including shock, guilt, depression, despair and loneliness.

Consequences of Fatigue

Fatigue is one of the most critical safety issues. While not all of the physiological reasons for fatigue have been fully quantified and categorised, one thing is clear—fatigue has a detrimental impact on human performance. Additionally, it has been recognised that the lack of basic knowledge or misconceptions about fatigue among the management, employees, and government regulators has prevented implementing substantial changes in existing attitudes concerning the critical relationship between fatigue and safety.

While physical fatigue is a major concern in industry, managers and executives largely suffer from cognitive fatigue. It is defined as the degradation of mental capacities with respect to decision-making, reasoning and judgement, and the ability to remember and process contextual information. This degradation can be caused by either inadequate rest or acute or cumulative loss of meaningful sleep. Hence, fatigue is more than being tired.

- Conflict between work schedules and the normal circadian cycle
- Continuous circadian disruption
- Extended and/or unpredictable work periods
- Prolonged wakefulness
- Fatigue from continuous operations
- Boredom/complacency

Overcoming fatigue

Fatigue is a physiological condition, which, in an operational environment cannot be eliminated, but can be managed if the proper set of tools is put in place. Sleepiness is not an indicator of laziness; sleep is a physical requirement just like eating, drinking and breathing. Failure to recognise this requirement and effectively manage it results in a degradation of human performance and an increased risk of incidents (i.e., rule violations, collisions, personal injuries, fatalities etc). Individuals can improve their alertness on the job by learning more about the science of sleep and by developing good sleep habits. Organizations can improve the alertness of their workforce by developing, in partnership, scientific measures and programs to counter fatigue. They should ascertain and implement suitable methods that would be effective in their operational environment. There is no quick fix or magic bullet. Organizations need to build a package of measures to manage fatigue.

Boredom

Boredom is a condition characterised by the perception that one's environment is dull, tedious and lacking in stimulation. There is an inherent anxiety in boredom; people will put considerable effort to prevent or remedy it. Yet in many circumstances, it is accepted as a suffering to be endured. Common passive ways to escape boredom are to sleep or to think creative thoughts (daydream). Typical active solutions consist in an intentional activity of some sort, often something new, as familiarity and repetition lead to the tediousness.

The first record of the word *boredom* is in the novel, *Bleak House*, by Charles Dickens, written in 1852, although the expression *to be a bore* had been used in the sense of 'to be tiresome or dull' since 1768.

Definition

There is no consensus on the definition of boredom, although some common themes exist which include the following features:

- **The environment**: A monotonous, repetitive, environment with low stimulation (perceived or real)
- **Arousal**: Less than optimal (low) levels of physiological arousal
- **Affect**: A dissatisfying emotional state
- **Cognition**: Poor concentration, attention deficit
- **Perception**: One-dimensional perceptual tendencies
- **Time**: Inefficient use of time and perception of time as passing slowly

Consequences of boredom

Workplace boredom can have a major negative impact on people. It hurts people's sense of self-worth, which can cause them to work less effectively or to not work at all. On the other hand, boredom may be beneficial in some ways. Boredom is a natural feeling that comes about when the person feels as though there is nothing new or nothing to inspire him or her. To relieve boredom, then, that person may take up a new hobby or come up with an interesting idea by thinking creatively.

Monotony

The word monotony is related to boredom. Monotony is defined as lack of variety, dullness or tedium arising from the fact that nothing different ever happens. It is an unvarying condition of work (repetitiveness). Since the root of monotony is the boredom at workplace, job enrichment may be the best option to avert monotony at work. Among others, job enrichment requires adding new varieties of job, so that an employee can get respite from the monotonous daily routine.

Hazards and Safety Issues

A hazard is a source or potential source of human injury, ill health or disease. There is a range of hazards, which needs to be identified, assessed and controlled before starting the relocation or closure process. These include physical, psychological and social hazards.

Physical hazards

These are perhaps the most readily identifiable and will increase during a relocation or closure process. There are many of these and include the following:

- Clutter from boxes, furniture and trolleys
- Obstruction of thoroughfares where corridors and passageways are used as temporary storage areas
- Manual handling risks associated with lifting, shifting, packing and moving
- Cleaning products

Typical example of workplace hazards

During the packing process, the office environment can become cluttered with boxes and additional waste disposal bins. It is important to ensure there are designated areas for these items so that they are easily accessible (to reduce manual handling hazards) but do not obstruct traffic flow or emergency exits and fire-fighting equipment.

Social or psychological hazards

Social and psychological issues, contribute to psychological hazards, which stem from the employees' perception that they would lose their jobs when relocated or redeployed, or when they are required to adjust to the organizational changes. The organization can support its employees through the various processes, as outlined below to help them to overcome psychological hazards.

- Ensuring lines of communication are open
- Ensuring there are consultative mechanisms in place
- Recognising and addressing staff uncertainty, and
- Creating an atmosphere of support in the workplace

Management of Hazards

Hazard management aims to reduce the risk of injuries and illnesses associated with work. It is a systematic, sequential process for making the work environment as safe as possible. The steps in the process are:

1. Identify the hazard by determining the factors that have the potential to cause injury or illness.
2. Assess the risk by understanding the hazard, injury or illness and its consequences.

3. Control the risk by duly identifying health and safety issues and by establishing the control systems to eliminate or minimise the same.
4. Monitor and evaluate, to ensure that the control measures are effective.

Scenario

Let us assume that your organization wishes to identify the hazard involved in moving archive boxes and you have been asked to do the job. Suggest ways in which you would perform the job.

Solution

1. Assess the risk to determine the likely weight and the number of boxes to move.
2. Control the risk by hiring or borrowing a trolley suitable for the task.
3. Monitor and review the hazard on a regular basis, taking stock of the number of archive boxes that are being moved to minimise double handling. Also ensure that the type of trolley acquired is the right one for the job and can resolve the entire manual handling risks.
4. Evaluate the controls by determining whether the trolley will be available whenever the boxes need to be moved, and the staff are aware of safe loading and handling practices and that it is the most appropriate way to do the job.

Common Hazards and Control Measures

Some of the examples of control measures for common hazards are given below.

- Physical control measures like controlling of bending and stretching while packing/unpacking; such bending or stretching control during the process of packing and unpacking can be ensured using following preventive actions:
    - ➢ Reduce the excess load prior to the move
    - ➢ Use surfaces when packing/unpacking to eliminate the need to bend
    - ➢ Ensure appropriate aids, e.g., step ladder to reach items above shoulder height

➢ Ensure adequate storage space at the new location which enables storage between knee and shoulder heights
➢ Provide training for relevant staff

- For lifting or moving boxes/equipment/furniture, allocate adequate resources to pay for professional handlers where appropriate.
- To minimise exposure to dust, arrange for monitoring of the area. If dust is an issue, ensure quality cleaning. While doing this, it is important to deploy only those staff members who do not have respiratory complaints. Provide dustcoats and gloves to the staff members.
- Control of psychological factors include measures such as (i) Consultation, communication and access to an Employee Assistance Program (ii) Transition program including application/interview skills, financial and vocational advice.

Hazard audit

Managing hazard at workplace requires systematic managerial intervention, more particularly from the industrial psychologists. The principal action in managing the hazards of closure or relocation is to undertake a hazard audit. It is a formal examination and documentation of the hazards identified and the control measures selected. A small team of suitable staff should undertake the hazard audit.

Accidents and Safety Issues

Accidents and safety issues in organizations both in India and abroad are major areas of concern for HR professionals. Accidents cannot be measured only in terms of frequency, i.e., number of times they occur. They are also assessed for severity. Accidents increase the number of man-days lost and compensation to be paid (both statutory and voluntary, more on humanitarian ground due to pressure of trade unions).Therefore, prevention of accidents by adopting appropriate safety measures is very important for organizations.

Before we analyse how accidents are caused, let us try to define accidents. An accident is an event, which occurs without any predictable reason and leads to personal injury of workers and damage to the equipment or property of an organization. Industrial accidents arise directly out of the work situation, which may be due to faulty equipment or inadequate performance of an individual worker or group, complexity of process and methods (for example, hazardous operations) etc. Whatever may be the reasons for accidents, we can classify them based on three important dimensions, i.e., the nature of accident, the causes and the impact. Table 6.2 shows some illustrative features of the three dimensions of an accident.

Table 6.2 Features of an accident

Nature of the event (assuming the accident occurred during movement of materials in a forklift inside the factory)

- ✓ Collision with workers walking by
- ✓ Collision with other forklifts, light vehicles and trucks moving through the factory
- ✓ Collision with other objects

Causes of the event (assuming a machine operation)

- ✓ Fingers or other body parts, clothing etc trapping into machine parts
- ✓ Tools or machine parts coming off or getting stuck
- ✓ Flying objects or particles especially in non-machine operations
- ✓ Falling objects and objects lying around

Whatever may be the nature, causes and effects of accidents, results of accidents principally involve costs, psychological or behavioural problems of workers, social consequences etc.

Prevention of accidents

Accident prevention requires investment for both employees and employers. Accidents are not only expensive, but they also lower the morale of the workers and in addition result in lower production rates. As a group, companies with excellent safety records probably have more satisfied workers than those that have severe and frequent accidents. There is an interaction here. Just as accidents lower morale, poor morale appears to be a cause of accidents. Any accident prevention policy requires consideration of the human element in the occurrence of accidents. Causation of accidents, like any problem of causation is a complex matter. Human error is an important element that causes accidents just as mechanical failures. Two most important aspects of the human element in accident prevention are equipment design and training.

Definition of Safety

The word safety can be defined as freedom from danger. Any workplace needs to be safe and without risk to health. Although there are various legal provisions for safe workplaces, normally we consider a workplace as safe, when it satisfies the following conditions:

- Fool-proof maintenance of equipment, devices and systems in the work place
- Effective and suitable provision for ventilation

- Provision for maintenance of a reasonable temperature
- Provision and maintenance of suitable and sufficient lighting
- Cleanliness of the workplace, furniture, furnishings and fittings
- Provision of adequate facilities for storage and disposal of waste
- Prevention of overcrowding in the workplace
- Provision of suitable workstations and seating
- Maintenance of safe floors and traffic routes
- Measures to prevent falls of people and objects
- Installation of safe windows, doors and gates
- Ensuring safety of windows, skylights and ventilators
- Ensuring control of movement of materials using forklift
- Safe doors and gates
- Safe escalators and moving walkways

Organizations develop a safe system of work by integrating people, machinery and materials to produce and maintain an acceptable standard of safety. To understand whether safety requirements are adequate, organizations routinely conduct safety audit. It is the systematic measurement and validation of an organization's management of its health and safety program against a series of specific and attainable standards. The audit subjects each area of an organization's activities to a critical examination with the principal objective of minimising loss. It is an ongoing process that ensures effective management of health and safety issues.

Safety culture

To ensure a safe workplace, every organization has to promote the safety culture. Some of the important ways to promote the safety culture are given below.

- Leadership and commitment from the top, which is genuine and demonstrable
- Accepting safety as a long-term strategy, which requires sustained effort and interest
- A policy statement of high expectations and conveying a sense of optimism about what is possible supported by adequate code of practice and safety standards
- Health and safety should be treated as other corporate aims and adequately resourced
- It must be a line management responsibility.
- Ownership of both health and safety must permeate at all levels of the work force—involving employees, adequate training and communication.
- Realistic and achievable targets should be set and performance measured against those.
- Incidents should be thoroughly investigated.

- Consistency of behaviour against agreed standards should be achieved by auditing and good safety behaviour should be conditional to continued employment.
- Deficiencies revealed by an investigation or audit should be remedied promptly.
- Management must receive adequate and up-to-date information to be able to assess performance.

Legal provisions for occupational health and safety

Workplace safety is related to employee motivation and morale as also the productivity. With poor safety management, organizations not only suffer financial loss, but also are deprived of the benefits of high productivity. Thus, safety issues are now considered a voluntary and strategic initiative of an organization. However, Indian organizations still lack in their safety initiatives. Indian labour laws have laid down certain provisions, requiring organizations to comply with those to ensure a safe workplace, free from occupational health hazards. The Factories Act, 1948, to give effect to some of the ILO conventions and recommendations, in its 1976 amendment, made compulsory appointment of safety officers. The stringent requirements have further been reinforced with the 1987 amendment to the Act, extending the safety issues even outside the premises of the organization. All organizations are now bound to disclose information about their safety preparedness to the authorities.

Similarly the Mines Act, 1952 also spelt out provisions to tackle occupational health and safety issues. Likewise the Dock Workers (Safety, Health and Welfare) Act, 1986, Plantation Labour Act, 1951, Shop and Establishments Act, Explosives Act, 1884, Petroleum Act, 1934, Insecticides Act, 1968, Indian Boilers Act, 1923, Dangerous Machines (Regulation) Act, 1983, Environment (Protection) Act, 1986, Indian Atomic Energy Act, 1962, etc have provisions concerning occupational health and safety issues in organizations.

Whistle-blowing

Whistle-blowing is raising an alarm or revelation of actual conditions usually by the members of the organizations, who are presently serving or who had served earlier against the illegal, immoral or illegitimate practices, detrimental to the interests of the organization in the long run. The concept is often institutionalised by the organizations with a documented policy, in the interests of both the organization as well as the whistle-blowers. In organizations, many sensitive issues may encompass the role of some employees, even in their day-to-day work. For example, internal auditors, inspectors, etc play the most crucial role in a company's finance functions. Even marketing managers' unethical campaigning go against the interests of the organizations. Sometimes, managers and executives may be biased in many employment-related decisions, like recruitment, promotion, transfers, compensation design, and even in decisions pertaining to dismissals. It may not always be possible for the management to gauge the justification of decisions, as many such decisions are subjective, and often influenced by the personal prejudices and bias of the managers and executives. In such cases, whistle-blowers can play the most effective role in giving the warning signals. But they often require revealing their observations to the managers who are outside their normal chain of command. Even at times they go out of the organizational hierarchy and make such information available to various regulatory bodies for positive action. In such situations, whistle-blowers may even have untoward experience, to the extent of threats to their security and safety. It is for this reason, organizations that believe in good corporate governance always prefer the structured whistle-blowing policy.

Factors that influence whistle-blowing

A whistle-blower in organizations perceives the following factors:

- When some misdeeds or illegal activities happen, the whistle-blower perceives such things could be prevented by the top management of the organization.
- They believe that action by the top management can control such illegal or immoral activities.
- They follow a process to expose the problems to the top management, expecting corrective measures to prevent such activities.

Careful examination of the above factors indicates that whistle-blowing involves organizational and individual dependence. Often, we observe in organizations that some employees play the role of whistle-blowers. This may be partially attributable to the accessibility to information, which is obviously restricted to some employees. Other reasons may be the prevalence of organizational culture that dissuades employees from indulging in whistle-blowing. Whatever may be the reason, employees do whistle-blowing, out of their sense of moral responsibility, guts and concern for the organization and society.

In organizations, whistle blowing per se was all along the domain of trade unions, but this was often construed as a perennial opposition of managerial activities. With a more institutionalised approach, today whistle-blowing has become the responsibility of all sections of employees that have access to sensitive information. Every whistle-blowing disclosure need not lead to detection of some disorder in the activities of the organizations. Therefore, organizations that believe in good corporate governance must not discourage whistle-blowers, whose information leads to no results; rather they should appreciate their concern for the organizations. At the same time, organizations must also take positive steps for the security and safety of the whistle-blowers, after the information leads to results.

In the Enron case, the whistle-blower Sharon Watkins had to face lot of opposition from the coworkers, top management and so on. Therefore, by promoting the right culture in the organization, it is possible to get better results from whistle-blowing.

Ethics and Values

Values and ethics are two moral principles which today's organizations need to integrate with the behaviour of all sections of employees, so that their actions are in consonance with those principles. To ensure this in organizational practices, most of the organizations adopt certain code of ethics. Both the terms are used interchangeably and construed as the science of conduct or values of management. Moreover, values are considered as the important constructs of ethics. In organizations, moral values are reflected through mutual respect, honesty, fairness, sense of responsibility etc. Through some documented code of ethics, organizations make their employees aware about right or wrong in their decision-making and in all other organizational practices. Operationally, therefore, we can define ethics as the framework of values for moral behaviour. Again, ethics encompass both the business and profession. While business represents application of ethics in our decisions and actions, profession requires adherence to certain code of ethics specific to the profession. Historically, in India guild systems laid down the ethics of business or profession. Codes of ethics are documented guidelines for compliance, and employees, by virtue of their membership with the organizations are expected to comply with such code of ethics. Code of ethics and so also the perceived values vary between individuals and across cultures. We have four key ethical principles, like egalitarianism, utilitarianism, individual right and distributive justice. With a utilitarianism approach in ethics, organizations take decisions based on the perceived decisional outcomes.

Code of ethics is different from code of conduct. The former is the statement of values and beliefs, while the codes of conduct translate the values into some specific behavioural standards. Thus, code of conduct is the outline of some fundamental set of principles.

Ethical values are critical to the performance of individual employees and so also for the organization as a whole. Ethics and values are now being integral part of organizational functioning, perceived ethical values have an influence on the following aspects of an organization:

- Efficiency and effectiveness of individual and organizational performance
- Decision-making process
- Commitment and job satisfaction
- Stress at workplace
- Employee turnover

Through ethical practices, organizations can also get the benefit of a favourable public image. People always repose their confidence in ethical organizations and buy their products and services without question. Many Indian organizations like the Tatas, Birlas, ITC, Murugappa group, Grasim etc. are today favourably considered for their focus on ethical business practices and social responsibilities.

Stress

Stress occurs when we perceive a threat. Our nervous system while perceiving a threat releases hormones. Thus, stress can be defined as the normal physical response to some events that make us feel threatened or that create imbalance in our way of life. Some of the signs and symptoms of stress are shown in Table 6.3.

Table 6.3 Symptoms of stress

Type of symptoms	Signs
Cognitive symptoms	Memory problems, lack of concentration, poor power of judgement, nurturing of negative thoughts, always racing with ideas and always worrying
Emotional symptoms	Fluctuating mood, frequent irritation, agitating, inability to relax, overwhelmed, feeling of isolation and loneliness, depression and unhappiness
Physical symptoms	Aches and pains, diarrhea, constipation, nausea, dizziness, chest pain, frequent colds
Behavioural symptoms	Overeating, poor eating, oversleeping, poor sleeping, deliberately isolating from others, procrastinating, smoking, addiction to alcohol, always feeling nervous

It is important to understand that some of the symptoms of stress may be for reasons other than stress. It may be more for medical reasons.

All stresses need not be always harmful. Some of the workplace stresses may also be positive. With stress in workplaces, we try to achieve our goals, and with such goal achievement we feel a sense of accomplishment. Good corporate practices demand helping employees even to perform in stressful situation.

In another way, we can define stress as a non-specific response of our body to some demand. Such non-specific response increases our heart beat, leads to faster breathing, tightened muscles and dilated pupils.

Managing Stress in Organizations

To manage stress at work, a leading unit with Japanese collaboration engaged in producing industrial chemicals, adopted a policy, delineating the responsibilities of the managers, individual employees and the organization The main thrust of the policy is to adopt proactive approach in matters of stress management, rather than waiting for the problem to arise. The policy document spells out that management of stress in the workplace is inseparable from the duties and the job roles of managers and supervisors. Being in the business of hazardous chemicals, stress in the workplace of the company also occurs due to occupational health hazards, in addition to the work-related stress. To guide the managers and supervisors, the policy document categorised the possible reasons for stress as under:

- Culture
- Demands
- Control
- Relationships
- Change
- Role
- Support

After categorisation of possible stressful issues that are likely to occur or have occurred, through brainstorming, managers and supervisors decide the possible course of action and recommend the same to the top management, who after review recommends its implementation within a day or two. Reviewing the initial pilot testing report on the suggestive approach to stress management, managers and supervisors, streamlined it as policy documents. To help the workers to self-manage the workplace stress, and so also the stress that may be exogenous to organization, a detailed FAQ (frequently asked questions) has been hosted by the company, and prominently displayed in canteens, shop floors etc.

This approach to stress management helped the company to reduce the workplace stress significantly. Backup support of counselling also helped the company to reduce stress exogenous to the organization, like family matters, relationship problems etc.

Stress Management for Individuals

At individual level, we manage stress taking charge of our thoughts, emotions, schedule, environment and the way we deal with problems. We do all these to ensure a balanced work life, better interpersonal relationships, relaxation, successfully coping with the work pressure and challenges. Stress management is the process of identifying the sources of stress in our life, and our subsequent efforts to cope with such stress, so that it does not impair our work capabilities. It is important to understand that we do not suffer from stress always for organizational work pressure. It often occurs due to our thoughts, feelings, and behaviours. Such nurturing of self-inflicted thoughts ultimately cascade to our workplaces, where we start delaying or procrastinating the work, leading to our inability to meet the deadline and accordingly suffer from stress.

Successful stress management largely depends on the way we manage ourselves, i.e., our habits and attitude. Following the same approach, organizations also help their stressful employees, explaining to them the following things:

- Stress is temporary and you can overcome it soon.
- Stress is an integral part of our work and family life. We cannot avoid it, so we need to manage it successfully.
- Diffuse stress attributing it to some external reasons.
- Consider stress as normal and unexceptional.
- Understand how to accept responsibility for your own role. This will not make you stressful, even when you fail to achieve the results.

At individual level, we can manage stress following certain strategies like, avoiding unnecessary stress, mastering the art of saying no, avoiding those people who create stress, taking control of our environment, avoiding unnecessary discussions on hot topics, altering the situation, expressing feelings rather than keeping the same with you, be willing to compromise, be assertive dealing with problems, being more assertive, effectively managing time, adapting to the stressor or stressful situation, reframing the problems, looking at the bigger picture, adjusting the situation to our standards, focusing on positive aspects, adjusting our attitude, and finally accepting those things that we cannot change.

It is not that one has to follow all the above strategies to manage stress. It depends on the type and nature of stress, based on which we select the appropriate strategies according to our situation. Setting aside time for relaxation and following a healthy lifestyle, helps us to reduce stress.

Job stress and performance

Job or occupational stress deters performance. If such negative effect is not managed by the organizations, their business may suffer. A holistic approach to management of job stress is necessary considering both the organizational factors and family reasons that contribute to job or occupational stress. Balanced physical and mental health can significantly reduce the job stress. The World Health Organization (WHO) apart from the emphasis on balanced physical and mental health, emphasised on social well-being to ensure proper management of stress in workplaces. The ultimate emphasis is helping people to lead socially and economically productive lives. Various research studies clarified that when individuals cannot endure job stress, their performance and productivity suffer. This ultimately leads to numerous health and psychological complications. Job stress levels vary with respect to the nature of the job or occupation, and also between organizations. With excessive job stress, people can experience burnout, when they can start relating their clients even as objects, and negatively feel about everything (including their colleagues, coworkers) as their objects that contribute to their stress. However, there are some interesting studies on positive aspects of job-related stress, which requires focus on positive health management and psychological movement. Obviously, there are different types of relationships between job stress and job performance. Among these, the most common one is the negative linear relationship, i.e., performance or productivity decreases with stress. The positive aspect is that productivity can also increases with stress, i.e., a positive linear relationship between stress and performance. Again there may be a curvilinear relationship (U-shaped) between stress and performance, which indicates, with stress productivity initially increases and reaches its peak level. It then starts reducing, when the individuals reach the state of distress. The final argument is that stress and performance do not have any quantifiable relationship.

The General Adaptation syndrome, i.e., the GAS model of stress pioneered by Hans Selye (1976) focused on certain phases of our stress experience, i.e., alarm, resistance and exhaustion, which ultimately cause diseases for obvious long-term chemical changes in our body systems. The GAS model is illustrated in Fig. 6.1. The model explains how slowly stress can render employees to perform less effectively affecting their performance and productivity at their workplaces.

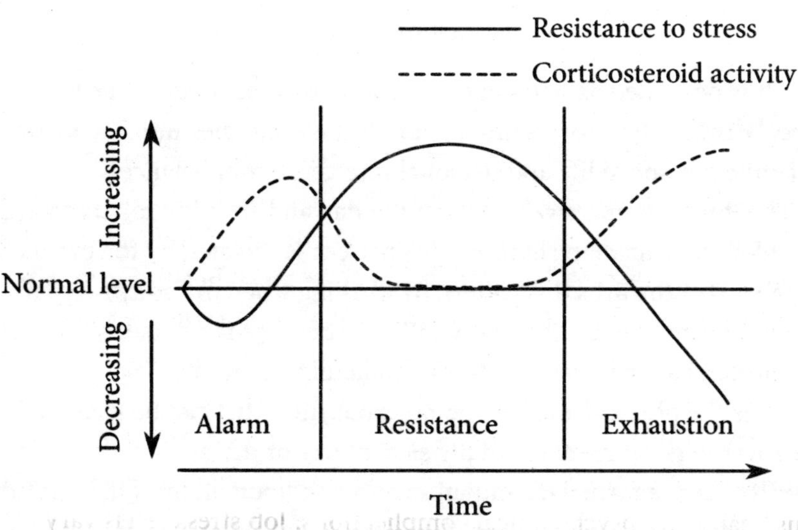

Fig. 6.1 The general adaptation syndrome (GAS)

Key Points

- Industrial psychologists should understand several work environment issues to create the right work environment.
- Positive work environment can increase the productivity and efficiency of workers. On the contrary, negative work environment may be counter-productive.
- Industrial psychologists must understand the organizational environment in the context of internal and task-related issues and external environmental issues.
- Work environment issues may contribute to employees' fatigue, monotony, boredom, accidents, safety, hazards, stress etc.
- Industrial psychologists can understand such environmental issues and counter the negative behavioural implications.

Important Terms

Burnout: It is described as striving too hard in one area of life while neglecting everything else. 'Workaholics', for example, put all their energies into their career, which puts their family life, social life and personal interests out of balance.

Circadian rhythm: Being awake during the day and sleeping for six to eight hours at night is called the circadian rhythm. This pattern is dictated by the brain's circadian clock. A shift worker disturbs this pattern by working when the body is programmed to sleep. Sleeping during the day is usually difficult, because the person's brain chemicals (neurotransmitters) are naturally set to the 'wakefulness' mode.

Fatigue: It is the physical and/or mental exhaustion that can be triggered by stress, medication, overwork, or mental and physical illness or disease.

Hazard audit: It is a formal examination and documentation of the hazards identified and the control measures selected. A small team of suitable staff should undertake the audit.

Illumination: It refers to maintaining natural light or equivalent brightness in the workplace. Sunlight is the best source of illumination for work.

Music at work: It is the most popular element in the work environment. Industrial psychologists help in taking a decision on intensity and variety of music at workplaces.

Noise level at work: Any sound unpleasant to ears is considered as noise. It is generally an annoying sound, which distracts our attention and interferes with our work.

Social or psychological hazards: Social and psychological matters contribute to psychological hazards, which stem from an employee's perceived feeling that he is going to lose his job, or when there is relocation or redeployment, or when he should adjust to organizational changes.

Whistle-blowing: It refers to the revelation or disclosure of illegal practices in an organization, often by those presently or in the past associated with it. Whistle-blowers act out of a sense of moral responsibility towards the long-term interests of the company. Good corporate governance practices have a code of action for instances of whistle-blowing.

Workplace stress: This can be caused by a wide range of factors including job dissatisfaction, heavy workload, conflicts with bosses or colleagues, bullying, constant change, or threats to job security.

Self-assessment Questions

1. Define the term work environment. List the internal work environment factors that influence employees' performance and productivity.
2. What is work-related fatigue? How can it be managed in an organization?
3. Explain the term boredom. Is it different from monotony? How can boredom be avoided in an organization?
4. For industrial psychologists, how are safety issues important? What steps do you recommend to avoid industrial accidents in an organization?
5. What are the internal task environment issues?
6. Explain the causes and symptoms of fatigue.
7. Explain how fatigue is diagnosed in the workplace?
8. What are the psychological causes of fatigue? What are the steps to overcome fatigue?
9. What is boredom at workplace? What are the features of boredom?
10. What is monotony at workplace? How it is managed?
11. Explain the various hazards and safety issues in workplaces.
12. Explain how hazards at workplaces can be managed.
13. Briefly explain the accident and safety issues in workplaces.
14. What is safety culture? What are the issues considered in developing a safety culture?
15. Explain the concept of stress. How can stress be managed in workplaces?
16. What is whistle-blowing? What are the factors that influence whistle-blowing?
17. What are the implications of ethics and values in workplaces?
18. Write short notes on the following:
    i. Music at work
    ii. Shift work
    iii. Safety culture
    iv. Hazards audit
    v. Workplace stress

Select Bibliography

1. Bhattacharyya DK (2006). *Human Resource Management*, 2nd edition. New Delhi: Excel Books.
2. Bhattacharyya DK (2009). *Organizational Behaviour: Concepts and Applications.* New Delhi: Oxford University Press.
3. Bhattacharyya DK (2011). *Industrial Management.* New Delhi: Vikas Publishing.
4. Goleman D (1998). *Working with Emotional Intelligence.* New York: Bantam Books.
5. Jex SM and TW Britt (2008). *Organizational Psychology.* New Jersey: John Wiley and Sons.
6. Muchinsky PM (1999). *Psychology Applied to Work,* 6th edition. Belmont: Wadsworth.
7. Seley H (1976). *The Stress of Life.* New York: McGraw-Hill.

7 Organizational Culture and Organizational Development

Learning Objectives

After reading this chapter, you will be able to:

- **Define organizational culture**
- **List the various national and international influences on organizational culture**
- **Understand the impact of organizational culture on its functioning**
- **Outline the diagnostic mechanism for cultural elements of an organization**
- **State the appropriate strategy for changing the organizational culture**
- **Discuss the behavioural impact of cultural change**
- **Outline the use of organizational development tools**

Overview

Industrial psychologists need to understand the culture of organizations. This is especially important for the new generation of knowledge workers, who are from diverse social and economic backgrounds. Culture is the moral, social and behavioural norms of an organization. It creates impact on beliefs, attitudes and priorities of organizational members. Building culture through continuous learning is now a global practice. This is primarily more important for globalisation and cross-border mergers and acquisitions. Movement of people from one country to another renewed our attention on building organization-specific corporate culture to bring order in behaviours and attitudes. To build corporate culture of their own, many global organizations have now started their own universities. These universities not only focus on competency building through renewal of knowledge and skill, but also transmit the organizational culture deeply into the minds of their employees. In our country, hardly few organizations focus on building corporate culture of their own. Indian organizations limit their efforts through general induction programs at the time of recruitment. A few also have an extended period of induction ranging from three to six months to orient their employees. However, they restrict it to job- or function-specific domain knowledge. Whether it is done or not, every organization has its own unique culture or value set. For some, it may be consciously created through induction while for others it may be unconsciously created, primarily based on the value systems of the top people or the promoter.

When in Rome, do as the Romans do! This is what we learn from Prof Greet Hofstede. After surveying more than 100,000 employees of IBM with operation in 50 countries he found five continuums of culture, which organizations around the world translate as culture of their own. Whether it is the focus on individualism or collectivism or power–distance approach, depends on organizational value system. Globally, collectivism is a more desired practice as it promotes team culture by developing common and consistent goals, organizational commitment, mutual accountability, team leadership and above all shared rewards. Power–distance focuses on distribution of power and adherence to formal channels. Uncertainty avoidance culture on the other hand hinges on the relative importance of rules to the employees, long-term employment and steady progression through well-defined career ladders. Dominant values focus on quality of relationships and job satisfaction and flexibility, while short-term versus long-term culture gets reflected in the relations between the organization and its employees. All these are the primary concern for industrial psychologists.

Organizational Culture

Every organization continuously interacts with its environment. This, therefore, requires balance between the internal features and the characteristics of the external environment, which is part of the contingency theory in organizational science. The theory suggests that an organization has to understand the dynamics of its environment in order to be able to adapt to the changing demands of the outside and inside (internal to the organization) world. There are many different ways of scanning the organizational environment. After scanning the organizational environment, it is imperative to go for organizational development (OD) in order to match with the requirement to stay updated in a competitive environment. However, to understand the OD, it is imperative to understand various other issues.

The concept of 'organizational culture' has become popular since the early 1980s. There is no consensus about its definition but most authors agree that it is something holistic, historically determined, related to the things anthropologists study, socially constructed, soft and difficult to change. It is something an organization has, but can also be seen as something an organization is.

Variations in national cultures

Organizational cultures should be distinguished from national cultures. Cultures manifest themselves, from superficial to deep, in symbols, heroes, rituals and values. National cultures differ mostly at the level of values; organizational cultures vary at the levels of symbols, heroes and rituals, together labelled as 'practices'.

Differences in national cultures have been studied by Hofstede for over 50 countries. They show five independent dimensions of values: power–distance; individualism versus collectivism; masculinity versus femininity; uncertainty avoidance; and long-term versus short-term orientation. National culture differences are reflected in solutions to organizational problems in different countries, but also in the validity of management theories in these countries. Different national cultures have different preferred ways of structuring organizations and different patterns of employee motivation. For example, they limit the options for performance appraisal, management by objectives, strategic management and humanisation of work.

Research into organizational cultures identified six independent dimensions of practices which are listed below.

- Process-oriented versus results-oriented
- Job-oriented versus employee-oriented
- Professional versus parochial
- Open systems versus closed systems
- Tightly versus loosely controlled
- Pragmatic versus normative

The position of an organization on these dimensions is determined in part by the business or industry the organization is in. Scores on the dimensions are also related to a number of other 'hard' characteristics of the organizations. These lead to conclusions about how organizational cultures can be and cannot be managed.

Managing international business means handling differences in national and organizational culture at the same time. Organizational cultures are somewhat manageable while national cultures are given facts for management; common organizational cultures across borders are what keep multinationals together.

Thus, the concept of organizational culture was born from early studies of organizational climate, intertwined with human resources and various sociological disciplines. The true definition is more a matter of perspective. Some authors like Bate believe that organization itself is a culture. This attributes organizational culture more as a metaphor for study through which meanings are constructed and expressed. A more modern view, like the one given by Wilson, however, considers organizational culture as a variable rather than a metaphor. Variables are different organizational practices, like performance management (Deal and Kennedy 1982), mechanism for effectiveness and control (Peters and Waterman 1982), recruitment and selection (Guest 1994), training and development (Schein 1968, 1991; O'Reilly 1989), knowledge management practices (Brown 1995), reward systems (Kerr and Slocum 1987) and overall human resource management practices.

Organizational culture in globalised scenario

The dictionary defines corporate culture as 'the act of developing intellectual and moral faculties, especially through education'. The other definition of culture is 'the moral, social, and behavioural norms of an organization based on the beliefs, attitudes, and priorities of its members'. Even though the first definition emphasises on building culture through the act of education, we find largely its relevance more in those organizations which have their unique system of emphasising on continuous learning. Many of them have their own universities, like Sears University, Hamburger, University of McDonald, Motorola University etc.

Hewlett–Packard

To illustrate, we can cite the example of Hewlett–Packard (HP). The company has been successful in creating a conscious corporate culture, which it calls 'The HP Way'. HP's corporate culture is based on (i) respect for others, (ii) a sense of community, and (iii) plain hard work as stated in the May 15, 1995 issue of the *Fortune* magazine. This culture is being sustained through extensive training of managers and all sections of employees. Today, HP's growth and success may be traced to its conscious corporate culture. The main features of HP's corporate culture are discussed here.

HP's culture is rooted in its commitment to diversity, inclusion and non-discrimination. Since its formation, HP has demonstrated ongoing commitment to people and to fair employment practices. As HP has grown and expanded throughout the world, its workforce has become more diverse. The company believes that this diverse workforce helps it realise its full potential. Recognising and developing the talents of the individual brings new ideas. The company benefits from the resulting infusion of creativity and innovation when HP people who have different experiences, perspectives and cultures work together. This is what drives innovation and high performance at HP. It also believes that a well managed, diverse workforce expands HP's base of knowledge, skills and cross-cultural understanding, which in turn, enables to understand, relate and respond to diverse and changing customers throughout the world, connecting them to the power of technology. The overall commitment is reflected in its philosophy of inclusion. The main elements of an inclusive organization are best seen in HP:

- A diverse, high-achieving workforce is the sustainable competitive advantage that differentiates HP. It is essential to win in the marketplaces, workplaces and communities around the world.

- An inclusive, flexible work environment that values differences motivates employees to contribute their best.
- To better serve customers, HP attracts, develops, promotes and retains a diverse workforce.
- Trust, mutual respect and dignity are fundamental beliefs that are reflected in HP's behaviour and actions.
- Accountability for diversity and inclusion goals drives HP's success.

General Electric company

Jack Welch, CEO, General Electric (GE), created a new corporate culture. The key elements of GE's corporate culture are as under:

- Redesigning the role of the leader in the new economy: creating followers through communicating a vision, and establishing open, caring relations with every employee
- Creating an open, collaborative workplace where everyone's opinion is welcome
- Empowering senior executives to run far-flung businesses in entrepreneurial fashion
- Liberating the workforce—making everybody a participant through improving vertical communication and empowerment of employees

Southwest airlines

Another illustration of corporate culture is Southwest Airlines. It is one of the profit-making airlines in the USA. Southwest's CEO, Herb Kelleher, defines the Southwest culture as under:

'Well, first of all, it starts with hiring. We are zealous about hiring. We are looking for a particular type of person, regardless of which job category it is. We are looking for attitudes that are positive and for people who can lend themselves to causes. We want folks who have a good sense of humour and people who are interested in performing as a team and take joy in team results instead of individual accomplishments. ....If you start with the type of person you want to hire, presumably you can build a workforce that is prepared for the culture you desire...

Another important thing is to spend a lot of time with your people and to communicate with them in a variety of ways. And a large part of it is demeanour. Sometimes we tend to lose sight of the fact that demeanour—the way you appear and the way you act—is a form of communication. We want our people to feel fulfilled and happy, and we want our management to radiate the demeanour that we are proud of our people, we are interested in them as individuals and we are interested in them outside the workforce, including the good and bad things that happen to them as individuals'.

Sears

An example of a more down-to-earth corporate culture can be of Sears, the second largest retail chain in the world. Sears emphasises the three Cs: Compelling place to work, compelling place to shop and compelling place for customer satisfaction. The company believes that these maxims of its culture when practised take into account overall growth and prosperity of their organization. Incidentally, they also align their performance management system with the three Cs. Similarly Wal Mart, the largest retail chain in the world also believes that all its employees are Associates and hence as a matter of corporate culture and practice, Wal Mart shares all strategic information with its employees to get the benefit of empowerment and motivation. This enables the company to achieve significant rate of growth every year.

Corporate Culture After Mergers

Mergers and acquisitions (M&A) also bring major changes in the corporate culture. There are many examples from around the world. Before discussing a case in detail, let us list certain cultural issues that were experienced by organizations around the world, during the post-merger phase.

- Disintegration of organizational value systems (Rent-to-own Store)
- Low employee morale that results in poor productivity and conflicts (Rent-to-own Store, Dell)
- Benefits of Synergy require time (IOC and IBP)—IOC's market share is 54% for POL products but in retail business its share is 40%. With IBP, IOC got 1540 outlets to its existing 7750 outlets (IBP's market share is 8%)
- HPCL, BPCL (together now enjoy 20%). Threat is from emerging new organizations like Reliance etc.
- Rationalisation and relocation of manpower may encounter problems (Blue Star)
- Generation gap may create conflict (CMC–Tata, Bank of Madura and ICICI)
- Flying of talent
- Different cultures (including cross-country culture)
- Rigidity to learn new things for the blue-collar employees
- Sentimental attachment
- Anxieties for the pink slip (as merger follows manpower rationalisation)
- Differences in HR style (Blue Star)
- Broken faith in management due the veil of secrecy in merger
- Stalemate in managerial positions (one has to leave or compromise for the new group which is taking over)

- Reduced employee enthusiasm
- To get a synergy of 2 + 2 > 4, cost control is implemented, which may affect the executive pay

Effective merger through cultural integration

Some of the good corporate practices to manage mergers and acquisitions would be possible through cultural integration. To ensure the same, organizations focus on:

- Ascertaining the differences in basic culture and procedures
- Pre-assessing the costs involved in integrating manpower from the merging organization.
- Plan for VRS for people rendered surplus
- Make provisions for increased HR cost for training and redeployment, relocation and VRS benefits
- Accommodate employees (including executives) of the merging organization in the new environment (Tata and VSNL)
- Develop an integrated culture with inputs from two organizations (Tata and VSNL)
- Focus on training and learning process (TCS executives handle mostly international projects while CMC executives handle mostly domestic projects)
- Develop a new organization chart and make it transparent
- Align the compensation package, if required even by redesigning (IMB and PwC)

Therefore, all these examples illustrate how developing and sustaining a conscious culture in the organization can contribute to its growth and prosperity. Organizational culture as a separate branch has received priority due to globalisation and the consequent mobility of people and cross-cultural influences, more particularly for multinational and transnational organizations.

Hofstede's cultural orientation model

To appreciate cultural diversity, Hofstede's cultural orientation model is considered as one of the best. Greet Hofstede, the Dutch researcher and author of *Culture's Consequences* elaborated his pioneering study of IBM affiliates in 50 countries. In fact, his work laid the foundation for the field of comparative management. This model has five elements.

- **Individual versus collective orientation:** At this level, behaviour is appropriately regulated.
- **Power–distance orientation:** It explains the extent to which less powerful parties accept the existing distribution of power and the degree to which adherence to formal channels is maintained.

- **Uncertainty avoidance orientation:** It is the degree to which employees are threatened by ambiguity, and the relative importance to employees of rules, long-term employment and steady progression through well-defined career ladder.
- **Dominant values orientation:** Dominant values like assertiveness, monetary focus, well-defined gender roles, formal structure, focus on quality of relationships and job satisfaction and flexibility are covered.
- **Short-term versus long-term orientation:** Through this concept we understand the time frame used, short-term (involving more inclination towards consumption, saving face by keeping up) versus long-term (involving preserving status-based relationships, thrift, deferred gratifications etc).

Quite often we debate how cross-cultural influence may persuade us to redesign the organizations, more particularly our human resource management policies and reward systems. The best example we find is in theory Z management, which combines American and Japanese management philosophies. Following are the requisites for changing a company's 'team culture':

- ➢ Common and consistent goals
- ➢ Organizational commitment
- ➢ Clarity in roles among team members
- ➢ Team leadership
- ➢ Mutual accountability with the team
- ➢ Complementary knowledge and skills
- ➢ Reinforcement of required behavioural competencies
- ➢ Power (real and perceived)
- ➢ Shared rewards

Culture applied at workplace

At the workplace, culture is important in the following areas:

- Mergers and Acquisitions
- Strategic alliances and partnerships
- Restructuring issues
- Change management
- Self-development processes
- People management skills
- Executive coaching
- Negotiation skills

- Multinational/remote/team-building
- Facilitating top performing teams
- Project teams
- Expatriate/inpatriate coaching/briefings
- Sales and marketing skills
- General management training and education
- Counselling
- Leadership
- Organizational influencing

Organizational structure

Organizational structure is also one of the central issues in organization theory in the 20th century. Three main subthemes of organizational structure have emerged: the archetypal bureaucracy, the stakeholder model and contemporary thinking, especially reflexive theories.

Archetypal bureaucracy theory stems from the theories of Max Weber. Its features are rationality, task specialisation, hierarchy and regularity and there is a strong emphasis on structure as a controlling force. In the stakeholder model, on the other hand, rationality is abandoned and structure becomes the framework in which the various stakeholders—leaders, internal parties, and external parties—seek to achieve their respective goals.

However, new research on organizational structure has focused on variables such as culture, metaphors, learning forms, dynamic organizational variants and fields such as total quality management, six sigma, lean manufacturing and the related paradigm shift. Both organizational theory and practice reflect on the significance and use of the concept of structure.

Managing Cultural Change

A need for cultural change does not always necessitate mergers and acquisitions. It may be also for developing the organization's capability to respond to the changing environment. Both Toyota and Honda of Japan had to change their corporate culture to suit conditions in the USA. But the other major Japanese company Mazda had to withdraw from the USA, due to their failure in adapting to a new culture, despite the fact, they entered the US market much before the other two. In India also we have experienced the cultural mismatch between Honda and Hero groups. But, Suzuki with Maruti in India, is a successful case of adaptive corporate culture. Many Indian organizations had to redefine their culture, keeping pace with globalisation.

Culture changes in organizations have to be personally led by the top management. This job cannot be delegated to people down the line. Primarily the top management exerts its power to influence for bringing about the necessary change. It requires dynamic leadership, an understanding of people's behaviour and the changing environmental cues. Often for restructuring, organizations may require to go in for skill change and changes in peoples' attitudes. These usually follow culture change. It encounters resistance and non-cooperation from people. But with sustained intervention from the top management, it can be achieved. Culture change also succeeds changes in internal practices. Making people innovative, empowered to take decisions, and capable to trouble-shoot the problems, is not so easy. Top management and the team require to lead the show and identify the change agents to further the process of cultural transformation.

Change in organizational culture is a constant challenge to broaden, deepen, or modify organizational capabilities and resource strengths in response to ongoing customer–market changes. Focus on customer relationship management (CRM) and developing people capabilities require organizations to undergo perceptive cultural change. Managers play the role of a teacher in cultural transformation; they send signals through practices, which people down the line emulate.

Building a strategy-fit corporate culture is important for successful execution of strategies, which produces a performing work environment and develops esprit de corps, as propounded by Henry Fayol.

Since culture sets the work climate, any change in corporate culture always encounters resistance. Organizations in a changing business environment always require taking an adaptive culture, which among others, necessitates being receptive to new ideas, experimentation, innovation, new strategies and new operating practices. Changing the prevailing organizational culture, therefore, requires competent leadership at the top. Apart from the symbolic actions from the top leadership, it also requires substantive actions, which demonstrate the degree of commitment from the top. With symbolic and substantive actions from the top management, behaviour of the people down the line can be changed automatically. Similarly, cultural change in organizations requires strong corporate ethics and values. Ethical norms develop business principles and moral values of people, which develop their capability to take socially responsive decisions. Ethical standards denote integrity, doing the right thing and genuine concern for stakeholders. To ensure practice of ethical standards, organizations conduct programs in ethics and values through training, form ethics committees, develop code of ethics and periodically conduct ethics audit. Above all, however, it is important for the top management to comply with those ethical norms that they expect people down the line to comply.

Another important enabler for cultural change is the top leadership. Leadership requires understanding of the organizational pulse through active listening and talking to people, coaching and mentoring, transparency in information sharing and encouraging people to be creative and innovative in their work. Since it exerts influence to elicit voluntary participation from organizational members, it requires leaders (top management) to be more proactive in their practices, so that people lower down the order can emulate them. Adopting a participative approach in planning and decision-making, developing problem-solving capability and supporting the people to mature are also important prerequisites for successful leadership in bringing cultural change in the organization.

Thus, implementing cultural change in organizations, requires a series of actions, without, however, any universally accepted practices. How it is done, therefore, depends on specific organizational constructs. In India, we have many such cases of successful cultural transformation as also in other countries. When Videocon, a traditional Indian organization, acquired a legacy-bound multinational like Philips, it had to pass through successive, often difficult, stages of cultural transformation. However, with the sustained efforts from the top management, mostly in line with the above stated courses of action, it could successfully achieve the results. In their initial phase of cultural transformation, the top management of Videocon even spent 80% of their time to listen to the people, playing a supportive role to infuse confidence to allay apprehensions. Organizational cultural change, therefore, is more situation-specific.

Organizational diagnostics for managing cultural change

Organizational diagnostics are measures that can apply to anyone in the organization, and can be aggregated to represent different levels of the organization, such as departments, branches, or the organization as a whole. These are useful diagnostics 'for gauging the morale of a company's workforce, testing the impact of new policies or procedures, monitoring long-term trends in the workforce, and determining where interventions are needed'. Here we shall highlight some of the measures which are essential for an organization's growth and development.

Attitudes towards work: Attitudes are the learned cognitive responses of an individual. Change in knowledge is followed by change in attitude. Diagnosis of attitude is done with the following areas of focus:

Job satisfaction: It denotes the degree to which employees are satisfied and happy with their jobs.

Sample item: *I am generally satisfied with the kind of work I do in this job.*

Role clarity: Knowledge of exactly what behaviour is expected in one's job

Sample item: *I know what my job responsibilities are.*

Role conflict: The extent to which two or more pressures occur together such that complying with one would make doing the other more difficult

Sample item: *I often have to bend a rule or policy in order to carry out an assignment.*

Autonomy: It describes the extent to which employees have a say in the scheduling of their tasks, as well as decisions regarding the procedures to be followed and equipment to be used in their work.

Sample item: *I am able to act independently of my supervisor in performing my job function.*

Participation in decision-making: It shows the extent to which employees participate in setting the goals and policies of the organization.

Sample item: *I can help in making decisions which affect my work.*

Job Involvement: The degree to which employees are committed to and involved in their job.

Sample item: *I don't mind working extra hours if I can finish a task.*

Organizational commitment: The major determinant of organizational success is the commitment shown by the employees. This can be measured using the following approach:

Job security: It refers to the ability to keep a job for as long as possible with satisfactory job performance.

Sample item: *I can be sure of my job as long as I do good work.*

Loyalty: It denotes the feelings of affection for and attachment to one's organization.

Sample item: *If another organization offered me more money for the same kind of work, I would almost certainly accept.*

Trust in the management: It is the indicator of the extent to which employees ascribe good intentions to, and have trust in, the works and actions of the management and the organization.

Sample item: *Management at my location acts with sincerity.*

Identification: It shows how much the employees adopt as their own, the goals and values of the organization.

Sample item: *I really feel as if the organization's problems are my own.*

Alienation: It is a measure of the extent to which employees feel disappointed with their career and professional development.

Sample item: *I don't feel a sense of pride or accomplishment as a result of the type of work that I do.*

Helplessness: It refers to the feeling among employees that they possess few opportunities within and limited alternatives outside their organization.

Sample item: *I feel I have too few options to consider leaving this organization.*

Organizational climate: The culture of an organization sets its climate. A positive organizational culture creates the right climate to make people feel comfortable to work. Organizational climate can be measured on the basis of the following attributes:

Fairness: It means employees perceive their workplace to be equitable and free of bias.

Sample item: *There is fair treatment of employees at my workplace.*

Safety: It shows how much the employees perceive their workplace to be safe and free of physical danger.

Sample item: *I am often in situations at work where I can easily get physically hurt.*

Support: It shows how the employees perceive their organization as providing emotional support to them.

Sample item: *Management here is interested in the welfare of its people.*

Communication: It denotes the accuracy and openness of information exchange.

Sample item: *I am kept informed about changes that affect my work.*

Tolerance for risk: It shows the degree to which the organization encourages bold action, risk and independence of thought from its employees.

Sample item: *Risk taking is a value supported by our corporate culture.*

Flexibility: It indicates the degree of adaptability and tolerance for ambiguity in an organization.

Sample item: *This organization adapts quickly to changes.*

Continuous learning: What are the opportunities for training and development available in the organization?

Sample item: *There are adequate opportunities to pursue professional development activities beyond the scope of my immediate job.*

Organizational Development

Organizational Development (OD) is understood to mean planned change based on the paradigm of action research. OD can, thus, be described as a learning process. The active development of an organization towards its desired corporate identity succeeds only if this change process is undertaken holistically. From a behavioural perspective this means, for example, that the behavioural conditions that lie within the person (qualifications, motivation) as well as those lying outside the person (organizational structure, technology) must be modified. The process of change is also described as a political process. That is, in which phases of change and for which reasons is the mobilisation of power salient? Lastly, the change process is often examined in terms of whether, and how, basic assumptions within an organization can be decoded through an analysis of symbols.

The types of intervention include the person-centred approach, structural approach and relationship approach. The first one requires the development of both a social competence that fosters cooperation and a general intellectual competence that promotes innovation. The second one is based on re-integrating hitherto segregated work sequences and attempts to decentralise decision-making. The relationship approach requires team development, role negotiation and survey–feedback methods.

Overall, evaluations of OD bear out the potential fruitfulness of its key approaches. But follow-up studies have thus far shown the outcomes to be widely variable, meaning that the degree of success or failure cannot be precisely forecast in each case.

A new approach to organizational transformation (OT) is beginning to gain acceptance in the literature. OT is a 'harder' concept, often associated with re-engineering, and there is some concern that this could be used, not as a contingency measure, but as a replacement for organizational development. Clearly there are dangers in a widespread adoption of such an approach.

Organizational Development Process

Organizational Development is a strategy or an effort, which is planned and managed from the top, to bring about planned changes for increasing organizational effectiveness through interventions based on social philosophy. The following statement by Alfred P Sloan amply clarifies the need for OD in an organization.

> *Circumstances of an ever-changing market and an ever-changing product are capable of breaking any business organization if that organization is unprepared for change indeed, in my opinion, if it has not provided procedures for anticipating change.*

Characteristics of OD

The important features of OD are discussed below.

Planned organizational change

It involves identification of the problem, diagnosis and development of strategies for improvement. The variables considered by OD programs are—values, attitudes, organizational culture and team development.

Planned intervention

It involves making an organization become more viable through planned intervention. It, therefore, examines present working norms, values and possible areas of conflict and develops alternatives for better health. The interventionist needs to diagnose different subsystems of the organization to develop alternatives. The important areas of intervention are planning and decision-making processes, goal-setting, team development, organizational structure, values and culture and skill upgradation.

Commitment of the top management to OD

Top management should feel interested in the program and its outcome and effectively support efforts in this direction. Unless mutual trust and collaborative relationships are developed between the change agents (which in most of the cases are consultants or professionals) and the management of the enterprise, efforts in OD may not succeed.

Social philosophy as a norm of change

The bureaucratic model of organization ignores the basic human factors and thereby reduces organizational effectiveness. The interventionist, therefore, requires knowledge of behavioural science to develop a system which is more humane and democratic.

Important Goals of OD

OD emphasises the need for changing from a closed system to an open one by inculcating various changes in the organization. Such changes inter alia, also include introduction of concepts of social philosophy in the organization which makes it socially more responsible and transparent.

- To supplement authority and hierarchical role with knowledge and skills, replacing traditional authority assigned to roles, which creates a more congenial work environment
- To build mutual trust and confidence in the organization for managing and reducing conflict
- To change structure and roles inconsistent with accomplishment of goals
- To encourage a sense of ownership and pride in the organization
- To decentralise decision-making staying close to the source of activity
- To emphasise on feedback, self-control and self-direction
- To develop the spirit of cooperation, mutual trust and confidence
- To develop a reward system based on achievement of goals and development of people

It is apparent from the above discussion that the goal of OD is basically to change the attitudes of people in the organization so as to enable them to identify the change areas and implement the desired organizational changes on their own.

Steps in Organizational Development

According to Robert Black and Jane S Mouton (1963), OD consists of six phases as shown below:

- Investigation by each member of the organization of his own managerial styles
- Examination of boss–subordinate relationship
- Analysis of team work action
- Exploration of coordination issues of interrelated terms
- Identifying and defining major organizational problem areas
- Planning for executing the solutions agreed upon that result in changes in the organization

OD passes through a series of well-defined stages that are discussed here.

Identification and diagnosis of the problem: The required changes in relation to various units in the organization should be identified and diagnosed by duly examining the feed-back from employees. Effective identification and diagnosis of the problem should be preceded by an employee survey.

Developing the strategy: While developing appropriate strategy, it is necessary to study people, subsystems and the organization as a total system. Strategy is the direction and scope of an organization in the long run, matching resources and the changing environment.

Implementing the program: The OD program should be implemented in a phased manner, i.e., it should be tried at the outset only in small parts of the organization and on getting positive results only it should gradually be implemented in the total organization. Since total organizational change precedes changes in attitude, values and beliefs of the people, the initial thrust should be given to training of employees, improvement of their skill, developing self-awareness, improving interpersonal relationships, reducing conflict etc.

Reviewing the progress of the program: Review of the OD program should be preferably done by a qualified person who was not involved in designing and developing it so that unbiased opinion can be obtained.

Key Points

- The term organizational culture generally refers to the shared meanings, beliefs and understanding held by a particular group or organization about its problems, practices and goals.
- Industrial psychologists need to know the organizational culture, as culture influences the behavioural pattern of employees, and cultural change also reflects on the behavioural change of employees.
- Organizational culture evolves from the social practices of the members of organizations and is, therefore, socially created realities that exist in the heads and minds of organizational members as well as in the formal rules, policies and procedures of organizational structures.
- Like organizational culture, corporate culture also refers to a company's values, beliefs, business principles, traditions, ways of operating and internal work environment. It is developed from a complex combination of sociological forces operating within organizational boundaries.
- Industrial psychologists need to understand that organizational culture can both be a positive contributor or a deterrent to organizational success. Ensuring a culture-fit organization requires proper initiatives for changing the culture through organizational development.
- Industrial psychologists need to understand the dynamics of the environment in order to be able to adapt to the changing demands outside and inside the organization, so that a culture-fit organization can be developed.

Important Terms

Archetypal bureaucracy theory: Its features are rationality, task specialisation, hierarchy and regularity. There is strong emphasis on structure as a controlling force.

Hofstede's cultural orientation model: Professor Greet Hofstede, after studying the differences in national cultures of more than 50 countries, has identified five independent dimensions of values: power–distance, individualism versus collectivism, masculinity versus femininity, uncertainty avoidance and long-term versus short-term orientation.

Organizational commitment: It emphasises on the emotional bonding between employees and the organization, continuance of commitment, cognitive dissonance (desire of individuals to reconcile internal inconsistencies and to maintain uniform behaviour) and normative pressures (which make employees feel committed to their organizations).

Organizational development (OD): It is understood to mean planned change based on the paradigm of action research. The development of an organization towards its desired corporate identity succeeds only if this change process is undertaken holistically.

Organizational diagnostics: It refers to measures that can apply to anyone in the organization, and can be aggregated to represent different levels such as departments, branches, or the organization as a whole.

Self-assessment Questions

1. Define corporate culture. Why do organizations across the globe try to create their own culture?
2. Explain Hofstede's cultural orientation model.
3. Discuss how an organization can create a team culture. What are the areas that an organization should change while endeavouring for a team culture?
4. Give a detailed account of the corporate culture at HP and Sears. Visit their websites for information and form your answer.
5. What are the important differences in work-related values? Give your answer from corporate examples.
6. What is Organizational Development? What are its important characteristics? How does it differ from management development?
7. Write a short note on culture-specific management.
8. Write short notes on the following:
   i. Individual versus collective orientation
   ii. Dominant values orientation
   iii. Uncertainty avoidance
   iv. Power–distance
   v. Masculinity and femininity
   vi. OD intervention

Select Bibliography

1. Albert M and M Silverman (1984a). Making management philosophy a cultural reality, Part 1: Getting started, *Personnel*, 61: 12–21.
2. Albert M and M Silverman (1984b). Making management philosophy a cultural reality, Part 2: Getting started, *Personnel*, 61: 28–35.
3. Bate P (1994). *Strategies for Cultural Change.* London: Butterworth Heinemann.
4. Bhattacharyya DK (2011). *Organizational Change and Development.* New Delhi: Oxford University Press.
5. Bhattacharyya DK (2010). *Cross-cultural Management.* New Delhi: PHI Learning.
6. Bhattacharyya DK (2009). *Organizational Behaviour: Concepts and Applications.* New Delhi: Oxford University Press.
7. Brown A (1995). *Organizational Culture.* London: Pitman Publishing.
8. Carr C (1996). *Choice, Chance and Organizational Change.* New York: Amacom.
9. Deal T and A Kennedy (1982). *Corporate Cultures.* Reading: Addison–Wesley.
10. Guest DE (1992). Right enough to be dangerously wrong: An analysis of the 'In search of excellence' phenomenon, *In* G Salaman (ed), *Human Resources Strategies.* London: Sage.
11. Hampden-Turner C and F Trompenaars (2000). *Building Cross-cultural Competence: How to Create Wealth from Conflicting Values.* New Haven: Yale University Press.
12. Harrison JR and GP Carrol (1991). Keeping the faith: A model of cultural transformation in formal organizations, *Admin Sci Quart*, 36: 552–82.
13. Hofstede G (1980). *Cultural Consequence: International Differences in Work-related Values.* Beverly Hills: Sage.
14. Kerr J and JW Slocum (1987). Managing corporate culture through reward systems, *Acad Man Exec*, 99–108.
15. Kotter JP and JL Heskett (1992). *Corporate Culture and Performance.* New York: Free Press.
16. Peters T and R Waterman (1982). *In Search of Excellence.* New York: Harper and Row.
17. Schein EH (1969). *Process Consultation: Its role in Organizational Development.* Reading: Addison–Wesley.

18. Schein EH (1990). Organizational culture, *American Psychologist*, 45: 109–19.
19. Sloan AP (1964). *My Years with General Motors*, J McDonald (ed). New York: Doubleday.
20. Spradley JP (1972). *Culture Cognition: Rules, Maps and Plans*. San Francisco: Chandler.

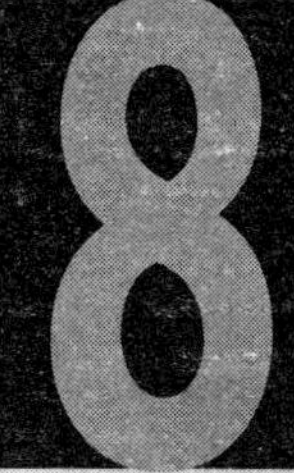

Theories of Leadership

Learning Objectives

After reading this chapter, you will be able to:

- **Outline the different theories of leadership**
- **Understand the difference between a leader and a manager**
- **Appreciate the different styles of leadership**
- **Discuss why leadership is essential for managing organizational behaviour**
- **List the process of development of leadership abilities in the organization**

Overview

Industrial psychologists, besides their other roles also contribute to leadership development among the employees. Development of leadership qualities requires two factors: employees who understand their respective strengths and weaknesses and support from the management in terms of training and development programs, so that employees can gain confidence in playing the leadership role.

It is now widely recognised that leadership is an essential quality for managers and employees. In any work situation when two or more people join together to work for a goal, a structure or a group develops and the leadership emerges. The difference between success and failure in business, sports or any movement can be attributed to leadership. Reviewing the existing literature on leadership, it can be defined as an activity which influences people to strive willingly for group objectives. It exists only in relationships and only in the imagination and perceptions of the 'followers'. *Leadership is something that goes on among people; it is not something within a person.* Leadership makes a substantial difference to organizations. It is typically a solution for most of the organizational problems.

Definition

Let us first examine some definitions of leadership. We shall then go on to identify different attributes and traits of good leadership. Raven (1976) defined a leader as 'someone who occupies a position in a group, influences others in accordance with the role expectation of the position and coordinates and directs the group in maintaining itself and reaching its goal'. Sears (1988) defined the leader as '...... the one who initiates action, gives order, makes decisions, settles disputes between group members, offers encouragement, serves as a model, and is in the forefront of group activity'. Therefore, the leader is the person who has the most impact on a group's behaviour and beliefs. Avery (1990) further expanded this concept as a 'process of influence between a leader and his followers to attain group, organizational and societal goals'.

Let us now consider a few more definitions of leadership. According to George Terry (1977) 'Leadership is the relationship in which one person, the leader, influences others to work together willingly on related tasks to attain that which the leader desires'. McFarland states that it is 'a process of interpersonal influence by which the executive or manager influences the activities of others in choosing and attaining the given ends'. Harold Koontz and Heinz Weihrich defined leadership 'as the art or process of influencing people so that they will strive willingly and enthusiastically toward the achievement of group goals'. Robert Tannenbaum, IR Weschler and F Massarick defined it '.......as a process of interpersonal relationships, through which a manager attempts to influence the behaviour of others toward the attainment of predetermined objective'. Keith Davis, on the other hand, defines it as '....the ability to persuade others to seek defined objectives enthusiastically. It is the human factor which binds group together and motivates it towards goals'.

Characteristics of Leadership

It is clear from the above definitions that leadership is a process of influencing people for achieving intended goals in a given situation. Therefore, we can list the characteristics of leadership as follows.

- **It is a personal quality**: This is what makes other people follow a leader. The quality of a leader is the aggregation of his intelligence, communication skills, emotional balance, inner drive, energy and other managerial skills (like conceptual, technical, human relations etc). To make others follow or exert themselves on the job, requires these qualities in different proportions depending on the practical situations.
- **It is a process of influencing others**: Only through influence can a leader make others work towards achieving goals. People may lack initiative or the urge to work or be de-motivated. Such behavioural characteristics may seriously impede the achievement of organizational objectives. But a good leader through his influence can turn the situation in his favour and motivate people towards high performance.
- **It regulates individual behaviour**: Individual behavioural attributes may stand against achieving group goals. A leader through his process of influence can regulate the individual's behaviour to submit to group norms. To illustrate, following an approach of 'discipline without punishment', as advocated by John Huberman, a leader can correct the indiscipline of an individual and transform him as a good performer.

- **Relationship between leaders and followers**: A leader succeeds by developing good relationship with the followers. He or she cannot flourish in a vacuum. That is why we call leadership also as followership. In order to develop such a relationship, the leader has to gain the confidence of the followers. This is done by developing a two-way relationship, through effective interpersonal communication and also through participative decision-making, that is taking decision by group consensus.
- **It is a continuous process**: Leadership is not a one-off process. In order to be a good leader, the manager should sustain the process continuously. Hence, it is not true that once a leader, always a leader.
- **Leadership is situational**: Leadership is exerted in a situation, which varies time to time. Responding to varying situations requires different leadership approach. One situation may require taking a lenient view, while another may otherwise. Since organizations need to respond to changes in order to remain competitive, leaders also require to tailore their approach. This requires leaders to develop multiple skills and abilities, so as to come out as winners.

Bolman and Deal have listed four important characteristics of leadership as under:

- Ability to get others to do what the organization wants (power)
- Motivate people to get things done—mostly through persuasion
- Provide a vision
- Empower people to do what they want

Leadership and management

A good leader may be a poor manager and a good manager need not be a leader. Bennis and Nanus suggested that 'managers do things right and leaders do the right thing'. Yet the terms managers and leaders are used interchangeably. However, leadership and management are not the same. We find the presence of leadership in unorganized groups also. But management exists only in organized and structured groups. A manager is more than a leader. Due to his positional role, a manager has to organize and control the activities of people towards the accomplishment of objectives. As a manager, one has to perform all functions of management but as a leader one is more related to the directing part, i.e., influencing people to achieve goals. Therefore, leadership is a part of management but not the whole of management. That is why, it is often said 'All managers are leaders but all leaders are not managers'.

To stretch the debate further, let us examine views of major contributors in this regard. Their main contentions are that leaders and managers vary in their orientation towards goals, perception about work and interpersonal style. French (1987) while distinguishing between a leader and a manager opined that:

> *'Leaders ... are often dramatic and unpredictable in style. They tend to create an atmosphere of change, ferment even chaos. They are often obsessed by their ideas, which appear as visionary and consequently excite, stimulate and drive other people to work hard to create reality out of fantasy. ... managers are typically hard-working, analytical, tolerant and fair-minded. They have a strong sense of belonging to the organization, and take great pride in perpetuating and improving the status quo'.*

Another opposing view, states that leadership is just one aspect of what a manager does. Leaders are only involved in influencing subordinates towards the achievement of organizational goals.

Vecchio (1988) pointed out that **'leadership can exist on a formal or informal basis'**.

We can summarise the differences between leadership and management with a quote from John Kotter (1991):

> *'Leadership is different from management, but not for the reason most people think. Leadership is not mystical and mysterious. It has nothing to do with having charisma or other exotic personality traits. It is not the province of a chosen few. Nor is leadership necessarily better than management or a replacement for it. Rather, leadership and management are two distinctive and complementary activities. Both are necessary for success in an increasingly complex and volatile business environment'.*

Management functions include planning, organising, staffing, directing and controlling. In order to direct his subordinates a manager must motivate, communicate, supervise, guide and lead them. Thus, it is in his directing function that a manager becomes responsible for effectively and successfully leading his subordinates. Managing can be more effective if those who manage are also the leaders, because leadership can substantially influence the results. Since a part of the manager's job involves getting things done through the efforts of other people, he will be more successful in the job if he is also skilful leader. Following are the important favourable results produced if managers are also good leaders:

- The leader guides and directs by eliminating uncertainties as to what should be done and thus coordinating individual efforts to make them move in a unified direction.
- The leader motivates people and integrates individual needs with the needs of the organization.
- The leader represents the group to the outside world and vice versa. He or she is looked upon by the group as a source of information and satisfaction.

Table 8.1 Differences between leaders and managers

Leaders	Managers
A manager is more than a leader.	A leader need not be a manager.
Leadership is a narrow term.	Management is a wider term.
A leader may also be in an informal group.	A manager fits in an organized structure.
A leader exerts influence on people to voluntarily achieve group goals. A leader does only one aspect of the management functions, i.e., directing.	A manager exercises different functions to achieve group goals. Therefore, a manager's influence is more holistic.
A leader earns his/her authority by virtue of his/her skill.	The authority of a manager stems from his or her professional role, delegated from the top.
Leaders need not be managers.	To be a successful manager, one has to be a good leader.

Three things provided by the leader as mentioned above are also referred to as direction, drive and representation, and sufficient to prove that leadership is an essential part of successful management. It is, however, argued that since managers have the authority to provide incentives, reprimand, fine, deprive or otherwise punish people in the organization, management leadership is more potential than real. Discipline and conformity can be maintained through the hierarchy and fear of loss of employment. However, leadership should not be emphasised so as to make it synonymous with management. It will improve the results if the manager is also a skilful leader. But a leader need not be a good manager as managing involves more than mere leading and a manager can do reasonably well even when he is not a leader. Leadership, therefore, is considered as one of the significant pre-requisites to managerial effectiveness. Table 8.1 lists some of the important features that differentiate leadership from management.

Formal and informal leaders

Structure of the organization is characterised by the hierarchy of positions which are manned by individuals in the scalar chain. Officially every manager enjoys power to lead and secure support of his subordinates. Managers are more than leaders because they have the formal authority to direct, motivate and lead people. This kind of leadership is known as formal or managerial leadership. Informal leaders are not delegated any authority to lead; rather they acquire such authority to guide and lead. Informal leadership is spontaneous and is part of an informal organization. If properly handled, the informal organization offers a good training ground for formal leaders to develop and test their leadership skills.

Significance of Leadership

From the meaning, characteristics and differences between leadership and management, we can understand how the former is important to an organization.

- **It improves motivation and morale of employees**: A successful leader influences the behaviour of an individual which enhances the involvement of individual employee to work. By creating confidence in employees and sustaining their enthusiasm and involvement in achieving organizational goals, it enhances their motivation and morale. Even during a crisis in an organization (viz., low profitability due to market slow down or other reasons), a leader can sustain a high level of commitment and motivation from employees. This may ultimately help in turnaround of the organization.That is why good leaders are considered as turnaround agents for the organization.
- **It leads to higher performance**: Leadership pulls the group to strive for results, i.e., achieving organizational goals. With increased level of commitment and motivation, a good leader, therefore, leads to higher performance of employees. This leads to increased productivity, which results in increased profitability, even in a competitive market.
- **It is an aid to authority**: Leadership is a process of influencing others. Mere use of authority by managers may not lead to results. But when managerial authority is enriched with good leadership, employees start cooperating. Therefore, formal exercise of authority may not bring success. Authority with leadership only can bring success to the organization.
- **It determines organizational success**: In the process of unification of group efforts to achieve organizational goals, leadership enhances organizational effectiveness. A good manager alone cannot achieve this.
- **It helps to respond to change**: Organizations today need to quickly respond to changes. A change in technology, process, methods, plans (including strategic plans) always encounter resistance from people working in organizations. Leadership can play a great role in implementing change in organizations by creating a conducive environment. People follow leaders; like to emulate the examples set by their leaders, which therefore makes the change process smooth and successful.
- **It inculcates values in organization**: A value-based organization gets increased commitment and loyalty from employees. A good leader being inspirational, he or she can also successfully percolate values, which shape the attitude of the employees towards work.

Principles of Leadership

The basic principles of leadership can be grouped as under:

- **A leader must know himself/herself and continuously seek self-improvement**: To know the self, one has to understand attributes like: be, know and do. Seeking self-improvement means continually strengthening such attributes which can be accomplished through reading, self-study, classes etc.
- **Be technically proficient**: As a leader, one must know both his own job and that of his followers.
- **Leader must seek responsibility and accept responsibility for his actions**: The leader must guide the organization to new heights and may not be successful at all times. This must not lead to blaming others. He or she should accept responsibility, analyse the situation and take corrective action.
- **The leader must make sound and timely decisions.** Using the various tools for problem-solving, planning and decision-making, a leader must make sound and timely decisions.
- **The leader must set the example.** A leader is a role model for his followers. He must not only hear what he is expected to do, but also see.
- **Knowing people and thinking about their well-being**: The leader must have empathy for his followers and should be caring towards them.
- **The leader must keep the followers informed**: Transparency in information enhances commitment from the followers. Hence, a leader must know how to communicate and keep his followers informed.
- **The leader must develop a sense of responsibility in the followers**: Development orientation requires inculcating good character traits within the followers, which will help them to carry out their professional responsibilities.
- **The leader must ensure that tasks are understood, supervised and accomplished**: This can be achieved only through transparent communication with the followers.
- **The leader must train the followers to work as a team**: Inculcating team spirit and culture, enables a leader to accomplish the goals. Hence, this is also considered one of the important principles of leadership.
- **The leader should develop full capabilities of the organization**: A leader can help in developing an organization to its fullest capabilities by fostering team spirit.

Factors of leadership

The four major factors of leadership are as follows.

Follower: Different people require different styles of leadership. For example, a newly recruited person requires more supervision than an experienced one. Similarly, a follower with poor motivation requires a different approach than one with a high degree of motivation. Thus, the starting point is having a good understanding of human nature: needs, emotions and motivation. Leader must know his followers' be, know and do attributes.

Leader: One must have an honest understanding of what one is, what one knows, and what one can do. Moreover, it is the followers, not the leader who determine whether a leader is successful. If a follower does not trust or lacks confidence in a leader, then he will be uninspired. Hence, to be successful a leader he or she has to convince the followers, not the self or superiors.

Communication: A leader leads through two-way communication. It need not always be verbal, it may be non-verbal also. For instance, through personal selling (his own behaviour) a leader 'sets the example'. The leader should not ask the followers to perform anything that he would not be willing to do himself. What and how a leader communicates either builds or harms the relationship between him and his followers.

Situation: Every situation is different. What one does in one leadership situation may not always work in another. A leader must use his judgement to decide the best course of action and the leadership style needed for each situation. For example, one may need to confront an employee for inappropriate behaviour, but if the confrontation is too late or too early, too harsh or too weak, results may be disastrous.

Environment and Leadership

Every organization has a particular work environment that dictates to a considerable degree how its leaders respond to problems and opportunities. This is brought about by a heritage of its past and present leaders. They exert influence on the environment by three types of actions:

- The goals and performance standards they establish
- The values they establish for the organization
- The business and people concepts they establish

Successful organizations have good leaders who set high standards and goals such as strategies, market leadership, plans, presentations, productivity, quality and reliability. Values reflect the concern the organization has for its employees, customers, investors, vendors and the community. These values define the manner in which business will be conducted and what type of business the organization will engage in. Concepts define what products or services the organization will offer and the methods and processes for conducting business. These goals, values and concepts make up the organization's 'personality' or how it is observed by both outsiders and insiders. This personality also defines its roles, relationships and rewards.

Roles are the positions that are defined by a set of expectations about behaviour of any newly recruited person. Each role has a set of tasks and responsibilities that may or may not be spelled out. Roles have a powerful effect on behaviour because money is paid for the performance of the role, there is prestige attached to a role, there is a sense of accomplishment or challenge and so on.

Relationships are determined by tasks. Some tasks are performed alone, but most are carried out in relationship with others. The tasks will determine who the role-holder is required to interact with, how often, and towards what end. Moreover, greater the interaction, more the liking. This in turn leads to more frequent interactions. In human behaviour, it is hard to like someone whom we have no contact with, and we tend to seek out those we like. People tend to do what they are rewarded for, and friendship is a powerful reward. Many tasks and behaviours that are associated with a role are brought about by these relationships. That is, new tasks and behaviours are expected of the present role-holder because a strong relationship was developed in the past, either by him or his predecessor. There are two distinct forces that dictate how to act within an organization: organizational culture and the climate for leadership.

Organizational culture

Each organization has its own distinctive culture. It is a combination of the founders, past and current leadership, crises, events, history, and size. It results in rites: the routines and rituals—the 'way we do things'. These rites impact individual behaviour on what it takes to be in good standing (the norm) and direct the appropriate behaviour for each circumstance. Culture is a long-term, complex phenomenon. It represents the shared expectations and self-image of the organization. Things are done differently in every organization. The collective vision that defines the institution is a reflection of its culture. Individual leaders cannot easily create or change culture because it is an integral part of the organization. Culture influences the characteristics of the climate by its effect on the actions and thought processes of the leader. But, everything a leader does will affect the climate of the organization.

Climate for leadership

Organizational climate represents the 'feel' of the organization, the individual and shared perceptions and attitudes of its members. While culture is the deeply rooted nature of the organization that is a result of long-held formal and informal systems, rules, traditions and customs, climate is a short-term phenomenon created by the current leadership. Climate represents the beliefs about the 'feel' of the organization by its members. This individual perception comes from what people believe about the activities that occur in the organization.

Organizational climate is directly related to the leadership and management style of the leader, based on his values, attributes, skills and actions, as well as the priorities. The ethical climate then is the 'feel' of the organization about the activities that have ethical content or those aspects of the work environment that constitute ethical behaviour. The ethical climate is the feel about whether we do things right; or the feel of whether we behave the way we ought to behave. The behaviour (character) of the leader is the most important factor that impacts the climate.

Functions of Leadership

Leadership is a means of directing and represents that part of executive activities by which he guides and influences the behaviour of the subordinates and the group towards some specified goals by working with them and understanding their feelings and problems. In recent years, management experts, psychologists, sociologists and behavioural scientists have tried to identify the functions of leadership in varied ways and from different viewpoints.

Sociological view: Among the work of sociologists who studied the functions of leaders, the opinion of P Selznick may be considered as appropriate. He viewed the leadership function in setting goals, shaping and reshaping the organization and reconciling the internal and external forces. In fact, it is the creative function of the leader that calls for viewing and reviewing organizational environment, work accomplishment and determining near and remote goals in the above perspective.

Review of the work of other sociologists highlights that the leader is supposed to build goals and determine policies into the social structure of the enterprise. It is his fundamental duty to see that the enterprise does not merely survive, but grows in stature. Leaders should be in a position to read the desired changes and direct the movement and functions of the enterprise to get it placed in the industrial complex. Another important function, however, is to manage and mitigate internal conflict. It is a hard fact that conflict is imminent in big organizations due to diverse opinion, views, beliefs and values. The effectiveness of leaders lies in their endeavour to win the consent of several groups and put them to work in accomplishing the objective and the enterprise's mission in the ultimate analysis.

Psychological view: In the opinion of psychologists people will best respond in terms of output if the organization provides opportunities for them to appraise and appropriate their basic, social and ego needs. As a matter of fact, one of the basic functions of the managers and executives, leaders in their words, is to devise the necessary motivational system to meet their needs. It should, however, be kept in view that though the above arrangement is sound from the viewpoint of motivation, it is not adequate to specify the scope in precise for the exercise of leadership on the part of the management.

Other views: Management experts, of late, have given a lot of attention in identifying the exact function of leadership. From the study of management experts, the leadership function can be viewed as: (i) directing, (ii) responding, and (iii) representing. The eminent scholar Leonard Sayles viewed directing as the primary function of leadership. In big organizations where divergent views and a number of groups exist, it is essentially through the means of directing that all of them are unified and coordinated for a central purpose. In this matter, of course, managers and executives have to take the required initiative with intelligent approach and rational attitude.

Management experts consider responding as the second function of leadership. It signifies responsiveness to the initiatives of subordinates. It may often be noticed that subordinates off and on ask for guidance, assistance, advice and help from their superior. Moreover, subordinates always want to be assured about their service rendered. Leadership quality helps superior to appraise the needs of their subordinates and meet them intelligently.

The other essential function of leadership is representing. It signifies that superiors would properly and effectively represent the interests of the total group among their peers and to the higher levels in the managerial hierarchy. This aspect of subordinate thinking may very commonly be observed where subordinates initiate action that requires to be accomplished by their superiors or higher level personnel. In fact, leadership quality enables the executives to represent such group effort and get positive response.

Effective leadership undoubtedly creates a well-to-do environment among the employees not only by influencing but also by responding to their problems, feelings, aspirations and ambitions. Further, it enhances the image of the organization to the outside world.

From the above discussions, we can list the functions of a leader as under:

- Develop team work in organizations
- Act as an important change agent in organizations
- Balance the use of power
- Act as a representative of the subordinates
- Be a counsellor to employees
- Help the employees to optimally utilise their time
- Help in achieving organizational effectiveness
- Enhance the level of motivation and morale of employees
- Inculcate human values within the organization
- Increase the level of commitment and loyalty of employees towards the organization

Leadership and power

Power, in the case of leadership, is divided into six categories that are interrelated. **Expert** and **informational** power is concerned with skills, knowledge and information, of which the holders of such abilities, are able to utilise, to influence others, for example, technicians and computer software professionals. **Reward** and **coercive** power, involves the ability to either reward or punish persons being influenced, in order to gain compliance. **Legitimate** power, is that which has been confirmed by the role structure of the group or organization and is accepted by all as correct and without dispute, such as in the case of the armed forces or the police force. **Referent** power, on the other hand, involves those being influenced, identifying with the leader, for example, rock stars or film personalities using their image to enter the political arena.

Most leaders make use of a combination of these six types of power, depending on the leadership style used. **Authoritarian** leaders, for example, use a mixture of legitimate, coercive and reward powers, to dictate the policies, plans and activities of a group. In comparison, a **democratic** or **participative** leader would mainly use **referent** power, involving all members of the group in the decision-making process.

Leadership Styles

The problem of leadership style is basically concerned with deciding the extent to which a manager should be dictatorial and the extent to which he is supposed to be participative or consultative. Different leadership styles can be categorised as follows: (i) Authoritarian or leader-centred or autocratic style (ii) Democratic or participative or consultative or group-centred style (iii) Laissez faire or free rein style (iv) Paternalistic leadership.

Autocratic style of leadership

This type of leader is characterised by centralisation of authority and decision-making and very limited participation by subordinates of the group. The autocratic leader accomplishes the results through use of authority, fear of deprivation, punishment and other coercive measures. Since it is negative in character, authoritarian approach will succeed only in the short run and will fail to induce subordinates for better performance in the long run. Resentment, absenteeism and higher turnover rate for employees are some of the most natural consequences of this approach. Still autocratic style deserves consideration because of the following reasons:

- There may be very little time for participation, particularly in a crisis.
- Confidential matters may not permit normal consultation.
- The leader may have more knowledge to compensate for participation.

Democratic style of leadership

Also known as consultative or participative style, it is characterised by allowing substantial participation by members of the group in management and decision-making process of the leaders. Subordinates are frequently consulted by the manager on wide ranging problems and are allowed sufficient freedom to communicate with the leader and also with their fellow subordinates. This style is based upon positive assumption about human beings. It encourages cooperative spirit and development of subordinates for higher responsibilities. This style of leadership substantially provides satisfaction to the subordinates.

Laissez faire style of leadership

Under this style, the leader depends largely upon the group and its members to establish their goals and make their own decisions. The leader is passive and assumes the role of just another member of the group. Tasks are assigned in general terms. Laissez faire approach is meant for selective application. If the subordinate is intelligent, highly qualified and experienced, and desires self-fulfilment, a manager may follow this approach without much risk. This style of leadership is, therefore, confined to a small creative or development group.

Paternalistic leadership

This type of leader assumes his function like a father. He treats his followers as members of the family and guides them as its head. He likes to help his followers to do the work, guides, protects and keeps them happy. This type of leader always tries to provide his followers good working conditions, fringe benefits and employee services. Obviously, because of difference in style, followers under this style of leadership work harder to accomplish the job.

A manager is not always free in the choice of leadership style most appropriate to him under a given situation. Feelings and attitudes long cherished are difficult to change. Though democratic style of leadership works better as a pattern of general purpose, the manager should occasionally be autocratic to lead people effectively. Thus, leadership style varies with different leaders, subordinates and situations. In general, the choice of the style of leadership depends upon the following factors:

- Skill, personality and values of the manager
- Forces dominating the subordinates like their expectations, aspirations, needs and values
- Situations such as type of structure, clarity or ambiguity in defining work and objectives, nature of the problems and time pressure
- People in the group, e.g., differences in education, interests, motives, loyalty and so on.

Attitudes and Skills for Leadership

In order to improve the manager's ability to lead, certain attitudes need to be cultivated. These are generally identified as empathy, objectivity and self-knowledge.

Empathy: It is generally described as the ability of a person to look at things or problems from another person's point of view. It involves projecting oneself into the position of the subordinates who are being directed and led. The manager should not assume that subordinates will understand the issues as he himself perceives them. People differ in their experiences, abilities and understanding of things. Each has his own value system and attitudes. Thus, in order to understand their feelings and problems, to lead them successfully, the manager should put himself in the position of his subordinates.

Objectivity: In his task of leading, the manager should not be guided by any preconceived notions about the attitude and behaviour of his subordinates. Problems and their causes should be observed objectively. Thus, a manager should not be annoyed with his subordinates simply because results are poor or change is resisted. He must observe the things as they are and analyse them carefully. It is only when a manager is objective and detached in his behaviour towards members of the group would he be able to assess their feelings and problems and guide them properly. But, this behaviour needs to be learnt.

Self-awareness: A manager may think of himself as being fair and objective but his subordinates may think otherwise. He should, therefore, know for himself how he appears to others and the effect of his attitude and behaviour on the subordinates which would help him lead in a pattern as perceived by those who are being led. Self-knowledge will help the leader to improve and cultivate those habits and attitudes that produce favourable response from the subordinates. For instance, if self-awareness leads him to learn that instructions are not properly understood, the manager can attempt to improve his ability to communicate.

Leadership skills

As a leader, one has to play many roles in the organization to achieve the intended goals and objectives. What skill sets are important is difficult to define. But from a general perspective, we can classify them as: (i) Human skill (ii) Conceptual skill (iii) Technical skill (iv) Personal skill.

Human skill: In order to get the cooperation of his followers, a leader has to successfully resolve more people-related issues than job-related ones. He must understand human behaviour, know their needs, sentiments, emotions, motivation and their contemplated actions and reactions to a particular situation. Therefore, without human relations skill, which emphasises understanding of the people, one cannot be a successful leader. We have already discussed two essential human skills requirement, i.e., empathy and objectivity, while explaining leadership attitude. These apart, a good leader should also have communication, teaching and social skills, which form part of human skills.

In order to persuade, inform, stimulate, direct and convince the followers, a leader should have good communication skills. Communication is the transfer of information in the form of understandable legible message. It helps in establishing and disseminating the goals of an enterprise, and enables the leader to create a climate in which people want to perform. Expecting the followers to perform would not be possible, unless the leader successfully demonstrates how to accomplish a particular task. Teaching skill, therefore, is also an important component of human skills. Similarly to win the confidence and loyalty of followers, leaders also should have the requisite social skill. This requires a leader to understand the followers and be helpful, empathetic and friendly with them.

Conceptual skill: This skill requires understanding the organization from an overall perspective. A leader should have the ability to look at the organisation as a whole. He should be able to relate various functions of the organization and how changes in one affect others. Understanding of the organization, its competitors, financial status, the functional nitty-gritty and their interrelationships are the essential requirements of conceptual skills.

Technical skill: This skill involves specialised knowledge, analytical skills and competence (which is the aggregation of skill, knowledge and abilities) for doing a job. These apart, principles, procedures and operations of a job also add to technical skill. Therefore, leaders without the necessary technical skills cannot expect the followers to do the jobs.

Personal skill: To get the best from the followers, the leader should also have the personal skills like intelligence, emotional maturity, motivation, integrity and flexibility of mind.

Theories of Leadership

There are four major categories of theories of leadership. **Contingency theories** basically argue that the 'right' or an effective leadership style varies according to the context (e.g., Blake and Mouton's managerial grid which has been very influential in organization development practices). **Instrumental theories** on leadership lay stress on task- and person-oriented behaviour (e.g., participation, delegation) by the leader to gain effective performance from others. **Inspirational theories**, on the other hand, include charismatic leaders and transformational leadership. The leader of this category appeals to values and vision and inspires others for raising their confidence and motivating them for change. This leadership comes from a compelling vision that draws in commitment and acceptance of change, and offers a potential for anyone to grow and develop with the vision. Words used are trust, loyalty, devotion, commitment, inspiration, admiration, outstanding and exceptional. According to House and Shamir, it represents the ability of a person to get an intense moral commitment and a strong identification from subordinates. They list a number of behaviours ranging from articulating the vision, passion, self-sacrifice, risk-taking, symbolic behaviours etc.

Informal leadership looks at behaviours associated with those who are not appointed to authority but assume leadership in other ways. **Path-goal theory** looks at what leaders must do to motivate people to perform well and get satisfaction from work. It draws on the expectancy theory of motivation and it has four leadership styles: supportive, directive, participative and achievement-oriented.

Fielder, one of the pioneers of the contingency school, offered a continuum ranging from task-focused to people-focused leadership. He argued that the most effective style depended on the quality of relationships, relative power position between the leader and the led and the nature of the task. He also argued that the style adopted is relatively stable and a feature of a leader's personality could therefore be predicted. He distinguishes between task-oriented and relations-oriented leaders.

Hersey and Blanchard's situational leadership dimensions are linked to task and relational behaviour. Task behaviour focuses on defining roles and responsibilities whereas relational behaviour is more about providing support to teams. The extent to which either is used depends on the person's job maturity and psychological security. Their test looks at elements like delegation, participation, selling (telling).

Good leaders are made, not born. With one's desire and willpower, one can become an effective leader. Good leaders develop through a continuous process of self-study, education, training and experience. Leadership influences others to accomplish a mission, task, or objective and directs the organization in a way that makes it more effective. A leader accomplishes this by applying leadership attributes (belief, values, ethics, character, knowledge and skills). Authority to carry out certain tasks and objectives in the organization does not make one a leader. By virtue of power, it simply makes one the boss. Leadership makes people to achieve goals and objectives, while, on the other hand, bosses tell people to accomplish a task or objective.

According to Bass, there are three basic ways to explain how people become leaders. These are:

- Some personality traits may lead people naturally into leadership roles. This is the Trait theory.
- A crisis or important event may cause a person to rise to the occasion, which brings out extraordinary leadership qualities in an ordinary person. This is the Great Events theory.
- People can choose to become leaders. People can learn leadership skills. This is the Transformational Leadership theory. It is the most widely accepted theory today.

The basis of good leadership is honourable character and selfless service to the organization. In the eyes of the employees, leadership is everything one does that affects the organization's objectives as well as their own well-being. A respected leader concentrates on what he/she **is** *[be]* (beliefs and character), what he/she **knows** (job, tasks, human nature), and what he/she **does** (implement, motivate, provide direction).

What makes a person want to follow a leader? People want to be guided by those who have a clear sense of direction and command respect. To gain respect, the leader must have impeccable integrity. A sense of direction is achieved by conveying a strong vision of the future.

We shall now discuss some widely acclaimed studies on leadership.

- **Iowa studies (1939)**: Ronald Lippitt and Ralph K White under the supervision of Kurt Lewin conducted this study at the University of Iowa forming hobby clubs for 10-year-old boys. Each club was put under three different styles of leadership, i.e, authoritarian, democratic and laissez faire. The authoritarian leader was very directive and did not allow any participation. The democratic leader encouraged discussion and participation and the laissez faire leader gave complete freedom. Under such experimental conditions, satisfaction, frustration and aggression of the boys were studied giving them the task of making masks, model aeroplanes, murals and soap carvings. Results of the study showed that boys under democratic leadership performed well than those who were under authoritarian and laissez faire styles. However, the study was considered not comparable to the formal organizational environment due to the type of the sample (pre-adolescent boys) and for not adequately controlling the variables. Even then the study is considered pioneering and this was the first attempt to determine experimentally the effects of leadership styles on a group.
- **Ohio state studies (1945)**: Business Research Group of Ohio State University with an interdisciplinary team (psychologists, sociologists and economists) of researchers analysed the influence of leadership on different groups using a structured Leader Behaviour Description Questionnaire (LBDO). 'Consideration' and 'Initiating' structure of leadership was found to be widely accepted by different heterogeneous groups like air force commanders to school superintendents.
- **Michigan studies (1961)**: In this study, Rensis Likert and his group identified two major styles of leadership—employee participation and production orientation. Employee-centred style resulted in high performance compared to production-centred style.

Directive, authoritarian or autocratic style of leadership is based on the assumption that the leader's power is derived from the status or position he occupies and the subordinate is inherently lazy and unreliable. Democratic or non-directive style of leadership has greater concern for human relationship and it considers that men are basically

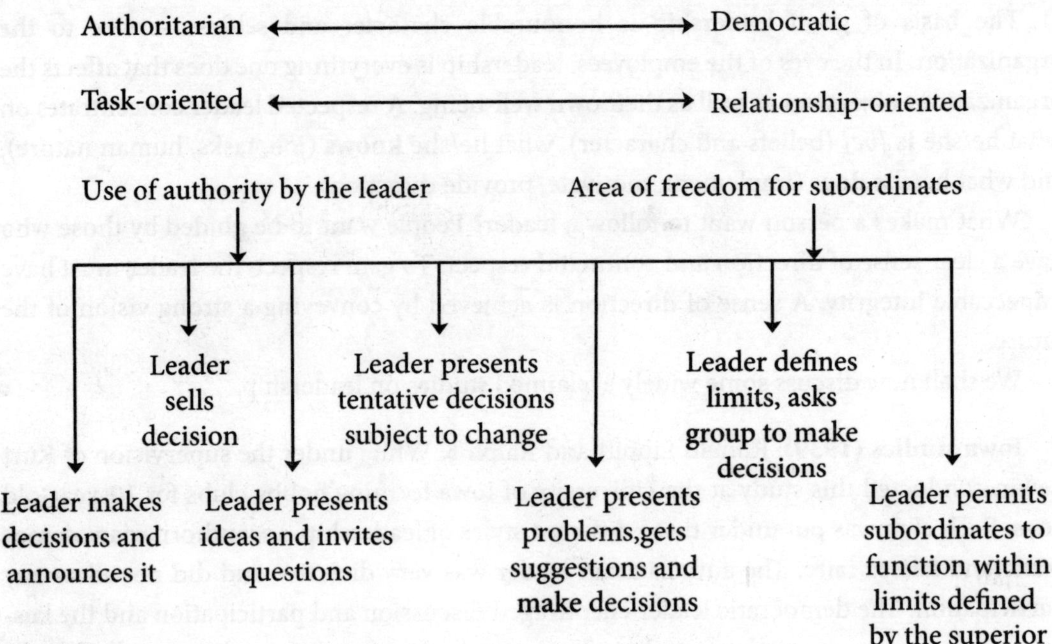

Fig. 8.1 Various styles of leadership

self-directed and can be made creative at work, if properly motivated. In between these two extremes, there are, of course a wide variety of leadership styles as shown in Fig. 8.1. The third leadership style, i.e., laissez faire permits the members of the group to do whatever they want to do. No policies or procedures are established and everyone is left alone. No one attempts to influence anyone else. Practically speaking, this style does not develop any leadership at all in the group.

- **Managerial grid (1978)**: Robert Blake and Jane S Mouton have unified the authoritarian and democratic concepts into the Managerial Grid. They recognised that leadership style is not either authoritarian or democratic but is a mixture of the two philosophies and the relative proportion will vary according to the specific situation. In the managerial grid, five different types of leadership based on concern for production (task) and concern for people (relationships) are located in the four quadrants as shown in Fig. 8.2.

Here, concern for production is represented on the horizontal axis. Production becomes more important to the leader as his rating advances on this horizontal scale. A leader with a rating of 9 on the horizontal axis has a maximum concern for production. Concern for people is taken on the vertical axis. People become more important to this leader as his rating

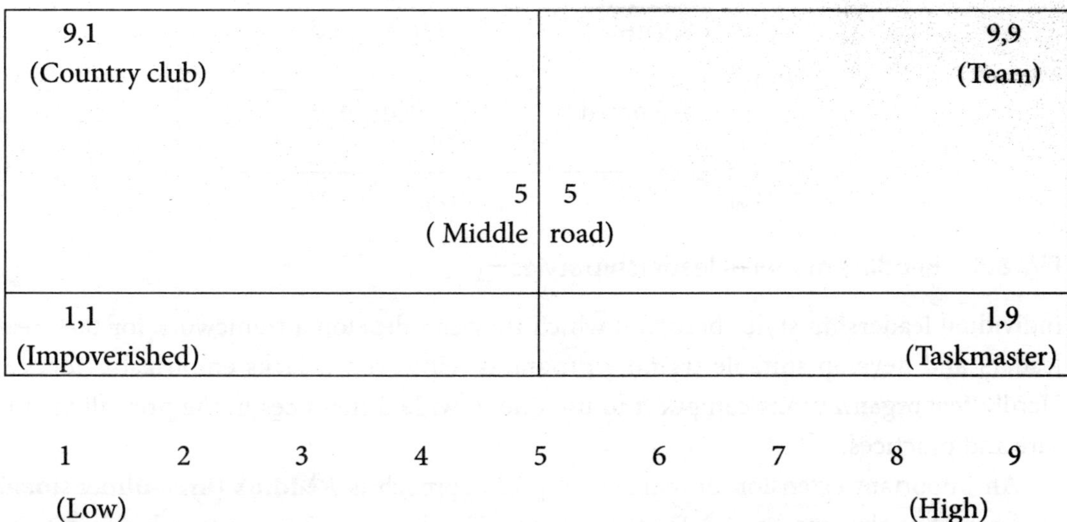

Fig. 8.2 The managerial grid

moves from 1 to 9 on this vertical axis. At 9, he has maximum concern for people. The five leadership styles are described as follows.

Impoverished (low–low, 1, 1): The leader exerts minimum effort, avoids controversy and confrontation and takes the position of an observer to just meet the situation.

Country club (low–high, 9,1): The leader expects highest attention to the needs of the people for keeping harmonious relationships. This leads to a comfortable, friendly work atmosphere.

Task-oriented (high–low, 1,9): This model has the authoritarian and task-oriented leader with poor orientation for human relations. Efficiency in operations results from arranging conditions of work in such a way that human elements interfere to a minimum degree.

Middle of the road (middle, 5, 5): This type of leader compromises between high production and employee satisfaction at optimum level for effective performance by the group.

Team (high–high, 9,9): This is the style of a team leader. Such a type of leader is extremely concerned about the task as well as people. He is concerned about accomplishment of work from committed people, interdependence through a 'common stake' in the organization and also strives for a relationship of trust and respect.

Theoretically there are 81 possible positions on the grid and each such position reflects one leadership style. But an analysis of the grid focuses on these five basic styles. The grid approach is widely accepted in organizations as it helps managers to identify their

	Related	Integrated
RO		
	Separated	Dedicated

TO

Fig. 8.3 Reddin's model of leadership styles

individual leadership styles based on which they can develop a framework for the ideal leaders and develop suitable training programs. However, it lacks empirical evidence. Hardly few organizations can put it to use due to wide differences in the prevailing culture and practices.

An important extension of managerial grid approach is **Reddin's three-dimensional grid,** which is also known as 3-D management. The three axes represent task-orientation, relationship-orientation and effectiveness. By adding the effectiveness dimension, Reddin had actually tried to integrate leadership styles with the situational variables. Task orientation (TO) is defined as the leader's direction to the followers to achieve their goals. It is concerned with planning, organising and controlling. Relationsnip orientation (RO) is defined as the extent of personal relationships of leaders with followers. It is achieved through mutual trust and respect for ideas from the followers. If the style of a leader is appropriate to a given situation, we call it effective and vice versa. Effectiveness and ineffectiveness is measured in terms of the appropriateness of behaviour in a given situation. Figure 8.3 shows the four styles of leadership according to this model.

These four styles represent four basic types of behaviour. A separated leader is concerned with correcting deviations. A related leader accepts others, not bothered about time, looks to the organization as a social system, loves to work with others and receives cooperation from others (followers) by setting an example. The dedicated manager dominates and is interested only in production. He never identifies himself with the subordinates. He only works with power. The integrated leader gets himself and his followers involved with the organization and emphasises on team work. Any of these styles may be effective in one situation but not in another. We can illustrate these styles by classifying them into 'less effective' and 'more effective' (Fig. 8.4).

- **Continuum of leadership behaviour**: Tannenbaum and Schmidt (1973) have explained a range of possible leadership styles on a continuum from authoritarian to free rein.

Basic style	Less effective style	More effective style
Integrated	Compromiser	Executive
Dedicated	Autocrat	Benevolent autocrat
Related	Missionary	Developer
Separated	Deserter	Bureaucrat

Fig. 8.4 Measure of effectiveness of Reddin's styles of leadership

Boss-centred ←——————→ Subordinate-centred

On the left side of the continuum, leaders enjoy a high degree of control and believe in less delegation of authority. On the right side, leaders give their followers freedom and show their authority in work-related matters. A leader moves along the continuum based on three forces, i.e., forces of the leader himself, forces of the followers and forces in the situation.

Forces in the leader: These forces are influenced by the value system of the leader, his confidence in his followers, his inclinations and finally his level of tolerance.

Forces in the followers: These forces are influenced by the followers' need for tolerance for ambiguity, their readiness to assume responsibility for decision-making, interest in understanding problems, level of understanding organizational goals and finally their experience with and expectations from leaders.

Forces in the situation: These forces include type of organization, its problems, group effectiveness and the time pressure.

The continuum theory provides a wide range of leader behaviour and its success depends on the behavioural modification of leaders as per the needs of the situation. However, the basic drawback of the theory is that it supports unidimensional thinking. Increase or decrease of any particular type of behaviour may decrease or increase the other type of behaviour. Another important aspect of this theory, which has been highlighted by the researchers is that employee-orientation and task-orientation are not opposite ends on a continuum (i.e., mutually exclusive). That is, if a leader became more employee-oriented, he need not necessarily become less task-oriented. This was also corroborated by the Ohio studies.

- **Four framework model**: In the *Four Framework Approach,* Bolman and Deal (1991) suggested that leaders display leadership behaviours in one of the four types of frameworks: structural, human resource, political or symbolic. The style can either be effective or ineffective, depending upon the chosen behaviour in the given situation.

Structural framework: In an effective leadership situation, the leader is a social architect whose leadership style is analytic and well designed. In an ineffective leadership situation, the leader goes into the details and reflects the behaviour of a typical bureaucrat. Structural leaders emphasise on structure, strategy, environment, implementation, experimentation and adaptation.

Human resource framework: A leader with HR framework acts as a catalyst. He supports, advocates and empowers his followers. He believes in people and also communicates the message accordingly. By sharing information, he enhances participation of his followers and involves them in decision-making. On the other hand, a leader with less HR framework acts as a push over; he abdicates and we even call him a fraud.

Political framework: An effective leader with this framework is an advocate, his leadership style is coalition and team-building. An ineffective leader, on the other hand, is a hustler with a manipulative style. Political leaders clarify what they want and what they can get; they assess the distribution of power and interests; they build linkages to other stakeholders; use persuasion first, then use negotiation and coercion only if necessary.

Symbolic framework: In an effective leadership situation, the leader is a prophet, whose leadership style is inspiration. In an ineffective leadership situation, the leader is a fanatic or fool, whose leadership style is smoke and mirrors. Symbolic leaders view organizations as a stage or theatre to play certain roles and create impressions. These leaders use symbols to capture attention and try to frame experience by providing plausible interpretations of experiences. They discover and communicate a vision.

This model suggests that leaders can be put into one of these four categories and there are times when one approach is more appropriate as compared to another. Any one of these approaches alone would be inadequate. We should be conscious of all the four approaches and not just rely on one. For example, during a major organizational change, the structural leadership style may be more effective than a visionary leadership style; while during a period when strong growth is needed, the visionary approach may be better. Leaders also need to understand themselves as each tends to have a preferred approach. They should also be aware of the limitations of their favoured approach.

- **Other theories of leadership**: Some other theories are Taylor's scientific manager's style (1911), Fielder's (1967) contingency theory, Hollander and Julian's (1969) group and exchange theories, RK House's (1971) path-goal theory, J Kelly's (1974) trait theory, RA Bandura's (1977) social learning theory and Blanchard and Zigarmi's (1990) situational leadership approach. Out of all the above, the situation approach is more preferred for its relevance to real-life work situation and more particularly for its applicability in service sector also. Hence, situational leadership has been discussed in detail here.

The different theories of leadership are classified into the following four categories: (i) Trait theory (ii) Behavioural theory (iii) Situational theory and (iv) Great man theory.

Trait theory of leadership

This theory seeks to determine personal characteristics of effective leaders. It points out that the personal traits or characteristics of a person make him an effective or successful leader. Charles Bird examined 20 lists of traits attributed to leaders in various surveys and found that none of the traits appeared on all the lists. Leaders were characterised by a wide variety of traits ranging all the way from neatness to nobility. Leaders are presumed to display better judgement and engage themselves in social activities. The study of the lives of successful leaders reveals that they possessed many of these traits. According to the trait theory, the persons who possess the following traits or personal characteristics could become successful leaders:

Good personality: Physical characteristics and level of maturity determine the personality of an individual. The success of a leader to a great extent depends on good personality.

Intellectual ability: A leader should have a level of intelligence higher than his followers. Intellectual ability enables a leader to analyse the situation accurately and take decision accordingly.

Initiative: A leader should have the initiative to undertake activities on time.

Imagination: It is also an essential trait for a successful leader. He must be able to visualise trends and adopt the right course of action to achieve results.

Maturity: A leader should have emotional maturity and balanced temperament. Maturity is reflected through tolerant behaviour.

Desire to accept responsibility: Accepting responsibility for his actions (irrespective of the results) creates a positive impression in the minds of the followers. A leader should have this trait also.

Self-confidence: A leader should be self-confident. This will motivate his followers and boost their morale.

Flexibility and adaptability: To become flexible and adaptable, a leader should have an open mind to accept the viewpoints of others. This will foster innovation and creativity in the organization.

Objectivity and fairness: In dealing with followers, a leader should be objective and fair. This trait requires a leader to be honest, fair, impartial, unbiased and have integrity.

Considerate: To be considerate to the followers ensures cooperation from them which adds to the success of a leader.

Limitations

The main limitations of this theory are shown below

- It assumes leadership to be a natural, inborn quality. This is not always correct. Leadership quality can also be developed through training. Even by successful handling of a crisis situation, one can emerge as a leader. This happened for Mr Russy Mody in 1947 when he successfully pacified the workmen who indulged in violent disruption at the Jamshedpur plant of the Tata Iron and Steel Company.
- A particular trait or some traits may help a leader to successfully manage a situation but he may fail in others. It is also difficult to find a leader with all such listed traits.
- There is no quantitative tool to measure one or many traits. Presence or lack of traits could only be understood when a leader manages a situation.
- The list of personal traits are only indicative and not exhaustive. A successful leader may have other traits like: foresight, vision, methodical thinking, thoroughness etc.
- Personal traits are only a micro part of leadership. In order to be a successful leader, one must have other qualities also. Hence, measuring leadership quality only on personal traits may be wrong.

Behavioural theory of leadership

According to this theory, a particular behaviour of a leader provides greater satisfaction to the followers. Such behavioural attributes enable the followers to recognise a leader. This theory is based on the premise that a leader plays a role behaviour, using his conceptual, human and technical skills, which influences the behaviour of his followers. Behaviour is not a trait, it sets a particular role pattern. For example, a leader may have a nurturing parent behaviour, which appreciates the problems of followers and even cajoles them when they fail to deliver. While a leader may also have a critical parent behaviour, which depicts critical nature in dealing with such situations. He never appreciates, but only reprimands.

Limitations

The main limitations of this theory are given below.

- The behavioural theory could not justify why a certain leadership behaviour is effective in one case but fails in others. For example, the nurturing parent behaviour may be effective to stop recurrence of failure on the part of subordinates in one case while it may not work in another case, where followers may take advantage of this behaviour on the part of the leader and repeat the deviant trend. Critical parent behaviour could have been better in the second situation.

- This theory does not recognise the traits of leaders. Certain traits, however, do help in making a successful leader.

Situational theory of leadership

This theory states that attributes of leadership emerge from a situation. It is the circumstance that determines how the leader will perform. A leader who is capable of fulfilling the aspirations of the followers in a given situation commands a following. A leader performs duly recognising the needs of the situation; hence his style may differ. Russy Mody's response is a perfect example of this style.

Limitations

- A major limitation of this theory is that it emphasises leadership with respect to a given situation. If the situation changes, there is no mention whether a person would still continue to be a leader. The best example here is that of trade union leaders. Followers may reject the leadership, if a trade union leader fails to meet their expectations in a different situation.
- As the situation changes, the same style may not guarantee success. In fact, the style of leadership is influenced by the particular traits and behavioural role of a leader.

Great man theory of leadership

This theory emphasises that leaders are born and not made. Hence, great leaders are natural leaders. It is partly true that some leadership qualities cannot be acquired even through training; for example, a commanding personality, charm, courage, intelligence, persuasiveness and aggressiveness. This theory, therefore, emphasises that leadership qualities are inborn. Therefore, ordinary people cannot become leaders.

Limitations

- This theory is not scientific and also has no empirical basis. In many cases, we can prove this theory as absurd.
- It also does not explain what leaders are and how they emerge, how they behave and turn into achievers.

Language of Leaders

The lexicon of leaders can be considered in the following maxims.

The six most important words: 'I admit I made a mistake'.

The five most important words: 'You did a good job'.

The four most important words: 'What is your opinion?'

The three most important words: 'If you please'.

The two most important words: 'Thank you'.

The one most important word: We

The least most important word: I

Key Points

- Several management thinkers have offered definitions of leadership. These range from personality theory to process orientation and situational approach. The evolution of this spectrum represents the movement from operational to behavioural models.
- Characteristics of a good leader include the ability to influence others, skills and judgement to read a given situation.
- Important principles of leadership are communication, empathy and self-awareness.
- There are four main styles of leadership: authoritarian, democratic, laissez faire and paternalistic.
- Several important studies were carried out to assess the optimal style of leadership. The general consensus is that the style of leadership most suitable for a given situation is determined by the situational variables.
- The important theories of leadership are the trait theory, behavioural theory, situational theory and great man theory.
- Industrial psychologists need to understand the organizational climate and culture so that they can assess the appropriate style of leadership. Further, they also need to know the attitudes and skills required so that leaders can be groomed in the organization through appropriate training programs.

Important Terms

Conceptual skills: It refers to the ability of the leader for holistic understanding such as an organization-wide perspective, analysis of competitors, appreciation of financial status and so on.

Entrepreneurial leadership: This type of leadership demonstrates entrepreneurial creativity, and always explores new opportunities, takes risks, ventures into new areas, and provides strategic direction and inspiration to people. The leader also takes responsibility for the failures of the team members.

Fiedler's contingency approach: It rests on the premise that people become leaders not only on the strength of their personality attributes, but also on the strength of different situational factors and the interactions between the leaders and the followers. Fiedler identified three critical dimensions of leadership, which determine the style of leadership—position power, task structure and leader–member relations.

Impoverished leader: This type of leader exerts minimum effort, avoids controversy and confrontation and takes the position of an observer to just meet the situation.

Paternalistic leadership: This type of leader assumes his/her functions like that of a head of the family. They treat followers as members of the family and guide, protect and keep them happy at work.

Team leader: This leader is extremely concerned about the task as well as people. He/she is concerned for work accomplishment from committed people, interdependence through a 'common stake' in organization and also strives for a relationship of trust and respect.

Self-assessment Questions

1. Briefly state the history of leadership. Why leadership is important in today's organizations?
2. Is leadership different from management? Explain.
3. What are the important characteristics of leadership?
4. State the significance and principles of leadership.
5. How does environment affect leadership styles? Can culture and climate of an organization also affect leadership?
6. Describe the important factors of leadership.
7. List out the functions of a leader. What are the principal objectives of a leader in an organization?

8. Is leadership merely exertion of power? Explain the relationship between leadership and power.
9. Discuss the different leadership styles. How do leadership styles differ between organizations and within an organization?
10. What are the important attitudinal elements of effective leadership?
11. Explain the important skills of leadership. Do you think the degree of such skill sets is uniform in every situation?
12. Briefly explain the theories of leadership.
13. *Leaders are born and not made!* Do you agree with this statement? Justify your answer.
14. Discuss the theory of managerial grid. How is it different from the 3D leadership model?
15. What is continuum leadership behaviour?
16. Explain the leadership framework. Is it necessary for all leaders to follow a particular framework of leadership in every situation?
17. What is the trait theory of leadership? How is it different from behavioural theory?
18. Explain the relationship between situational theory and great man theory of leadership.
19. What is formal and informal leadership? Does an informal leader follow any particular style of leadership?
20. Write short notes on the following:
    i. Leaders and followers
    ii. Communication and leadership
    iii. Laissez faire style of leadership
    iv. Transformational leader
    v. Paternalistic leader
    vi. Leadership and empathy

Selected Bibliography

1. Bass BM (1990). *Bass and Stodgill's Handbook of Leadership.* New York: Free Press.
2. Bhattacharyya DK (2010). *Organizational Behaviour: Concepts and Practices.* New Delhi: Oxford University Press.
3. Fiedler FE (1967). *A Theory of Leadership Effectiveness.* New York: McGraw-Hill.
4. Hersey P, KH Blanchard and DE Johnson (2001). *Management of Organizational Behaviour—Leading Human Resources,* 8th edition. New Delhi: Pearson Education.
5. Likert R (1961). *New Patterns of Management.* New York: McGraw-Hill.
6. Robbins SP (2005). *Organizational Behaviour,* 11th edition. New Delhi: Prentice-Hall India.
7. Selznick P (1957). *Leadership and Administration.* New York: Harper and Row.

Group Dynamics

Learning Objectives

After reading this chapter you will be able to:

- Appreciate the concept of group
- List the types of groups
- Understand the effectiveness of groups
- Analyse the group decision-making process and its influence on organizational culture
- Outline the methods for team development and managing group conflicts

Overview

For industrial psychologists, group dynamics is yet another area of prime focus. In this chapter, we have discussed the process of group dynamics to facilitate core understanding, so that in workplaces the principles can be applied.

Development of Groups

Tracing the origin and development of social life of human beings, it is evident that right from the beginning, in order to survive, people tended to be collective. This process of collectivism developed mutual interaction, and this *per se*, later developed language and behavioural norms. Extension of such collectivism and subsequent formation of social groups is what we study today in organizational behaviour. In organizational behaviour, the study of work groups has significant meaning, because of behavioural dynamics of people. Through the historical process, we have understood that to sustain, group formation is a necessity to accomplish tasks, to establish a sense of identity, and to exchange ideas. Characteristically, we study groups in two forms: primary group and secondary group. Primary groups develop emotional attachment, culture of their own to differentiate them from others and have their own normative systems. Secondary groups, on the other hand, are developed, detaching personal feelings and attachment, to get the work done or to achieve the desired level of performance. A work group in organization is an example of secondary group. Primary group is a social group, which can also be an informal group in an organization. Study of work group in organization is important to understand the psychology of people, when they are in a collective. Since work process in organization is now managed through work group formation, before fitting an individual to a particular work group, we try to assess the degree of compatibility, or else, the purpose of the organization may be defeated. Failure of Mazda of Japan in USA is attributable to such incompatibility, which literally forced Mazda to withdraw, despite being the first (much before Toyota and Honda) to enter the American market. Toyota's current recruitment practice focuses more on assessment of such compatibility, which allows them to get the right fit and reduce the attrition rate.

Despite such logic behind group formation, a group is often misconstrued as merely a collection of people. Every collection of people cannot be a group because it does not have any interaction, cohesion and common goal. Therefore, a collection of people (two or more) can only be a group, when they have a common purpose or goal, there exists a stable structure (usually hierarchical with a leader), and some established set of roles, a standard pattern of interaction and members in the group identify themselves with the group. Many organizations use the terms team and group interchangeably. Although the difference between the team and group in today's organization hardly exists, the concept of group is more traditional, as it is the outcome of principles of division of labour, based on job specialisation and putting them under one supervisor. The team concept is more modern as the test of a team does not essentially require functional commonality, but members strive to achieve a common goal. In a team, members interact interdependently and adaptively to achieve specified, shared and valued objectives. Members in a team believe in shared commitment. In this chapter, however, we will not make any distinction between the terms group and team. However, to keep pace with the organizational practices, team work issues have been separately dealt in the later part of this chapter.

Need to Study Groups

It is important to remember once again that people in a group behave differently compared to their personal or individual behaviour. The subject of organizational behaviour primarily focuses on issues of managing people in a group, as organizations essentially represent a form of secondary group (though informal primary groups may exist).

Understanding the group process in an organization, helps us to assess how people work together and accomplish the results. The most unfortunate part in today's organizations is that while we all spend adequate time and efforts to formulate strategies, we neglect the group process and dynamics, resulting in failure in achieving our results. Today's managers must know and appreciate how people behave in an organization, interact among themselves and share common goals. Understanding this aspect facilitates the managers to integrate the new recruits, prepare them for their job roles, make them aware of the norms and thus achieve group cohesiveness. Managers need to appreciate that people not only play their formal roles in the organization but also play different informal roles to develop better understanding among themselves. Norms need not always be explicit, but also implicit. We have seen the significance of such group norms in the Bank wiring experiment by Mayo, where group norms persuaded workers to contain productivity despite availability of incentives and the opportunity to earn more. Thus, group norms can be both positive and negative. While positive norms bring a sense of order in an organization, the opposite can have an adverse impact on the people and the organization.

Similarly, study of group cohesiveness is also important in an organization. Cohesiveness factors bind all members of the organization together to achieve the results. It is achieved when group members can align their individual needs and goals. This is what Henry Fayol referred as **esprit de corps**. A cohesive work group is a precursor for the success of the organization. The manager as a leader of the group should focus on achieving group cohesiveness.

Thus, apart from the study of the group development process, the analysis of group conflicts, the group decision-making process, elements of group dynamics etc are all important areas in an organization. Organizational success largely depends on effective management of workgroups.

Definition

We now know that in organizations, a group represents a collection of two or more individuals, who work for a common goal and are interdependent. Members interact with each other to achieve group objectives or goals. Since such interaction among group members entails managing many issues like personality and attitude, emotions and individual interests of the people, the manager's task in managing the group becomes more complex. Managers always need to endeavour for effective management of the group behaviour to achieve the results. Freud Luthans suggests that an effective group in an organization makes its members motivated to join, perceive the group as a unified entity, contribute to group process and reach agreement and disagreements through various forms of interaction.

Like many other managerial terms, the definition of group is better understood, once we explain the essence of a group. This is primarily due to a lack of consensus on a common definition as well as the use of term in in various other disciplines. The essence of a group can be defined as two or more individuals who share any or all of the following aspects:

- **Interpersonal interaction**—Individuals do not form a group merely by being in the same place; there has to be some interaction between them.
- **Perception of membership**—Individuals should perceive that they are members of the group.

- **Interdependency and mutual influence**—Any event that affects a group member affects all; each member influences and is influenced by every other member.
- **Mutual goals**—Individuals come together in pursuit of a mutual goal.
- **Motivation**—Group members are motivated to accomplish their goals through their joint association.
- **Structured relationships**—Interactions are structured by a set of role definitions and norms.

Group dynamics

As with the definition of a group, there is no consensus on the definition of group dynamics, even though Kurt Lewin advocated the term in the 1930s. One normative view is that group dynamics describe how a group should be organised and conducted. Democratic leadership, participation by members and overall cooperation are stressed. Another view of group dynamics is that it consists of a set of techniques. Here, role playing, brainstorming, the Johari window, transactional analysis and team-building are equated with group dynamics. A third view, which is closest to Lewin's original concept is that group dynamics should be viewed as the internal nature of groups, how they form, their structure and the organisation.

Types of Groups

We have earlier classified groups into two types: primary and secondary. However, ideally we can classify groups according to two elements viz., size and cohesiveness.

On the basis of size groups are classified as small and large or primary and secondary. In terms of cohesiveness, groups can be classified as coalitions, expert groups or in and out groups. The generally accepted notion is that the group to which any person pledges complete membership and loyalty is a primary group. In the event of a conflict of interest, the group's well-being would be paramount. Although there is no attempt to assign precise numbers to the size of primary groups, the criterion is that the group must be small enough for face-to-face interaction between the members.

Individuals may assume membership of groups other than primary ones; such membership may be limited by time, task or location. As an individual's affinity to such a group becomes higher, it is quite possible that this group may move up to becoming a primary group. In general, however, it is accepted that primary groups are socialising groups and have a very high degree of affinity and interdependency among members.

Based upon an individual's membership status, groups could be classified as membership/reference groups or as in-group/out-group. The criterion here is that the image of the group is very powerful and it attracts individuals to become a part of the group. Until he gets full membership of the group, an individual looks to it as a reference group, the values and activities of which have to be imitated.

The Hawthorne studies (1924) attempted to examine the relationship between intensity of illumination on the shop floor of manual work sites and employee productivity. A test group and a control group were used. The test group in an early phase showed no increase or decrease in output in proportion to the increase or decrease of illumination. The control group with unchanged illumination increased output by the same amount overall as the test group. Subsequent phases brought the level of light for the test group down to moonlight intensity: the workers could barely see what they were doing, but productivity increased. The results were baffling to the researchers.

It is fortunate that those responsible for the Hawthorne studies had enough foresight and spirit to accept the challenge of looking beneath the surface of the apparent failure of the experiments. The unanticipated results of the illumination experiments are generally regarded as the beginning of structured studies of human behaviour at work. Anthropologists had earlier demonstrated the tremendous impact that a primary group (a socialising group such as the family and the peer group) has on individual behaviour, regardless of context or environmental conditions. With the Hawthorne studies, came the important recognition that workgroups have primary group qualities, even if they were not initially conceived as socialising groups.

The Hawthorne studies provided an impetus to the study of human behaviour, specifically the impact groups have on organizations and individuals. A series of experiments were carried out following the illumination experiments. From organizational practices, we find the following types of groups.

Formal group

This group is defined by the organizational structure. After planning, organizations group the activities and put those under a formal structure, deciding their goals and objectives and strategies to achieve the same. Formal group members report to their superior and interact with each other to achieve the common goals. Usually a formal group contains members with more or less homogeneous nature of job. In a shop floor, a gang engaged in doing the same job represents a formal group. Similarly, in a call centre all outbound callers handling the same customer account, represent a formal group. Thus, a formal group is formed based on job specialisation and similarity of skill sets, to reap the advantages of division of labour.

Command group

This group is also known as task group. A task is defined as cross-functional activities, carried out by group members to accomplish a common goal. A command group can be formed drawing members from various formal groups. For example, to achieve success in launching a new product, the company may form a command group. Once the task is achieved, group members may be sent back to their specific formal groups.

Committees

Organizations often form permanent or temporary committees, drawing members from various formal groups. They also include cross-functional members. In a command group, goals may be specific, but they may vary for committees. For example, various members drawn from the user sections, finance, marketing, HR and others, may comprise a Tender Purchase Committee to ensure better transparency and accuracy in purchase decisions. Such committees may be permanent in nature. Again there may be temporary committees that may be entrusted to achieve short-term goals like enquiry into a case of embezzlement or fraud.

Informal groups

These groups are formed within a formal organizational structure. Members primarily meet their social or affiliation needs through membership of such groups. Thus, informal groups are not organizationally determined but by the members themselves to fulfil their need for social interaction. In a particular organization, functional proximity primarily determines the formation of an informal group. These apart, like-minded people, i.e., those who have the same personality and attitude constructs or those belong to similar status (in terms of hierarchy or economic status) also form informal groups. Constructive use of informal groups may benefit an organization. However, inefficient management may render informal group to be counterproductive.

Theories of Group Formation

Some of the important theories of group formation are: propinquity theory, balance theory and exchange theory. These are described in detail here.

Propinquity theory: It is based on the most basic assumption that individuals form groups out of 'propinquity', meaning spatial or geographical proximity. While this may explain why people travelling in the same coach of a train or the same bus every day form a weakly bonded group, it cannot explain other complexities involved in group formation.

Balance theory: This theory states that persons are attracted to one another on the basis of similar attitudes towards commonly relevant objects and goals. Individuals X and Y will interact and form a relationship because of common attitudes and values (Z). Once this relationship is formed, the participants strive to maintain a balance between the attraction and the common attitudes. If an imbalance occurs, an attempt is made to restore the balance. If it cannot be restored, the relationship dissolves. Both propinquity and interaction play a role in balance theory.

Exchange theory: The exchange theory of groups is based upon reward–cost outcomes of interaction. A minimum positive level (rewards greater than costs) of an outcome must exist in order for attraction or affiliation to take place. Rewards from interactions gratify needs, while costs incur anxiety, frustration, embarrassment or fatigue. Propinquity, interaction and common attitudes have a role in exchange theory.

Stages of Group Development

Being living entities, groups go through a process of evolution, beginning with their birth, maturity and decline. These stages are by no means water-tight or even sequential. The stages of group formation as suggested by Tuckman B (1965) are shown in Fig. 9.1.

Forming: The group defines expectations from members, the environment in which it operates and the reason for its existence. The members get oriented to each other and share their ideas about what the group is seeking to achieve.

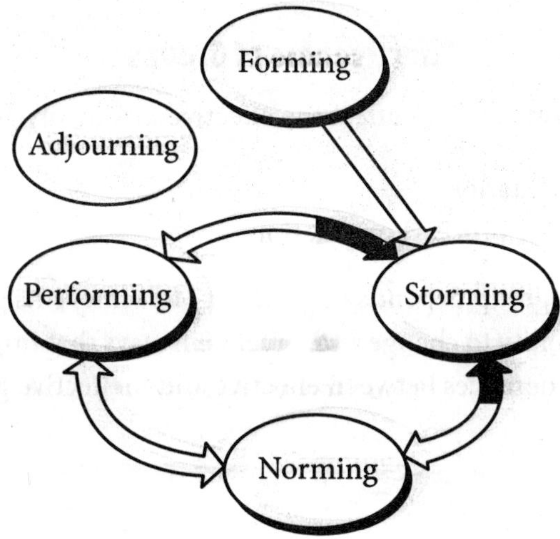

Fig. 9.1 Stages of formation of groups

Storming: Members strive or lobby for influence and positions and try to impose their will on other members in the group. Differences arise over all kinds of issues—group structure, agenda, work allocation etc. There may be rebellion against perceived leaders or against suggested structures.

Norming: Members begin to recognise the need for mutuality and interdependence. Differences are negotiated and workable approaches are arrived at keeping in mind the interests of the group. Intangible, unwritten norms are established for the group members.

Performing: Having arrived at a consensus on all the issues facing the group, the members work towards the goals in the manner specified by the group norms.

Adjourning: As a result of completion of task in the previous performing stage, emotional dependency between the members is reduced and work behaviour terminates.

It is interesting to note here that the first three stages take a while, during which, apparently, there is not much progress. But it must be recognised that these stages lay the foundation for performance. Without these stages, the group will be trapped in trying to come to terms with it. Also, effective groups are constantly on the lookout for renewal. As the operating environment or the goals change, the group goes through the first three stages, thereby rediscovering itself. Ultimately, the group terminates. This happens when the group is unable to satisfy the needs of the members within the boundaries that it had set for itself. Members look to other groups to satisfy their needs. The group's existence becomes redundant and it fades away.

Effectiveness of Groups

There are two major parameters that affect the effectiveness of any group:

- The degree of task orientation
- The degree of people (or process) orientation

The effectiveness of a group depends on its ability to achieve its goals, maintain itself as a cohesive unit and the ability to change and develop in ways that improve further. Table 9.1 highlights some of the differences between effective and ineffective groups.

Table 9.1 Differences between effective and ineffective groups

Effective groups	Ineffective groups
Goals are clarified and changed so that the best possible match between individual and the group's goals can be achieved.	Goals are competitively structured, imposed and accepted by members.
Communication is open and accurate expression of both ideas and feelings is emphasised.	Communication is restricted and only ideas are expressed; feelings are suppressed or ignored.
Participation and leadership are distributed among all group members.	Leadership is delegated and based upon authority. Members' participation is limited.
Ability and information determine influence and power. Contacts are built to make sure individual goals and needs are fulfilled.	Position determines influence and power. Power is concentrated in the authority positions and obedience to authority is the rule.
Different decision-making procedures are used according to the situation. Consensus is sought for important decisions. Group discussions are encouraged.	Decisions are always made by the highest authority. There is little group discussion.
Controversy and conflict are seen as a positive key to members' involvement, the quality and originality of decisions, and the continuance of the group in good working condition.	Controversy and conflict are ignored, denied, avoided or suppressed. Internal maintenance and development are ignored as much as possible. Stability is affirmed
Members evaluate the effectiveness of the group and decide how to improve its functioning.	The highest authority evaluates the group's effectiveness and decides how goal accomplishment may be improved.

Decision-making in Groups

Decision-making is the process to select a course of action from a number of alternatives. Decision-making is all pervasive, and is an important part of planning. For any organization, policy documents helps in taking managerial decisions. But these are decisions of routine nature, which we also call operational decisions. Strategic or important decisions obviously are taken considering different alternatives. In order to be a successful manager, one has to necessarily develop decision-making skills. The process of decision-making is similar to strategic planning. It involves the following steps:

i) Diagnosing, defining and identifying the source of the problem
ii) Gathering information and analysing the facts required to solve the problem
iii) Developing and evaluating alternative solutions to the problem
iv) Choosing the best decision alternatives
v) Communicating the decisions
vi) Implementing the decisions

Forecasting tools

Various forecasting tools help us in decision-making. But the most important tool is the **decision tree**, which is a graphic representation of the sequence of decisions required in determining the expected values of alternative courses of action. Each decision alternative is weighed by developing a pay-off matrix, which depicts the probable value of each of the decision alternatives by quantifying the various outcomes and probabilities of their occurrence.

Probability is the degree of likelihood that a particular event will occur. It varies from zero (no chance of occurring) to one (certain chance of occurring). Outcomes are quantified in terms of Expected Value (EV) and then based on EV, decision alternatives are selected.

Apart from the pay-off matrix and decision tree, queuing theory, inventory and distribution models and game theory are also used. The queuing model helps us to reduce waiting time to ensure better service to customers. Distribution model helps us to determine the cost-effective way of distribution of products and services. Inventory models help us to determine the optimum inventory level for both inputs (raw materials and spares/components) and output (finished goods). Game theory measures the decision outcomes under different situations of uncertainty. The Delphi technique and nominal group technique are examples of group decision-making.

In a large majority of organizational situations, decision-making boils down to choosing between alternatives. Recently, there has also been considerable research on how groups can enhance effectiveness of decision-making by enlarging the range of alternatives available so that a wider choice is available.

Phases in decision-making

The three major phases are discussed here.

- **Identification or intelligence activity phase:** This phase is characterised by searching the environment for conditions calling for decision-making. There is a formal recognition of a problem or an opportunity and a diagnosis is made. Normally, immediate, severe problems do not have an extensive diagnosis, but mild problems do.
- **Development or design activity phase:** In this phase inventing, developing and analysing the possible courses of action takes place. There may be a search for existing standard procedures or solutions, or a new solution may be arrived at. At this stage, the decision-makers only have a vague idea of the ideal solution.
- **Selection or choice activity phase:** In this phase, the particular course of action is selected. This could be on the basis of judgement (intuition or experience), by analysis (logical or systematic) or by bargaining (when some compromise needs to be made for an optimal solution).

Ideally, the decision taken by the group should be acceptable to all members. This will be possible only when the group is mature, has a common goal and has sufficiently strong processes to handle differences of opinion. The time available to the group to arrive at a decision also has a very strong influence on the quality of the decision.

Groups use several methods to arrive at a decision. Minority, autocratic decision, majority voting, expert decision, averaging and consensus are some of the common techniques used. By and large, it is recognised that decision-making by consensus is the most effective method. It satisfies all the five conditions required for an effective decision, which are:

- The resources of the group members are fully utilized.
- Time is well used.
- The decision is correct, or of high quality.
- The decision is implemented fully by all the required group members.
- The problem-solving ability of the group is enhanced (or at least not lowered).

Decisions by consensus, however, take a great deal of time and require a high degree of maturity of members. But, in terms of the future ability of the group to make high-quality decisions, consensus productively resolves controversies and conflicts—which none of the other methods can achieve. Research shows that the more effective groups tend to have designated leaders who allow greater participation and more differences of opinion and who express greater acceptance of different decisions. Group members who feel that they have had little influence over a decision not only fail to contribute their resources to it, but usually are less likely to carry it out when action is required.

The Delphi technique

The Greek word *Delphi* refers to an oracle who was believed to get advice from Apollo. The priests then interpreted the pronouncements of Delphi.

In modern times, this method is essentially a group process to achieve a consensus forecast. This method calls for the selection of a panel of experts either from within or outside the organization, whose comments are crystallised from a series of responses to questionnaire and then used as the basis for forecast. The questionnaire is prepared from the responses received from a prior set of questions in a sequencing manner. At every stage, information obtained from previous questionnaire is shared among the participating members, without, however, disclosing majority opinion as this may otherwise have peer-group influence on minority opinion.

The procedure in Delphi technique is as follows :

1. To start with, it requires selection of a coordinator and a panel of experts from both within and outside the organizations.
2. The coordinator then circulates questions in writing to each such expert.
3. The experts then write their observations.
4. The coordinator then edits those observations and summarises, without, however disclosing the majority opinion in his summary.
5. On the basis of his summary, the coordinator then develops a new set of questionnaire and circulates among the experts.
6. Experts then answer the new set of questions.
7. The coordinator repeats the process till such time he is able to synthesise from the opinion of the experts.

The success of the process depends on the following factors :

- Experts should be so chosen that they have the requisite knowledge and skills to give the best answers.
- Questions should be relevant to the objective.
- The criteria for evaluating responses should be consistent, unbiased and befitting with the objectives. Although there is no universal set of criteria for evaluating responses, the following are considered necessary:
  - ➢ Consider the assessment made by the experts in terms of their knowledge in the area.

- ➢ Consider the assessment in terms of feasibility, objectives, requirement of time and resources.
- ➢ Consider the assessment in terms of desirability.
- ➢ Consider the assessment in terms of extraneous factors.

Nominal group method

Like the Delphi method, this also involves a panel of experts. However, the major difference between the two is that in the former experts are not allowed to discuss among themselves, for assessing the questions. In the latter, experts are given the opportunity to discuss among themselves. Under this method, the coordinator assumes the role of a facilitator, allowing the experts to sit together to discuss their ideas. He also records such discussions are made on a flip chart. After this, experts are asked to rank their ideas according to their perceived priority through round table discussions. The group's consensus is then derived mathematically in terms of individual rankings. The process, therefore, affords creativity and facilitates scientific consensus unlike that by qualification (as coordinator ultimately decides the best course of action) under the Delphi method.

Groupthink

While a high desire for consensus marks a group as being effective, it might become counterproductive for cohesive, mature groups. Having understood the benefits of consensus decision-making, such groups might become obsessed on reaching a consensus that there will be no realistic appraisal of alternative courses of action in a decision and deviant, minority or unpopular views go unexpressed. The intra-group pressures are so huge that it results in 'groupthink'—a deterioration of mental efficiency, reality testing and moral judgement.

The Groupthink syndrome was defined by Janis (1982) as '...a mode of thinking that people engage in. When the members' striving for unanimity overrides their motivation to realistically appraise alternative courses of action'. In highly cohesive groups, there is a tendency for group members to try to avoid disagreements or conflicts with one another. Informal group norms are established that apply pressure on individuals to preserve friendly group relations. As a result, the group avoids disagreements and does not seek out alternatives to critically evaluate. It has been shown by Johnson and Johnson (1994) that individuals try to avoid responsibility for their decisions by procrastinating on a decision or by rationalising their agreement as group loyalty. The groupthink syndrome produces poor group decisions.

A very formal approach to avoiding the pitfalls of groupthink has been put forward by Edward de Bono, the pioneer of the concept of lateral thinking. Called six thinking hats, this approach formalises the divergence of thinking processes necessary for high quality decision-making. The six hats, briefly described, are:

- **White Hat**—Objective look at data and information
- **Red Hat**—Legitimises feelings, hunches and intuition
- **Black Hat**—Logical negative, judgement and caution
- **Yellow Hat**—Logical positive, feasibility and benefits
- **Green Hat**—New ideas and creative thinking
- **Blue Hat**—Control of the thinking process

Such categorisation allows a legitimate expression of feelings and intuition in a meeting, without apology or justification. In addition, it requires all members to be able to use each type of thinking without sticking only to one type. All the hats, used in sequence will be able to bring out the various aspects involved in arriving at a high-quality decision, without having to contend with pressures of conformance to in-group norms; after all, the norm is now to think on all these lines! Some of the characteristics of groupthink process, as identified by Janis are as follows:

- Overestimates strength of the group
- Illusion of invincibility
- Unquestioned belief in group's morality
- Becomes close-minded
- Rationalisation
- Stereotyped view of opponent: consider out-group as too evil or too weak or too unintelligent
- Pressure towards uniformity
- Pressure on conformity to avoid disapproval: most people fall into line
- Self-censorship: people withhold their misgivings
- Illusion of unanimity

In groupthink process, the Abilene paradox happens when a group takes actions just opposite to what they really want to do, which means consensus occurs due to pressure from members to preserve group harmony. Members of the group generate fewer efforts than what they could when they perform the tasks alone. This syndrome is known as social loafing. One of the prime reasons for group formation is to enhance productivity. But when the group inhibits individual productivity, due to social loafing, it fails to achieve the results. However, social loafing is minimised when organizations emphasise on cohesive teams. Unique and challenging tasks also minimise social loafing.

Impact on group maturity: In a cohesive group, the groupthink process is more positive, as members of the group can ask questions and put their own arguments during decision-making. But when the group is not cohesive, it may be too imposing on the members to agree to the majority opinion. While deciding the annual business plan, many organizations engage some outside consultant, who moderates such discussions to arrive at rational decisions. Thus, in a cohesive group, groupthink by nature is not bad. It is undesirable only when the group feels constrained from openly discussing the issues. A cohesive group is considered to be a matured group, and in a matured group groupthink process works well. When the leader properly guides the groupthink process, the group also matures.

Groups and the Organizational Culture

Groups are subsets of larger systems. Because many groups are also a part of, or subsets of larger organizations, a part of the explanation for any group behaviour may be extracted from an explanation of the larger organization—its values, norms and culture. Whereas groups of software engineers may exhibit similar behaviours (attitudes and values) on the basis of their profession (behaviours often formed during college and university experiences), one may also expect differences in these groups' behaviours based on their larger corporate or organizational settings. Differences in behaviours between software engineers at IBM versus those at Microsoft have been well-documented.

Reasons for joining groups

The answer to the question, 'Why are groups formed?' lies in a number of general tendencies.
Similarity attraction effect: We like people who are similar to us in some way.
Hypothesis of complementary needs: We like people who possess qualities that fulfill our own needs.
Proximity attraction effect: We like people who are close by.
Exposure: We like people whom we have been exposed to repeatedly.
Reciprocity: We like people who like us.
Reflected glory: We seek to associate with successful, prestigious groups. We tend to avoid individuals who possess objectionable characteristics.

Some more reasons for joining groups are listed below.

- **Affiliation:** Humans are gregarious. Groups provide a natural way for people to gather in order to satisfy their social needs.
- **Goal achievement:** Problems and tasks that require knowledge tend to give groups an advantage over individuals. There is more information in a group than in any one of its members, and groups tend to provide a greater number of approaches to solving a particular problem.

- **Power:** Individuals gain power in their relationship with their employers by forming unions. Consumer rights groups fighting class action suits against large companies, confer power on the members that these members would not have as individuals.
- **Status:** In educational institutions, membership of a particular gang may confer status (perceived) on members. Similarly, membership in some service clubs or a political body may be seen to confer status on members.
- **Self-esteem:** As suggested by Maslow, people have a basic desire for self-esteem. Group membership may nurture self-esteem. If one belongs to a successful group, then self-esteem of all members may be enhanced.
- **Security:** Sometimes, individuals need protection from other groups or more powerful individuals: 'there is safety in numbers.' These individuals may seek security in group membership. Neighbours may form a 'Block Watch' group to ensure the security and protection of their neighbourhood.

Advantages and disadvantages of groups

Table 9.2 shows the advantages and disadvantages of groups.

Cohesiveness of Groups

Group cohesiveness means group togetherness, i.e., sticking together by the group members. In a cohesive group, members identify with each other, i.e., they feel proud to be a member of the group and identify themselves with the group goals and purposes aligning with their own goals. Some of the benefits of group cohesiveness are:

- Members value their association with the group.
- Members receive benefits from their participation in groups.

Table 9.2 Advantages and disadvantages of groups

Advantages	Disadvantages
Take advantage of a wider range of knowledge, expertise and ideas	Only one person can talk at a time (blocking)
Effective way to build consensus	The most talkative person talks 40%, next 20%, everyone else under 10% (exponential drop off)
Effective way of communicating complex information	Organizational status can create situations where the 'wrong' person does all the talking(status differentials)

- Members invest their time for the group; hence cannot forsake their membership.
- Member enjoy satisfaction.
- Members achieve group goals more effectively.
- Interpersonal communication among members is very high.
- The group leader can exert influence won a cohesive group to get results.

Some of the factors that affect group cohesiveness are:

- **Poor conformity:** Conformity indicates members' going along with their groups. Poor conformity may be for the pressure on group members to compromise, when members are persuaded too much to achieve the group goals, when they feel coerced, feel the time constraint and are frustrated. The end result of poor conformity is abandonment from group membership.
- **Unclear group roles and norms:** When group roles and norms are not adequately defined or clarified, members feel frustrated and group cohesiveness suffers.
- **Unhealthy competition and conflict:** Group leaders often unconsciously incite unhealthy competition and conflict among members. Although productive conflict (right to questioning) is helpful for effective group decision-making, group members often face the brunt, when group leaders impose their decisions. Similarly, provoking group members to unnecessary competition also dissuades them from enjoying harmonious relationships which compromises group cohesiveness.
- **Ineffective group leadership:** When group leaders are ineffective, they fail to exert influence on the group members, resulting in loss of group cohesiveness.
- **Lack of intellectual stimulation:** Group members often feel low intellectual stimulation, as they are not encouraged to think and use their creativity and inventiveness, causing problems in group cohesiveness.
- **Poor inspiration:** Group members need to feel inspired. When inspiration is less, they feel frustrated, and suffer from poor morale resulting in loss of group cohesiveness.

Group cohesion and performance

Numerous research studies have established the positive relationship between group cohesion and performance. Some of the factors for improved performance due to group cohesion can be listed as under:

Satisfaction of group members: With increased cohesion, group members feel satisfied, which enhances their performance.

Group conformity: A cohesive group enjoys high conformity, resulting in high performance.

Adherence to group norms: In cohesive groups, members adhere to group norms, by relating to them willingly.

Group Roles and Norms

Norms are expectations applying to all group members, while roles are the expectations regarding behaviour of a group member in specific positions. Group norms are unspoken rules which are agreed upon and which guide the behaviour of the members of the group. Norms represent shared ways of viewing the world. Norms, if written down, become formal rules of proper conduct. However, in most instances, norms are adopted implicitly as people align their behaviours during the group formation process until consensus in actions emerges.

Group roles

Roles are sets of shared expectations about who should do what under a given set of circumstances. Group structures provide for relationships among members and they influence group processes. Certain structures are common to virtually all groups. These structures provide an underlying framework for the role, status, attraction and communication relationships among members, and they influence a variety of group processes. Thus, individuals who occupy specific roles generally perform a specific set of behaviours in their groups.

Role differentiation takes place when group members interact with one another. Such role differentiation broadly encompasses task and socio-emotional roles. Task-oriented roles may again be categorised into the following types:

- **Initiator–contributor:** Suggests new ideas to solve group problem or new ways for the group to organise the task
- **Information giver/seeker:** Deals with information and facts about the group's task
- **Opinion seeker/giver:** Deals with the group's values regarding its tasks
- **Energizers:** Tries to keep up the group's energy level
- **Elaborator:** Explains in detail about how group plans would work
- **Coordinator:** Coordinates group activities
- **Orienter:** Keeps the group focused on its goals
- **Recorder:** Acts as the memory of the group

Similarly, socio-emotional or relations-oriented roles can be classified into the following types:

- **Harmoniser:** Tries to keep relations between group members harmonious
- **Compromiser:** Offers to compromise own position to keep the group harmonious

- **Encourager:** Praises and encourages group members
- **Gatekeeper:** Facilitates the participation of others in the group
- **Group observer:** Supplies the group with observations of its procedures

This apart, groups may have self-oriented roles and prescribed roles. Self-oriented roles again can be divided into following categories:

- **Blocker:** Disagrees with the group and revives old issues for discussion
- **Recognition seeker:** Seeks personal honour in the group
- **Dominator:** Attempts to manipulate the group and dominate others
- **Avoider:** Refuses to focus on the task or group relationship problems
- **Aggressor:** Attacks the group
- **Self-confessor:** Uses the group as a forum for inappropriate talk about self
- **Help seeker:** Looks for sympathy from others
- **Clown:** Shows non-involvement in group and engages in distracting communication

All the types of roles of the groups mentioned above evolve naturally. Organizations, however, may prescribe specific roles to employees. These roles are classified as prescribed roles in a formal organization, which are limited to position, title, job description and organizational directives.

Often the role of an individual conferred either by the group or the organization may be the source of problems. Some of these problems may be due to role ambiguity, i.e., lack of clarity regarding duties, responsibilities and/or authority. This may be due to the complexity of the job. Less capable or less confident group members often complain of role ambiguity.

Role conflict: It refers to the mismatch between the perceived role expectations and the actual role of the individual. Role conflict takes place either due to one specific assigned role (internal conflict) or due to assignment of several simultaneous roles with conflicting expectations (inter-role conflict). Inter-role conflict is 'a case of wearing too many hats'. We can illustrate these citing good examples from the corporate world.

Many organizations describe their mission as growing through customer satisfaction. This requires managers to focus on customer satisfaction and build corporate image, keeping in view long-term sustainability. However, this role runs into conflict of achieving short-term results. Many Indian organizations still believe in gaining strength in the short-run, neglecting the initiatives to build a favourable long-term image. Likewise achieving higher profits shows inter-role conflict with labour welfare. Thus, inter-role conflict emerges when an individual employee gets too many directives from different bosses, or when the employee concerned has to meet several ends in one go. Thus, apart from wearing 'too many hats', inter-role conflict may also emerge from having 'too many bosses'.

Group norms

These may be prescriptive or proscriptive. Prescriptive norms dictate behaviour that should be performed, while proscriptive norms dictate behaviours that should be avoided. As already stated, norms differ from rules and hence these are not formal or documented. Norms get intertwined with the organizational practices in such a way that group members remain unaware that they even exist. Organizations may have a disciplinary policy (i.e., documented norms) but complying with disciplinary issues may be more the force of group norms. Thus, norms govern behaviour in many areas. Like roles, norms also may be of different types:

- **Performance-related**—relates more to the task of the group
- **Appearance**—relates more to the attire
- **Demonstration of loyalty**—internalisation of loyalty
- **Informal social arrangements**—cliques, coalitions
- **Allocation of resources**—who gets what in a given situation

In organizations, norms develop in a number of ways, as shown below.

Primacy: Adoption of norms to ensure behavioural consistency by minimising ambiguity

Explicit statements: Statements or directives made by a group member

Critical events: These evolve over a period of time. Some critical events may require group members to reassess their existing rules, procedures, processes or relationships.

Carry-over behaviours: Members carry over past experiences. For example, occupational norms, ethical norms, athletic or social group norms etc.

Group norms are established to facilitate group survival. Some critical events may threaten achievement of group goals. This requires group members to re-assess their norms and make adjustments, so that group can survive and achieve success. Similarly group norms ensure predictable behaviour of group members, allow members to express the central values of the group (to demonstrate their distinctiveness), reduce interpersonal problems of group members etc.

Despite having group norms, we often encounter group conflict. Group conflict plays a significant role, as some 'essential' conflicts may promote creative decision-making. On the other hand, some group conflicts may be counterproductive. In terms of the effect, group conflicts may be either cognitive (task-oriented) or affective (relationship-oriented). Cognitive conflict generally plays a positive role, while affective conflict has the opposite effect as it mainly stems from personality mismatch. Organizations try to avoid group conflict by setting up group norms. Such group norms govern the relationship between group members, in a way that hardly incites conflict among them. This, however, can only limit intra-group conflict. Since conflict is also perceived as the most effective way to promote creativity and innovation in organizations, instead of having group norms to avoid conflict, they may adopt openness norms to encourage discussion.

Group Dynamics

Group dynamics is founded on Lewin's concept of action research. He felt that social problems, including conflict, leadership and adjustment, should be solved scientifically for there 'is no hope of creating a better world without a deeper scientific insight into the function of leadership and culture' and other essentials of group life' (Lewin 1948). Lewin's action research argues against the traditional distinction between basic and applied science by suggesting that scientific understanding will occur most rapidly if researchers and practitioner's efforts are unified.

Group dynamics may be defined as the behaviour of a group of people under certain conditions, and the way they change with the situation. Also it can be defined as the branch of social psychology that studies the dynamics of interaction in a small group.

In any organization, group processes are followed. Group process understands how an organization's members work together and get the things done. Some of the ways to understand a group process are group's morale, membership participation, decision-making style and how people get along with each other. By developing a group process, organizations can successfully develop self-confidence, refine skills and make friends. Not everyone in a group has the same expectations, does the same thing or has the same commitment level. Knowledge about how group members interact, share common goals and work with one another can help you to integrate newcomers and prepare them or the roles, norms, and cohesiveness of the group.

Team Development

The terms group and team are often used interchangeably, although theoretically and operationally these are different. A team is driven by a common goal, and represented by cross-functional people. A group, on the other hand, performs similar jobs under a common leader. A group, therefore, is relatively easier to form based on common functions or compatibility. A team, on the other hand, is difficult to form, as team members may subscribe to the common goal with their complementary skills. The success of a group is measured in terms of the output volume, while the success of a team's work is measured in terms of interpersonal dynamics to achieve the common goal. Because of this typical nature, conflict in a team is rarely possible, although it is quite common in groups. A team being dynamic can hardly be contaminated by the groupthink to arrive at some conclusions. A group is controlled by a designated leader; a team, on the other hand, is represented by shared leadership roles with mutual and individual accountability of team members.

Model of Team Development

The classical model of team development suggests that teams develop in a linear fashion, through a sequence of phases. Some recent investigations of workgroups indicate that teams develop through a variety of alternative paths rather than a single sequence of developmental phases. This line of research developed around studies of the lifespan development of naturally occurring task-driven workgroups in organizations.

In a modified model of team development, the stages of development are considered to be relatively informal, indistinct and overlapping, because sharp demarcations are not generally characteristic of the dynamic situations in which operational teams work and develop.

A team's progression through the stages depends on a number of factors:

- Team characteristics
- Member characteristics
- Members' past histories and experiences with one another
- Nature of the tasks and the technologies available to complete them,
- Environmental demands and constraints

Teams develop (generally) from initial ineptness and exploratory interactions to the final levels of skilled performance that are manifested as team members learn to cooperate and coordinate their efforts effectively. There are nine stages in the development of a team. These are listed below.

i) Pre-forming stage that recognises the forces from the environment that call for, and contribute to, the establishment of the team; that is, forces external to the team that cause the team to be formed.
ii) Formation of the team during its first meeting (forming)
iii) Members' initial, and sometimes unstable, exploration of the situation (storming)
iv) Initial efforts toward accommodation and the formation and acceptance of roles (norming)
v) Performance leading toward occasional inefficient patterns (performing-I)
vi) Re-evaluation and transition (reforming)
vii) Refocusing of efforts to produce effective performance (performing-II)
viii) Completion of team assignments (conforming)

ix) The team is disbanded. Team members leave the group and the team loses its identity and ceases to exist. Individuals return to the organizational sectors from which they were initially drawn or move to new territories and relationships.

The development of a team might be recycled from any of the final stages to an earlier stage if necessitated by a failure to achieve satisfactory performance or if adjustments to environmental demands are required or if problematic team interactions develop.

A modified team development model suggests that team development is characterized by the differential maturation of task work and team work skills. Individual task work skills, (no matter how great) may be relatively useless without the cooperative, coordinated, and supporting efforts of others where group or team performances are required.

Team development includes the progression of two distinguishable activity tracks: task work and team work.

- **Task work-oriented behaviours:** It involves activities that are tied to the specific task(s) being performed. These activities encompass operational skills and include interactions of the team members with tools and machines, the technical aspects of the job (procedures, policies etc), and other task-related activities.
- **Team work-oriented behaviours:** This consists of methods for enhancing the quality of the interactions, interdependencies, relationships, cooperation and coordination of the team. This track is important for generating group cohesion and organizational commitment and for sustaining the integrity and viability of the team.

The second track of activities

A substantial portion of the energies devoted to building better teams can be accounted for in terms of activities that are aimed at people (other team members) and relationships. Coordination in a team requires members to engage in person-to-person activities designed to enhance interpersonal communication, social relationships and interaction patterns (the maturation and maintenance of the team as a cohesive unit). As the team develops, its ability to communicate, coordinate and interact should improve, and this contributes to its enhanced viability as a group and to better team performance.

- **Interdependence of task work and team work behaviours:** In order for teams to achieve optimum levels of performance, the task work and team work lines of team development must be separately enhanced, progressively focused, and ultimately converged so that all activities contribute to improved team viability and performance. Team training should seek not only to improve the formally programmed task performance but also to enhance the team's ability to communicate, relate and interact.

Key Points

- Understanding the group process in an organization, helps us to assess how people work together and accomplish the results.
- Groups are classified as formal, command, committees and informal categories.
- The three important theories of group formation are: propinquity theory, balance theory and exchange theory.
- There are five stages in the formation of groups: Forming, Storming, Norming, Performing and Adjourning.
- Effective and ineffective groups differ on the basis of clarity of goals, level of communication and participation in decision-making.
- Decision-making in groups uses various forecasting tools like decision tree, Delphi technique and nominal group method. Statistical models based on queuing theory, game theory, distribution and inventory management are also popular.
- Groupthink is the phenomenon of conformity with the majority opinion. It is undesirable in immature groups as it could lead to 'social loafing'. It is very effective in mature groups.
- Some of the important reasons for joining groups are: affiliation, power, status, self-esteem and security.
- Groups need to be cohesive to achieve high performance. Group roles are explicitly stated while group norms are imputed to the behaviour of members.
- Teams are different from groups and have a distinct model of development with nine stages.

Important Terms

Command group: It is a task group, where tasks are defined as cross-functional activities and carried out by group members to accomplish a common goal. A command group can be formed drawing members from various formal groups.

Group dynamics: It is defined as the behaviour of a group of people under certain conditions, and the way they change with the situation. It is also considered as a branch of social psychology that studies the dynamics of interaction in a small group.

Groupthink syndrome: It is a mode of thinking by group members to strive for consensus. This thinking process at times may ignore the need for realistic assessment of alternative courses of action. It requires the group members to be more cohesive and friendly.

Mutual goals: Using a goal congruence model, organizations try to set mutual goals. When employees feel that their personal goals match with that stipulated by the organization for individuals, they pursue goal achievement voluntarily.

Role conflict: It refers to the mismatch between the perceived role expectations and the actual role of the individual. Role conflict takes place either due to one specific assigned role (internal conflict) or due to assignment of several simultaneous roles with conflicting expectations (inter-role conflict).

Team work-oriented behaviours: This type of behaviour enhances the quality of interactions, interdependencies, relationships, affection, cooperation and coordination of the team. This track is important for generating group cohesion and organizational commitment, and for sustaining the integrity and viability of the team.

Self-assessment Questions

1. Explain why people tend to form groups? Is it not possible to survive without groups?
2. What are the characteristic features of a group? How do such features contribute to its effectiveness
3. Explain the process of group decision-making. What are the problems encountered by an organization in group decision-making?
4. Elaborate the concept of group norms. How are group norms decided?
5. What are the group roles? How do group roles lead to a conflicting situation? How can group role conflict be resolved?
6. Write short notes on the following:
   - i. Tuckman's model
   - ii. Socio-emotional or relations-oriented roles
   - iii. Team-oriented behaviour
   - iv. Task-oriented behaviour
   - v. Self-esteemed group
   - vi. Power group
   - vii. Group cohesion
   - vii. Team development

Select Bibliography

1. Bednar RL and T Kaul (1978). Experiential group research: Current perspectives. *In* S Garfield and A Bergin (eds), *Handbook of Psychotherapy and Behaviour Change*. New York: Wiley.
2. Bhattacharyya DK (2009). *Organizational Behaviour: Concepts and Applications*. New Delhi: Oxford University Press.
3. Forsyth DR (1993). Building a bridge between basic social psychology and the study of mental health. *Contemporary Psychology*, 38: 931–32.
4. Forsyth DR and MR Leary (1991). Metatheoretical and epistemological issues. *In* CR Snyder and DR Forsyth (eds), *Handbook of Social and Clinical Psychology: The Health Perspective*. New York: Pergamon. 757–73.
5. Freud S (1922). *Group Psychology and the Analysis of the Ego*. London: Hogarth.
6. Klein RH (1983). Group treatment approaches. *In* M Hersen, AE Kazdin and AS Bellack (eds), *The Clinical Psychology Handbook* . New York: Pergamon. 593–610.
7. Le Bon G (1895/1960). The crowd (translation of psychologie des foules). New York: The Viking Press.
8. Lewin K (1936). *Principles of Topological Psychology*. New York: McGraw-Hill.
9. Lewin K (1948). *Resolving Social Conflicts: Selected Papers on Group Dynamics.* New York: Harper.
10. Moreno JL (1932). *Who shall survive*? Washington DC: Nervous and Mental Disease Publishing Co.
11. Tuckman B (1965). Developmental sequence in small groups, *Psychological Bulletin*, 63: 384–99.

10 Job Analysis and Job Design

Learning Objectives

After reading this chapter, you will be able to:

- **Define job analysis, job design and job evaluation**
- **Appreciate how job analysis is used by industrial psychologists**
- **Understand the process of job analysis and job description**
- **Outline job assessment and job pricing**

Overview

The importance of job analysis with the involvement of industrial psychologists can be understood in the context of the rising number of litigations throughout the world, over decisions on selection and promotions, particularly in public sector companies. Effective job analysis, to a great extent, can help in avoiding and save considerably the costs incurred by the organizations on such litigation. Having too many job titles complicates the issue; hence industrial psychologists help in scientific job analysis and thereby help to merge several job titles into a job family. This is done depending on the compatibility between the jobs. Job analysis encompasses various macro level organizational subsystems like personnel, technological, and other external environmental issues. Through job analysis, we try to match jobs with workers. Such analysis helps in understanding the safety, efficiency, technological development, and the mental and physical well-being of workers.

Results of job analysis help in personnel selection and placement, performance management, management of workplace safety, man–machine design, work design, and developing of various manpower inventories.

For effective human resource management, compiling job analysis information and documentation of the same is necessary as it subsequently helps in job description and job evaluation. With the active involvement of industrial psychologists, the process of identification of job requirements and suitable designing of the same with due indication of job families, soft skill sets, skill mapping and developing of skill inventories etc are done. This ensures meeting the manpower requirements for the present and future and placement of right people in the right jobs.

Job Information

Job information is one essential input for effective human resource planning. It not only facilitates job evaluation while designing the compensation, but also helps in disseminating information to employees about their duties and responsibilities. Imperfect knowledge of employees about their duties and responsibilities due to inadequate job information also affects their performance and overall organizational productivity. Disseminating job information in the 'Letter of Appointment' may not be adequate. Proper documentation and communication during induction training is the right approach.

Objectives of job information

- The first objective of job information is to communicate duties and responsibilities attached to a job to the employees to help them understand clearly their own roles and the organization's expectations.
- Another objective of job information is organizational analysis. It helps in work flow analysis with respect to a job and also helps in identification of redundant work elements in a job and thus facilitates in job restructuring.
- Job information helps in analysing the scope for internal hiring and the requirements of external hiring for staffing various positions in the organization thus facilitating the process of human resource planning.

In setting performance standards and establishing job objectives, job information is essential both in qualitative and quantitative terms. This also facilitates more scientific appraisal of the performance of employees against the set standards.

For other HR-related decisions like promotion, transfer, relocation, redundancy and compensation designing, job information provides critical inputs.

Job Analysis

Job analysis is the process of gathering information about the job and evaluating such information in terms of what is necessary and relevant. Essentially, job analysis involves three questions:

- What is a job?
- What should be analysed?
- What methods of analysis should be used?

A job is a group of essentially similar activities or tasks performed by a person or a group of persons. These activities or tasks together become a job. Obviously, tasks or activities of jobs need not be identical. It may be performed in different places, with different equipment or in a different sequence. Also, some employees may perform certain activities in addition to the main job. Or some employees may perform a job occasionally or temporarily, normally to fill in for persons who are absent or on vacation. This definition of a job is typically used in compensation designing and for other management practices. However, a more generic description of a job is used, which is identified by 'position' rather than 'job'. A position is a family of jobs in which specific duties vary but some interchangeability of work is possible and the functional nature of the work is similar. Examples include assemblers, clerk-cum-typists, and book-keepers. Broader definition of a job facilitates development of accurate job information and this accurately reflects the work of each employee.

Another basic issue for job analysis is whether the organization should measure work assigned or work actually performed. Some experts argue that unless job analysis considers work performance, the organization may not account for employees' credit for what they are actually doing. On the other hand, analysing work performance may imply that employees have been given latitude to assign work to themselves. In reality, it is the manager's responsibility to assign a job. The role of an analyst is essentially to gather job information and not to evaluate the logic of work assignments. He is primarily responsible for recording of those responsibilities that a manager has assigned to an employee.

Scope of Job Analysis

What should be the nature of job information for job analysis depends upon a number of considerations. Whether the analysis is required for evaluation or for other purposes, considerations like what job level is to be analysed, what type of evaluation plan is to be used and what job knowledge is held by the analyst who would conduct the evaluation are essential. Some basic details included in the preparation of job analysis report are:

- Fundamental purpose of the job
- Work elements in the job obtained from the study of specific tasks, areas of responsibility, and so on
- General importance of each job element and its relationship to the total operation i.e., how it is integrated with the total job
- Approximate time spent on each task or specific area of responsibility
- Scope of the job and its impact on the operation
- Inherent authority (not only formal delegation but also latitude of action) and formal or informal audits of work
- Working relationships (including supervision)
- Specific methods, equipment or techniques, that is required for the job

- Job climate, including objectives and work environment
- Job conditions like physical effort, hazards, discomfort, chasing of deadlines, travel requirement, creativity required etc

Methods of Job Analysis

The information required for job analysis can be obtained in various ways either by a staff analyst or by the individual line manager. Because of functional proximity, it is always better to involve the line managers in compiling job information. One relatively simple and inexpensive method of analysis is the questionnaire. Direct observation of work performed is another important method. Observation of work is essential to understand the job role. However, it is more costly and time-consuming. Valuable job information can also be obtained from the organization manual, time study reports, former job descriptions and method studies.

Position Analysis Questionnaire (PAQ)

A structured Position Analysis Questionnaire (PAQ) can quantify the job analysis. It was developed in the early 1970s by McCormick and others. It consists of 194 worker-oriented job elements divided into six major categories. The analyst rates the job elements on a scale of 0 to 5. Analysing the 189 behavioural items comprising the six categories, we can assess job performance. Job elements are also classified into information input, mental process, work output, interpersonal relationships, work situation and job context, and other job characteristics. These apart, it also requires the study of tools and equipment required for job performance, physical and perceptual requirements of the job, mathematical and communication requirements, decision-making and responsibility-decisions about methods, order of work, standards, job conditions and perceived job characteristics.

The other approach in PAQ consists of methods that match the profiles of jobs.

Job questionnaire

A job questionnaire is a special tool for consolidating job information. It is a printed form in which essential information about the job may be listed either by the employee or his supervisors. The major advantage of the questionnaire is that it uses the knowledge of those who are proximate to the job. In addition, it gives each employee an opportunity to participate and contribute by giving responses to the questionnaire, which facilitates immediate compilation of job information.

Another important advantage of job questionnaire is that the compiled information can be used as job descriptions. It, therefore, eliminates the requirement of further writing of job descriptions. Moreover, by using a job questionnaire, organizations also get the benefit of communicating up-to-date job information to the employees.

However, the major disadvantages associated with job questionnaire are that, its success depends on the understanding and writing ability of individual employees and supervisors. For perceptual incongruence, inconsistencies in the response pattern may arise. Such inconsistencies in the response pattern may multiply when more sections of people participate in the questionnaire response/survey. In addition, compiling job information from the questionnaire response again may suffer from the problem of exaggeration. These are the inherent problems of the quality of information through job questionnaire.

To eliminate such inherent problems of compiling job information through job questionnaire, it is always better to compile the information through a combination of direct observation and job questionnaire. This approach may be time-consuming and involve huge cost, but it is more scientific as it eliminates the chance of error by accounting for the differences between the respondents' perception and what they actually do.

Job description

The compiled job information is translated into job descriptions. They are written records of job duties and responsibilities and provide a factual basis for job evaluation. Job descriptions are recorded on a standard form.

For obvious requirement of writing skill in the preparation of job descriptions, many organizations assign this task to trained and professional job analysts. However, this by itself cannot guarantee flawless job description. This is because a professional job analyst may not have specific job knowledge. Therefore, despite engaging an analyst, the inclusion of the company staff is better for scientific description of jobs.

In terms of format, the job description should first name the job, using the title which accurately summarises duties assigned. While naming a job, it is always better to consider the job family. To illustrate, instead of naming a HR job as HR Manager, if the term 'Knowledge Manager' is used, it may give a contemporary or trendy job title but for the others (including members within the organization), it may be a misnomer. Secondly, job description should then document in a single form (frequently with short sentences or phrases) a list of duties assigned. What is to be included while listing the job duties and how those are to be written will depend on the level of the position and the purpose to be served by the description. For the top management level, a job description may be the description of the business goals and objectives. But, at the operational level, job descriptions may be limited to listing the specific duties performed, equipment used and procedures followed. The broader the use of the job description information and the higher the functional level, the longer the job description. Therefore for operational positions, job description may be about one page, while for higher management, it may run into many.

Job specifications

In addition to providing information about duties associated with job assignments, job descriptions also outline basic specifications of the job. Such specifications include education or experience required to do the job and special knowledge and skill set necessary to carry out the job. In addition, specifications also identify the soft skills like interpersonal skills, analytical ability, problem-solving and decision-making skills which are required to perform the duties assigned.

This exercise of processing job information is known as developing job specification. It helps in the evaluation of jobs and at the same time it defines the attributes required for a job position. This is required during recruitment. Therefore, job specifications list out all those attributes, like education, experience, age, physical fitness etc along with other soft skills required for performing a job. This also requires the special skill of the analyst, as any mistake in judgement may defeat the purpose, not only by selecting a wrong person for a job but also for wrongly evaluating a job, which is directly associated with job pricing.

Transparency in job descriptions

Today's organizations are dynamic and every now and then require restructuring, which also necessitates redesigning of jobs. Therefore, it is widely believed that showing a job description to employees may cause controversy and in future employees may resist doing work which is not specifically listed in their job descriptions. However, if job descriptions are well developed, there is nothing wrong in sharing them with the employees, as they spell out the list of duties employees are expected to perform. To eliminate the problem, an all inclusive statement like 'in addition to the listed duties and responsibilities, your superior may ask you to perform other tasks from time to time' can be considered.

By sharing job descriptions with employees, organizations can make their job evaluation process participative and avoid any dissonance with the results of job evaluation. This is also important, as organizations are also laden with employees' dissatisfaction on job pricing. Communication of job descriptions enhances acceptance of the same, as employees are not left with any doubts about their duties and responsibilities. Such communication with the employees should be an ongoing exercise, as employees also can understand their changed job duties and responsibilities, if any.

Uses of job description

Job descriptions help in the management in getting things done through people and to accomplish following objectives:

- Efficient organization of jobs
- Proper recruitment or staffing for the organization
- Assigning jobs to people by communicating to them their duties and responsibilities and by setting job standards
- Reviewing performance of the people
- Improving performance through appraisal and training
- Rewarding employees

Therefore, job descriptions play a very crucial role in key management activities. However, it is very important for the manager to ensure that job descriptions are correct and whatever jobs have been assigned are essential. He must ensure that essential tasks have only been grouped into jobs. Since job descriptions have interconnectivity, the analyst has to align it to decisions on recruitment, performance appraisal, training needs, promotion, transfer and relocation. From the point of view of the employees, it should mention clearly what is expected of them and how the assigned work should be done.

By listing the assigned duties in a job description, a manager can determine reasonable performance standard. Identification of such performance standards facilitate benchmarking the performance of an employee against the best performer.

Job descriptions also facilitate proper utilisation of manpower. By a periodic review of the listed duties, a manager can identify which jobs are time-consuming but require lower skill set. He or she can reassign such jobs accordingly to lower-paid employees. In addition, the manager can also study jobs in terms of workload and determine man-hours required. For low technology and low-skill jobs, he or she can consider the decision to offload the job to subcontractors. Therefore, it has tremendous implication for effective human resource planning in an organization. We may call this also an instrument for proper rightsizing of employees in an organization.

Finally, job descriptions, as a basic management tool, also influence operating procedures by identifying duplication of work, indicating a scientific work flow, suggesting better allocation of jobs and by pointing out possible job bottlenecks.

Figure 10.1 shows a central peripheral relational model of job analysis.

Fig. 10.1 A model of job analysis

Job Evaluation

Job evaluation originated in the United States of America in 1971. Much earlier, in 1909, the Civil Service Commission in Chicago and the Commonwealth Edison Company of Chicago pioneered the concept. In 1926, Merill R Lott wrote *Wage Scales and Job Evaluation*, describing methods used in his company, the Sperry Gyroscope Company Inc.

It is the process of determining the worth of one job in relation to that of another without regard to the personalities. It analyses and assesses the content of jobs, to place them in some standard rank order. The end result is used as the basis for a fair and logical remuneration system.

A properly devised job evaluation scheme provides the management with definite, systematic and reliable data for working out wage and salary scales. Thus, logical wage negotiation reduces wage grievances and dissatisfaction with wage differentials and ensures fair treatment for each employee. It also provides a logical basis for promotion. A survey by the British Institute of Management indicated the following reasons for the use of job evaluation.

- Reduce employee turnover rate
- Increase output
- Improve morale
- Reduce loss of time due to wage negotiation and disputes
- Reduce complaints regarding wages
- Reduce wage and salary anomalies

Steps in job evaluation

The steps in job evaluation are listed below.

1. Thorough examination of the job (job assessment)
2. Preparation of job description (recording its characteristics to suit assessment of method)
3. Preparation of job analysis to set out the requirements of the job under various factor headings
4. Comparison of one job with another
5. Arrangement of jobs in a progression
6. Relating the progression of jobs to a money scale

Types of Job Evaluation Schemes

There are four basic types of job evaluation. These are discussed in detail here.

Ranking: This is a simple system to judge each job as a whole to understand its relative worth by ranking one whole job against another. To start with, a job description is prepared in a narrative form, starting with duties, responsibilities and qualifications, required for the job. The jobs are then ranked in order of relative difficulty or value to the company and grade levels are then defined and wage levels are finalised. One of the disadvantages of this method is that the degree of difference between jobs cannot be indicated. Ranking, therefore, may be incorrect and suffer extraneous influence. The relative value of the employees (currently occupying the jobs) may be ranked rather than the jobs. The methods may be adequate for the easily defined jobs of a small number of workmen but it is regarded as impracticable for complicated jobs and a large number of workmen.

Classification: This is different from ranking because grade and wage levels are predetermined before jobs are ranked and descriptions are written defining the type of jobs that would fall into each group. Under this method, usually a committee allocates jobs to each group using job description. The system is simple but suffers from limitation similar to that of ranking system.

Points rating: Under this system, to achieve a higher level of accuracy, each job is broken down into its component factors or characteristics and then evaluated separately rather than evaluating the job as a whole. A narrative job description is prepared and supplemented by a statement of the various requirements (present in the job). Characteristics like experience and training, mental and physical effort common to the jobs are selected and a point value for each characteristic or factor is determined. Factors are defined objectively and points are given to each factor based on its estimated importance. Consolidated point values are finally converted into money terms.

Factor comparison: This method is also similar to the points rating system as here also each job is broken into factors. The only difference, is that in this method, five factors are used, i.e., knowledge requirements, skill requirements, physical requirements, responsibility and working conditions. After job descriptions, key jobs are judged and related to one another. The jobs are considered one by one and reviewed to understand how much of the current wage rate for the job is paid for each factor. Key jobs are arranged in a scale in order of their value for each factor. The remaining jobs are compared with the key job factors and a comparative money value is determined for each factor in each job. The total of the factor values so determined for each job represents its rate. This is a complex system but offers higher degree of accuracy.

Limitations of job evaluation

Job evaluation alone cannot establish a wage scale. For wage fixation, we need to take cognisance of statutory requirements, like Minimum Wages Act, 1948. Similarly, other factors of wage fixation like capacity to pay, inter-industry wage variation, inter-regional wage variation and collective bargaining agreement, if any, also need to be given importance. Job evaluation is highly subjective being based on estimate. Similarly, it cannot take into account the cyclical effect of market value of occupations. For example, finance jobs were highly priced in the market at one point of time (now IT and marketing have taken its place). However, with the failure of Non-banking Financial Companies (NBFCs), finance jobs are not that highly priced in the market at least at this point of time, even though no material changes in the job profile of finance professionals have taken place in between. Despite such limitations, job evaluation technique is considered very useful.

Job Design

Every job undergoes constant modification because of the impact of mechanisation and automation. Some jobs become redundant while others are created and still others are altered in content. This necessitates different types of education, experience and other attributes. Also for effecting job design, the organization needs to respect the unions, which otherwise may stall the move on one ground or the other.

While designing a job, the management must also be concerned with the practical considerations of quantity and quality of available personnel (both within the organization and in the labour market). Issues like personality conflict and friction, problem of human relations, boredom, obsessive thinking etc are also taken care of. The factors which are likely to affect job design can be enumerated as follows:

- Job specialisation and repetitive operations
- Changing technology
- Labour union policies
- Abilities of present personnel
- Adequate availability of potential personnel
- Interaction among jobs with the system
- Psychological and social needs that can be met by the job

Industrial psychologists design the job for effective structure and style of management to address the ergonomic and behavioural issues. Among others, job designing also helps in decision-making, delegation and formation of autonomous work groups, de-layer the structure by reducing the number and levels of managers, increase the span of control, increase the productivity levels, motivate employees etc. The concept of job design, therefore, suggests incorporating the following elements:

Variety + Responsibility + Control

Job design ensures that all jobs contain variety, some responsibility for decision-making and some control over the way the jobs are done.

To understand the effectiveness of a job design, we need to first understand the various job content factors, duly classifying them as dissatisfying and satisfying factors. Table 10.1 lists some of the job content factors accordingly.

Table 10.1 Dissatisfying and satisfying factors in job content

Dissatisfying factors	Satisfying factors
Administrative policies	Achievement
Supervision	Recognition
Working conditions	Work itself
Interpersonal relations	Responsibility
Salary	Advancement
Status	Growth
Job security	
Personal life	

Characteristics of Job Design

When jobs are interesting or satisfying to employees, we observe at least one or more of the following characteristics.

Task variety: The job with this feature facilitates movement of employees to different job verticals, and in the process employees through job change feel satisfied both mentally and physically.

Task identity: When the tasks fit with the complete job, i.e., when it is possible to establish job relatedness, employees can enjoy a sense of importance, as they can trace where their contributions fit. Therefore, employees can enjoy the sense of belonging and gradually make themselves a party to the overall organizational progress.

Task significance: By establishing task significance, industrial psychologists can also help employees feel a sense of pride, as they gain importance through an increase of their self-esteem.

Autonomy: Developing a sense of autonomy through job design is possible, when employees are told how their jobs are done, the order of tasks, the speed of work etc. Thereafter, employees should be given a free hand, reducing the extent of supervision and control so that they start realising that they are responsible for their jobs and they are the job owners.

Feedback: This characteristic of job design provides an opportunity to the employees to understand their strengths and mistakes, and in the process they mature and achieve perfection in the future.

Methods and Techniques of Job Design

Robertson and Smith (1985) recommended some of the strategies to analyse jobs as under:

- Review of literature and other existing data like prevailing job descriptions, training manuals, assessing job designs from the manuals of technology providers or vendors etc

- Interview immediate managers to understand about the responsibilities and tasks required for performing the job well
- Interview the current employees, who are presently doing the job, in the same line and assess the job requirements
- Observe employees while they do the job
- Try individually to do the job, wherever possible to rationalise the job requirements
- Write job descriptions, detailing all the findings and observations

These apart, while designing jobs; we also refer to organizational policies, incentives and feedback systems as all these largely affect the level of efficiency and motivation of employees. Some of the important techniques of job design are discussed in the following section.

Job rotation: It requires periodic vertical and horizontal movement of employees between a set of jobs or tasks. Through job rotation, employees get relieved of the boredom and monotony that they experience by doing the same repetitive jobs or tasks. However, this requires organizations to initiate multiskilling of employees through continuous training and learning activities. Job rotation becomes much easier where interchangeability of skills is high. Where it is low, multiskilling initiative is the first step. Among others, job rotation relieves employees from the physical strain, tiredness and muscle strain, and provides satisfaction. Through job rotation, organizations can also enhance the decision-making capabilities of employees.

Job enlargement: Through horizontal expansion of jobs, industrial psychologists can practice job enlargement. It involves grouping of job variety within rather than between. Job rotation may require employees to perform similar tasks with more responsibility. Hence, to some extent, it may increase the job load. But increased sense of responsibility may make the employees satisfied, as they get the sense of importance. For obvious horizontal integration of job, organizations can benefit from job rotation in terms of cost optimisation.

Job enrichment: Unlike job enlargement, job enrichment reverses the effect of repetitive tasks as it involves vertical job expansion. Employees feel tired doing again and again same the repetitive tasks or jobs. According to Leach and Wall (2204), boredom, lack of flexibility in jobs makes them feel dissatisfied. Job enrichment through vertical expansion of jobs enhances the scope of jobs and employees also feel more motivated and self-sufficient. It also helps in developing employees through exposure to new job verticals. From organizational point of view, job enrichment facilitates in succession planning, as tracking employees' performance, organizations can make out the future potential employees who can be groomed to top managerial positions.

Table 10.2 Job characteristics model

Job characteristics		Critical psychological state	Job outcomes
Skill variety		Experiences	Internal work motivation
Task identity	→	meaningfulness of work	Job satisfaction
Task significance			
Autonomy	→	Responsibility for outcomes	Growth satisfaction
			Low absenteeism
Feedback	→	Knowledge of results	High quality of performance

Since all skill varieties, i.e., conceptual, technical, human and business are properly addressed by the employees through job enrichment, they can also feel satisfied for opportunities for future growth and development.

Job characteristic model

Hackman and Oldham (1975) suggested the use of job characteristic model for job enrichment. The model suggests five core job characteristics and three psychological states, which can produce positive results through job enrichment. Table 10.2 shows the job characteristics model.

Job enrichment questionnaires

Another approach to make the job enrichment effective is the use of the questionnaire. Analysis of questionnaire response ensures proper alignment between workers' needs and organizational needs. Job design is done through job analysis, job information compilation, job descriptions etc.

> Do employees need jobs that involve responsibility, variety, feedback, challenge, accountability, significance and opportunities to learn?
>
> What techniques can be implemented without changing the job classification plan?
>
> What techniques would require changes in the job classification plan?

Job assessment

At this stage, information about each job is made available to the assessors. Every job, whether manual or not, is closely observed and inspected in actual operation by the assessors. If required, assessors question the operators and their supervisors to collect further details about the job to clear doubts, if any. To keep pace with the changing job content, due to technological changes, it is necessary to make periodic re-assessment of the job keeping in view the old job description.

Pricing Job Value

The purpose of job evaluation is to establish the relative job value within the organization in terms of points or rankings and in terms of pay levels. The next step is to translate these data into a pay structure through job correlation. This, therefore, involves first deciding the pay grades and then developing the pay ranges for each grade.

Steps in job pricing

The initial process of pricing the job and fitting it into a pay structure calls for translating the points into different job grades. Thereafter, jobs have to be grouped as per different pay grades and then relate the result with comparable jobs in other companies. However, this may not be possible for jobs which are unique in nature. When jobs are properly grouped, it is not difficult to price each such job group. After pricing each job group, pay structure can be developed on the mathematical principle that 'things which are equal to the same things are equal to each other'.

From the survey report of other companies, base salaries for each pay grade are established considering the average paid by the companies surveyed.

The next step in job pricing is to develop pay ranges around the base salaries. Once this is developed, individual compensation based on performance and other considerations can be worked out. Different pay ranges enable an organization to adopt a flexible approach (within the range) in hiring new employees, taking cognisance of the flexibility in labour market.

To illustrate, for a manufacturing organization, a fitter may have a pay grade ranging between ₹ 5,000–10,000 per month. This pay grade can be broken into different ranges like, fitter grade-I:₹ 8,000–10,000 per month, fitter grade-II: ₹ 6,000–8,000 per month, fitter grade-III:₹ 5,000–6,000 per month.

Key Points

- Job analysis helps in design, and therefore, it has direct impact on mental and physical health of employees and so also on their performance levels.
- Industrial psychologists are required to understand the physical aspects of jobs, considering the ergonomic issues. The mental aspects of the jobs are also studied using various tools and techniques.
- Effective job analysis facilitates practices of job rotation, job enlargement and job enrichment techniques, which not only reduces the physical strain in doing the jobs, but also provides satisfaction to the employees.
- Job analysis, therefore, through effective job design increases the performance and productivity of workers.

Important Terms

Ergonomics: It helps in designing a work system by considering all the human factors involved.

Factor comparison: This method is used in job evaluation. Five factors are used, i.e., knowledge requirements, skill requirements, physical requirements, responsibility and working conditions.

Job rotation: It involves periodic vertical and horizontal movement of groups of employees between a set of jobs or tasks.

Position Analysis Questionnaire (PAQ): It is used for gathering information for job analysis.

Task identity: Tasks fit together to make a complete job since this gives the employee a sense of doing a whole job from beginning to end with a visible output.

Task variety: It varies the tasks to be performed so that an employee can move from one job to another at various points of time.

Self-assessment Questions

1. Explain the process of job design.
2. Discuss how job analysis facilitates job designing.
3. What is the purpose of job evaluation? Discuss the steps involved in job evaluation.

4. Discuss different types of job evaluation techniques. Which type do you consider more suitable and why?
5. Distinguish between job analysis and job assessment. Select any job and analyse its individual content.
6. Write short notes on the following:
    i. Job characteristics model
    ii. Job assessment methods
    iii. Ergonomics
    iv. Job design

Selected Bibliography

1. Bhattacharyya DK (2009). *Compensation Management*. New Delhi: Oxford University Press.
2. Bhattacharyya DK (2007). *Human Resource Research Methods*. New Delhi: Oxford University Press.
3. Bhattacharyya DK (2006). *Human Resource Planning*, 2nd edition. New Delhi: Oxford University Press.
4. Brown R. Design jobs that motivate and develop people, http://www.media-associates.co.nz/fjobdesign.html. Retrieved on February 14, 2004.
5. Drucker P (1999). *Management Challenges for the 21st Century*. New York: HarperCollins.
6. Hemphill J K (1959). Job description for executives, *Harvard Business Review*, 37(5): 55–67.
7. Herzberg F (1966). *Work and the Nature of Man*. Cleveland: World Publishing Co.
8. Robertson Iand Smith M (1985). *Motivation and Job Design: Theory, Research and Practice*. St Paul: West Publishing Co.
9. Rush H (1971). *Job Design for Motivation: Experiments in Job Enlargement and Job Enrichment*. New York: The Conference Board.

Appendix

JOB ANALYSIS DATA SHEET

Job Title .... **CODE:**

Other Titles

Suggested Title ....

Department .... **Dept No.** .... **Dept Head** ....

No. on Job .... **Range** .... **Supervised By** ....

PERSONS INTERVIEWED ....

ANALYSIS **DATE** **LOCATION OF JOB**

OTHER IDENTIFICATION ....

JOB SUMMARY (Key phrases that cover job):

RELATION TO OTHERS JOBS:

PROMOTION FROM :
PROMOTION TO :
TRANSFER TO AND FROM :

WORK PERFORMED: WHAT – HOW – WHY (Use additional sheets if required)

MAJOR DUTIES :

OTHER TASKS :

EQUIPMENT, MACHINES :

SKILLS INVOLVED: PHYSICAL DEMANDS :

Experience (Type and amount) :

Education and training (Specific skills required) :

Responsibility for product and material :

Responsibility for equipment and machinery :

Responsibility for work of others :

Other Jobs directly affected :

Resourcefulness :

Monetary :

Visual efforts :

Physical efforts :

Surroundings :

Hazards :

JOB DESCRIPTION

FORM NO.2

JOB IDENTIFICATION DATA :
PRESENT JOB TITLE :
DEPARTMENT/SECTION :
SUGGESTED JOB TITLE : **DATE:**
JOB CODE :
EMPLOYEES INTERVIEWED :

JOB SUMMARY

(A) **REGULAR TASKS :**

1.
2.
3.
4.

(B) **CASUAL TASKS :**

1.
2.
3.

(C) **EQUIPMENT OR MACHINE USED :**

(D) **WORKING CONDITIONS AND HAZARD :**

FORM NO.3

JOB SPECIFICATIONS

JOB TITLE (Existing) : **JOB CODE NO.:**

JOB TITLE (Suggested):

DEPARTMENT/SEC **TOTAL POINTS CLASSIFICATION**

---

1. Education Points
2. Experience Points
3. Responsibility for Product or Materials Points
4. Responsibility for Machinery & Equipment Points
5. Responsibility for Works of Others Points
6. Responsibility for Safety of Others Points
7. Manual Skill Points
8. Physical Effort Points
9. Working Condition including Hazards Points

11 Recruitment and Selection

Learning Objectives

After reading this chapter, you will be able to:

- **Understand the recruitment functions in the organization**
- **Outline the process of recruitment**
- **Analyse the interview process and induction program**
- **Describe the placement of employees after recruitment**

Overview

Industrial engineers extend support to organizations in choosing the right candidates for the right jobs. Recruitment is one of the important strategic functions for the organizations, as effective recruitment ultimately enables organizations to sustain the competitive strength. For recruiting to various positions in the organization, we need to go for external hiring, as redeploying existing manpower through job restructuring (internal recruitment) may not be adequate. External hiring process succeeds Human Resource Planning (HRP). Through HRP, we can understand the extent of external hiring after adjustment of internal manpower.

Recruitment, selection, induction and placement are important tools for procuring and effectively using human resources in an organization. While recruitment involves employing suitably trained workforce, selection helps in choosing the right candidate for the right job. Induction and placement puts men to the right jobs. This chapter focuses on these four important organizational activities.

Recruitment

Recruitment functions in recent years have assumed importance for the increasing emphasis on human resources. Traditional approach to personnel management was to ensure routine human resources maintenance functions for the organizations. But recently, radical changes in human resource management, i.e., perceiving human resources like other important resources (physical and financial) of an organization have developed new areas for personnel management. The human resources are the people who are part of the organization. Broadly, they may be direct employees, part-time persons, temporary employees or consultants or any person or persons with a variety of other relationships to the organization. Within the human resources area, there are two major activities. The first is concerned with the recruitment, selection, placement, compensation and appraisal of the human resources (these are known as human resources utilization functions or personnel functions). The other functions are directed to work with the existing human resources, improving their efficiency and effectiveness. These are known as Human Resources Development (HRD) functions which are designed to enable existing human resources to learn activities for their effective functioning in the present jobs, future identifiable jobs and so also for future undefined jobs.

For increasing importance of human resources, it is now imperative for all organizations to retain the manpower and at the same time to recruit and select best possible talents in the country. Most of the organizations are now facing technological changes, resulting in radical change in the recruitment process. Such a technological change, *inter alia*, calls for hiring manpower having higher skills and knowledge, which were not so far available. However, when we consider the recruitment of manpower for unskilled jobs, there seem to be no apparent problems for the organization, as these people are abundantly available in our country for obvious high rate of unemployment. For high-technology employees, i.e., mostly those who are in managerial positions with professional skills, recruitment function is more complex and dynamic.

Definition and Functions

The term recruitment may be defined as the process to discover sources of manpower to meet the requirements or the staffing schedule and to employ effective measures for attracting that manpower in adequate number to facilitate the selection of an efficient working force.

The first important task of recruitment function is to frame a recruitment policy. Framing a recruitment policy calls for a review of manpower requirement i.e., it should be adequately supported by effective manpower forecasting. Manpower planning and so also manpower forecasting of an organization depends on many important factors like present nature of work, possible change in the future working of the organization, the manpower records and information available in the organization for the present strength, the diversification plans and programs of the organization, the environmental change and the change necessary in the organization to respond to such environmental change etc. Most of the organizations, in principle, believe in recruiting best possible manpower from outside. However, recruitment policy of some organizations considers recruiting the employees based on the recommendation of the present employees or recruiting employees from the wards of the existing employees.

For example, in the Tata group, there is a system to recruit employees for unskilled/low-skilled jobs, both technical and non-technical nature, from the wards of the existing employees. Such a policy of recruitment in theTatas has been accepted in principle and, in their manufacturing units, the group maintains a separate employment exchange records to enlist the names and other details of the wards of employees to offer them employment as and when a vacancy arises. But such type of recruitment policy is not followed while hiring manpower for managerial jobs. In such cases, companies are looking for the best available talents. Thus, they go either for advertising the vacancies in leading newspapers of the country, even in good professional journals or they may go in for recruitment of such managerial manpower through campus interview or by using the services of recruitment consultants. The latter maintain a separate data bank for the prospective job seekers, can make available the list of prospective managerial manpower to such companies. In addition to the framing of recruitment policy, each organization for making their recruitment a scientific process of selection, carries out regular forecasting of manpower recruitments.

Internal recruitment

In some cases, organizations also try to internally manage their higher managerial vacancies from their existing employees. In those cases, organizations need to develop their existing manpower adopting suitable training and development functions. Training and development may not necessarily always ensure availability of the best talents internally. Organizations are then compelled to recruit from outside sources mentioned above.

Differences between recruitment and selection

We use both the terms recruitment and selection interchangeably, though technically they are different. Some of the areas of differences between the two can be summarised as under:

- Recruitment is the process of searching the candidates and at the same time attracting the talent for employment in the organization. Selection, on the other hand, involves a series of steps that candidates are required to follow, to ultimately succeed in getting the job.
- The purpose of recruitment is to create a talent pool of candidates. Selection chooses the best-fit for the jobs.
- Recruitment is a positive process, as it is open to all eligible candidates to apply for the jobs, while selection is a negative process, because by screening through successive stages of interview and tests, it rejects many candidates, and ultimately selects the best-fits only.
- Recruitment is more like a search process, whereas selection is the process of elimination.

Recruitment policy

A sound recruitment policy calls for adopting a scientific process of recruitment, i.e., those techniques, which are modern and scientific. Recruitment policy also requires understanding of the high cost of managerial turnover. Unless a company adopts a suitable recruitment policy, it may not be possible for it to select the right candidate for the right job. A sound recruitment policy, therefore, needs to:

- Identify, at the outset, the recruitment needs of the organization
- Identify the preferred sources of recruitment
- Frame suitable criteria for selection
- Consider the cost of recruitment

The Recruitment Process

As has already been discussed, a particular organization may effect recruitment either from internal sources, i.e., by promoting the existing employees for higher positions, or it might go for outside sources. Thus, internal and external sources of recruitment can either be resorted to by any organization, subject to convenience and feasibility. Recruitment is an art of attracting applicants, from whom the most suitable ones may be selected for a particular job or jobs. Internal recruitment may often avoid the unpleasantness, but it is not necessarily effective because it does not allow the organization to get many alternatives to select the best available talent. The external sources being open, give an opportunity to tap the best or suitable candidates from widely dispersed areas. The requisition for recruitment contains a brief description of the post, qualification and experience required etc. Such requisitions are normally signed by the head of the Human Resource department. External sources of recruitment are resorted to keeping in view the type of personnel required. The workmen may be recruited at the gate itself or from the employment exchange. Management trainees are taken from the institutes and universities, effecting campus interview. Senior executives are attracted through advertisements in leading newspapers and magazines. The major sources of recruitment for different types of personnel, therefore, are as follows:

- Employment exchanges
- Consultants and private employment agencies
- Advertisements in periodicals and newspapers, radio and TV
- Deputation
- Universities and management institutes
- From the source of existing employees/referrals
- Trade unions
- Internet websites

The employment exchanges maintain a register of candidates seeking various types of jobs. Under Compulsory Notification of Vacancies Act, 1955, the employers are required to notify certain types of vacancies to the nearest employment exchange and recruit candidates from among the applicants registered with them. The skilled and unskilled workers and the clerical staff are mostly recruited through employment exchanges. Private consultants and agencies assist organizations in locating technical and managerial staff. They charge prescribed fees for their services to the organization.

Advertising in newspapers and magazines, radio and television, have now become the most effective sources for attracting the prospective candidates. It also helps in building the image for the organization because through such advertisements, the organization makes available certain information, like their product, market share, turnover etc to the public in general and target consumers in particular. Since written press insertions or verbal advertisements through audio and audio-visual methods give the first-hand information to the prospective job seekers, each organization is required to give as much factual information as possible regarding the job expectations from the candidates, their age group, qualifications and experience, salary and perks attached to the positions and important conditions of service, the time-limit and mode of applying etc. There are some agencies that help organizations in drafting, publishing and broadcasting advertisements.

Deputationists are mainly appointed in public sector undertakings. The civil servants are often deputed for many senior and mid-level positions for a specified time.

Recruitment from universities and management institutes are effected through campus interview. Almost all good private organizations select their management trainees through such method. Some organizations even sponsor the cost of prospective students during their learning to join them after completion of the course.

From the source of existing employees also, recruitment is done by many private organizations to ensure commitment and loyalty and at the same time to motivate the employees. Such type of recruitment, however, is restricted only to the clerical and unskilled jobs in most of the cases.

Trade unions also recommend candidates for clerical and unskilled jobs. This practice is not in vogue in many organizations. Only in technical training scheme, trade unions were found to influence the organizations to induct their recommended candidates as apprentices.

Recruitment through internet/job sites also have now become very popular for its wide reach to focused job seekers, immediacy and cost effectiveness. Because of its global reach, organizations also get the flexibility to attract the best talent. Many placement agents have now started this service to increase their business volume.

The next step in the selection procedure is to personify such attributes in candidates, i.e., developing a specification of persons, to define the background education, training, personality and characteristics of the candidates to suit the vacancy position. This, in reality, is an exercise to pre-portray an ideal candidate for a job.

Preliminary screening

The number of applications normally received against any advertised vacancy is usually high. This creates the problem of selecting the right persons from many. Moreover, conducting tests and interviews for all the candidates may not be always feasible and at the same time cost-efficient. To obviate such problems, most of the organizations sort out unsuitable candidates before going ahead with the selection process. There are many different ways to do such preliminary screening. Some organizations conduct short tests for all the applications, while the best method may be the checking of Application Blank. Each organization, before going for the selection process, develops its own standards or potential attributes for the prospective candidates. This helps it also to define the rejection standards. For example, for the post of a stenographer, a particular organization may define their rejection standards as below:

- Those having shorthand speed less than 100 words per minute and typing speed below 40 words per minute
- Those not having any work experience
- Those who are above 35 years age

By checking the Application Blank of the candidates, an organization may reject a good number of applicants based on the above rejection parameters. All the above processes, therefore, enable the organization to shortlist the candidates before going ahead with the subsequent stages of selection. The rejection standards, like the ones stated above, may also be mentioned in the advertisement itself so that the number of applicants is minimised.

Some organizations also adopt 'successive-hurdles' technique as an effective screening process. This technique calls for arranging all selection factors in order of importance. For example, if for a particular post, aptitude test is considered the most important; the first step should be to test the aptitude of the candidates, then the other successive tests, like qualification, job experience, personality etc may be conducted provided the candidates qualify these hurdles one by one.

Review of application blanks: The application blanks form is designed to have detailed information about the applicants. Some organizations have their own printed application blank, while others ask the candidates to give their particulars in a standard format to elicit information like:

- Personal data and biographical information, i.e., name, address, telephone number, age, gender, marital status, children, nationality, education (school, college, university attended, degree/diploma passed, year of passing, subjects, grade or division obtained etc), professional qualification and membership of professional bodies, languages known (read, write and speak) etc

- Chronological employment history for all jobs (with joining and leaving dates in each case of employment change), employer's name, address and nature of business positions held and duties, reason for leaving (if any)
- Personal circumstances, when available, prepared to serve anywhere or not
- Medical history, brief details of any serious illness, number of days absent during the last few years (in case the applicant served earlier somewhere) on medical grounds, record of hospitalisation (if any), disability, major operation etc
- Interest, hobbies, sports and other activities
- Anything else which the applicant may like to add in support of his candidature.

Several other items may be included in the application blank on the specific requirements of the organization and the job.

Weighted application blanks are also prepared by some organizations to record personal history items associated with job success. For each item of the application blank, weight factors are predetermined. Importance of weight factors for different jobs also varies. For example, for unskilled jobs, education may be given less weight, while for executive positions, education receives higher weightage. Application blank, therefore, helps in comparing the applications.

Reference checking

Some organizations ask for references from the applicants in the application blank itself to get information on the candidate's character and antecedents. Such references are preferred from earlier employers and schools/colleges/universities that have some acquaintance with the candidates. Organizations try to verify candidates' antecedents from the references either over phone, through correspondence or through personal visits. Most of the organizations send a brief questionnaire to such references along with a confidential note, requesting them to furnish such details.

Psychological testing

Generally, psychological testing is used for purposes like, determining training needs and evaluation of training programs, selection and placement, transfer and promotion, counselling and so on. However, such testing is primarily used for selection and placement. Such tests are of different types like, group or individual test, instrumental tests, aptitude or achievements tests, personality and interest tests etc. Group tests are designed to test a group of candidates simultaneously. Individual tests are for individual candidates at a particular point of time. Instrumental tests can be group tests or individual tests. When it is an individual test, it makes use of different tools to study individual candidates' familiarity and skills. But in case of its application for a group, it involves written test or paper-pencil test to study the written responses of the candidates. Aptitude tests are intended to assess the potential of the applicants to learn on the job, while achievement tests enable us to assess how effectively an individual can perform his job. Conventionally, aptitude tests are administered on freshers, i.e. those who are not having any past work experience, while achievement tests are intended for experienced candidates. For marketing jobs and managerial and executive positions, such tests have much relevance. However, psychological tests are mostly designed to measure the aptitude and skills of successful job performers. For selection and placement, most of the organizations retain the services of consultants and experts on psychological testing. This minimises the chances of error in selecting the wrong candidates for different job positions. Since psychological testing is a complex method and has wide divergence, we have briefly introduced the concept of attitudinal measurement with a simple example and illustrations together with some conceptual details about different types of measurement and scales.

Attitude measurement

Attitude is a mental state of an individual which tends to act or respond or is ready to respond for or against objects, situation etc, with which his/her vested feeling or affect, interest, liking, desire and so on, are directly or indirectly linked or associated. During the course of development, the person acquires tendencies to respond to objects. These learned cognitive mechanisms are called attitudes. Changes in knowledge are followed by change in attitudes. Attitudes are different from knowledge in a sense that attitudes are emotion-laden. Knowledge reinforces attitudes and reinforced attitudes in the long run reinforce individual and group behaviour. Hence, attitude is neither behaviour nor cause of behaviour but it relates to an intervening predisposition or a frame of reference which influences the behaviour of an individual.

When the interest, feeling etc of an individual is not connected in any way with the object or situation, his/her responses (towards the said object or situation) will then not be attitude but opinion. Attitudes or psychic state cannot be observed because psychological variables are dormant or latent. Attitude measurement is difficult. Inference, prediction from behaviour data, interviews with structured questionnaires and scales are the usual tools for attitudinal measurement.

Attitude survey

To recruit a new incumbent and to evaluate the human relation in the factories, industries and different organizations, attitude survey is indispensable. The study of attitude is also important in designing a training program, which is a core HRD function. Attitude surveys focus on feelings and motives of the employees' opinions about their working environments. There are three basic purposes for conducting attitude surveys:

- To compare results with those from other surveys
- To measure the effect of change that occurs and,
- To determine the nature and extent of employee feelings regarding specific organizational issues and the organization in general

Usually attitude surveys are carried out by interviewing a person with a structured close-ended questionnaire. The skill of the interviewer is all important here for correct measurement of attitude. While framing the questionnaire, the interviewer should be cautious, as simple opinion-laden questionnaire items will not depict the attitude of the interviewee. What is important is to put value-laden questionnaire items, use of behaviourally anchored statements, asking the respondents to rank any myth statements etc. A sample list of such myth statements and value-laden questionnaire items are given below:

Myth statements:

- Hard work ensures better result.
- Linking to work with subordinates for prompt results
- Never say no to anyone; listen to everybody's problems
- One, who is indispensable, is efficient.
- Maintaining the hierarchical structure while taking decisions very rigidly

Sample questionnaire for attitude measurement

1. Do you think the expenditure on training is wasteful? (Give your answer selecting any one from the given alternatives).
   (a) To a large extent
   (b) To some extent
   (c) To a very little extent
   (d) Not at all
2. What, to your knowledge, are the major barriers to effective implementation of flexible working hours in India? (Please arrange the factors in order of your perceived preference).
   (a) Lack of awareness
   (b) Difficulty in implementation

(c) Supervisory problems
(d) Lack of support from workers
(e) Lack of support from unions
(f) Production problems
(g) Any other (please specify)

The first questionnaire item (which reflects the attitude of a person regarding training) can be evaluated by adding the weighted value of individual responses.

Interview

In the literal sense of the word, an interview means a conversation with a purpose. Such purposes are classified under three categories i.e., obtaining information from the candidates, giving information to the candidates and finally to motivate the candidates. The first purpose is intended to get information from candidates regarding their background, experience, education, training and interests to evaluate their suitability as per the requirements of the organization. The second purpose is to provide the candidates information regarding the organization, its philosophy, personnel policies etc. The third purpose is to establish a positive relationship to motivate the prospective candidates to join the organization. However, all these purposes being successive stages of interview, the subsequent stages will be followed only when the interviewers are prima facie satisfied with the candidates in the first stage.

The Human Resource department of most of the organizations conducts preliminary interview for the candidates. However, for subsequent interview, a committee of executives is formed to select the right candidates. For managerial and executive positions, organizations prefer to retain the service of consultancy organizations with subject experts on the selection committee.

There are different types of interview as under:

- **Patterned interview:** This is also known as structured or standardised interview. It is intended to assess the candidate's emotional strength and stability, industry, ability to get along well with others, self-reliance, willingness to accept responsibility, motivation etc.
- **Indirect or non-directive interview:** This type of interview is meant for helping the candidates to feel relaxed and free to talk. Interviewers become listeners and allow the candidates to reveal their personality and in-depth knowledge in a free and relaxed atmosphere.
- **Direct planned interview:** It is a simple question-answer session to ascertain the suitability of the candidates.
- **Stress interview:** This interview assesses the candidates' emotional balance under a situation of tension and stress. Such tension is, therefore, deliberately created by interruptions, provocations, silence and criticism or even by firing questions. Interviewers in such a

situation deliberately become more unfriendly and even, at times, hostile. For selection of executives, who are required to work under stress, this method is often adopted.

- **Group interview:** This method is intended to assess the leadership ability of the candidates. Generally, a topic is given to the candidates to discuss among themselves. The interviewers remain in the background to assess the best leaders, their initiative, poise, adaptability, awareness, interpersonal skills etc.
- **Panel or board interview:** Several interviewers collectively interview a candidate to rate his/her attributes. Generally, such a panel consists of several experts and each of them interviews a candidate only in those areas on which they have the requisite expertise.

For conducting a successful interview, interviewers should be adequately competent and trained. Interview should be conducted in a suitable place. It should be well planned; job descriptions and information about the applicants should be adequately studied. Interviewers should be free from any conceivable prejudice. Interviewees should be allowed to feel relaxed, beginning and ending of an interview should be made in a best possible friendly manner etc.

The limitations of the traditional selection process like failure to select the right persons for the right jobs or too much emphasis on written tests and interview, resulted in the development of the psychometric method. This method enables us to quantify the attributes, adding which we can select the candidates in order of their merit. Many organizations today are making use of this method to ensure proper selection of their employees.

E-recruitment

E-recruitment is also known as online recruitment. Although its use is rapidly increasing, it is not free from defects. Some of the shortcomings are:

- Online processing of job seekers' details is time-consuming and also the results are debatable.
- Internet penetration is low and usage is yet to catch up to become a recognised method of job seeking.
- Often selection of the candidates cannot be validated through their subsequent performance, as candidates assessment is done more through the method of approximation.
- Full dependence on online or e-recruitment is not advisable for lack of web-enabled holistic selection technology.

However, advantages of e-recruitment are also many. Some are listed below:

- It involves lower costs.
- Job-seekers can directly interact with the company.

- It is less time-consuming.
- Overall process of recruitment becomes more efficient.
- It works 24 x 7 across the globe.

Outsourcing

Recruitment through outsourcing vendors is gaining importance day by day. Business volatility has made manpower requirement of organizations more time-independent than a well planned function, if not for all jobs, at least for some. Information Technology (IT) and IT-enabled services (ITeS) organizations being execute project-based assignments, depend mainly on outsourced manpower. For manufacturing industry, outsourcing is restricted to non-core activities, although many manufacturing organizations take the advantage of outsourcing for manpower cost optimisation. Nationally and internationally, we have many manpower supply vendors, who can make available people with any skill set even for a very short period.

Induction

After selection of employees, the first step is to orient them to organizational life. Induction or orientation program of an organization is a process to guide and counsel the employees to familiarise them with the job and the organization. This process helps an organization to clarify the terms and conditions of employment, specific job requirements and also to inculcate confidence in the minds of the new entrants.

Objectives

The general objectives of such a program normally are:

- To introduce new employees with the organizational environment, exposing them to the mission, history and traditions of the organization, its achievements and future challenges, its personnel policy and expectations from the new employees
- To create a positive attitude in the minds of the new employees
- To create proper awareness in the new employees enabling them to understand the business of the organization
- To provide opportunity to interact with fellow employees and also with other managerial employees of the organization

A good induction program should contain the following areas which are conveniently distributed under organization's point of view and employee's point of view.

For the organization: It should cover the following points.

- History, mission, objectives and philosophy of the organization
- Its product, production process, operations involved, state of technology
- Its past achievements, present status and future growth plan
- Structure of the organization and the functions of different departments
- Delegation of authority and decision-making process
- Personnel policies, other miscellaneous policies, practices and regulations
- Job descriptions and responsibilities
- Expectations from new employees

For the employee: It should have the following elements.

- Job responsibilities
- Office procedures
- Grievance handling procedures
- Salary and perks
- Service rules governing hours of work, overtime
- Rules covering probation, confirmation, promotion opportunities, transfer
- Retirement and superannuation benefits
- Employee services and welfare activities
- Employee's participation in small group activities, question schemes
- Performance evaluation

Steps in the induction program

An induction program essentially involves the following steps.

General orientation: It includes guided tours to different departments of an organization, introduction with fellow employees, supervisors and executives, information about the organizations' mission, philosophy, achievements and future plans etc. Some organizations have their printed manuals, which they give to their new employees to orient them with their induction training programs for a week or so. The purpose of such general orientation program is to build a sense of pride in the minds of the new employees and also to create an interest in them about the organization.

Specific orientation: This is intended to help the new employees to get acclimatised to their new work environment. The supervisor or the departmental boss of the employee takes him around to his place of work and imparts vocational guidance for his particular nature of work. He is also told about the technology, environment and other facilities available in the organization, prevailing practices and customs and specific expectations from an employee.

For executives and managerial employees, targets and key result areas for each of them are given to make them aware of what the organization expects from them.

Follow-up orientation: This orientation is conducted following the initial induction of an employee, i.e., preferably within six months or so. The purpose of such orientation is guide and counsel the employees to ensure that they are reasonably satisfied and gradually settling with the organization.

Socialisation

Orientation and induction is also called employee socialisation process. Socialisation, however, is a continuous process, in today's dynamic organizations. For the new employees Decenzo and Robins (1999) identified that socialisation process involves three distinct stages as under:

Pre-arrival stage: At this stage, individual employees come to an organization with certain values, attitudes and expectations. As this exercise is undertaken at the selection stage to enable an employee to understand to what extent his perceived mapping matches with organizational culture and systems, it is the duty of the persons involved in the selection process to facilitate this. Now-a-days because of availability of information about organizations through different media, including websites and Internet, an enthusiastic individual may also have some preconceived ideas about the organization. Therefore, it is better to first understand from the individual about what he understands about the organization and then help him to synchronise this information with the reality. This helps the individual to take the right decision.

Encounter stage: At this stage, perceptions earlier generated by an individual, are reaffirmed through a well-planned induction program. Any dichotomy between the employees' perceptions and those of the organization need to be properly identified and removed through increased socialisation process.

Metamorphosis stage: At this final stage of socialisation, employees understand the organizations and identify themselves with them. Employees develop a sense of belongingness and become a contributor to achieving organizational goals and objectives.

However, as explained earlier, socialisation is a continuous process, as organizations are now required to go for restructuring and re-engineering every now and then, keeping pace with the changing environment.

Placement

After the initial program is over, an employee is put to a specific job, for which he has been selected. Most of the organizations put new employees on probation for a specified period after which they are confirmed or made permanent, provided they match the organizational requirements. Personnel department periodically reviews the progress of such employees getting feedback on their performance from their controlling authority. Some organizations also have a system to extend the probationary period, if the employees fail to match to the organizational expectations. Such second placement is known as **differential placement**.

Placement is defined as assigning employees to the job for which they have been identified as suitable based on the selection techniques. But such definition would be meaningless, if a particular employee is recruited against a particular vacancy. Generally, the question of placement arises when a group of trainees are recruited. Organizations, to identify the true potential of an employee, in such cases, make provision for short-term placement, when the employees are allowed to work on different jobs, through a systematic job rotation program. However, at a later stage, permanent placement is effected matching the employees' competence, knowledge, skill and job interest.

Significance of induction and placement

Common use of higher technology, increased level of knowledge and skills of the new job entrants, production restructuring and flexibility coupled with perceptive change about human resources, which is now considered as most important resource of an organization, have now transformed labour as an item for competitive purchase and sale. However, despite the problem of unemployment in India, there still exists dearth of knowledge and skilled workers as also executives and managers. The recent economic liberalisation program of the Government of India has paved the way for entry of multinationals and foreign companies. Market globalisation has further intensified the competition. Development of Total Quality Management philosophy, *inter alia*, is also demanding a sea change in product mix and service mix of an organization. All these together have now increased the scope for job mobility for employees with knowledge and skills of appropriate type and degree.

Unfortunately, retaining employees after the recruitment and selection is an utterly neglected area in the Indian corporate sector. Many organizations spend several lakhs of rupees in terms of job advertisement, conducting tests and interviews, hiring the services of consultants and psychologists etc, for selecting a managerial employee. A weak induction program, without adequate emphasis on building self-confidence and a sense of belongingness in the the new employees, results in quick separation, leading to the wastage of colossal sums of money for the organization. Such experience is quite common in public sector units. Very recently, a leading Tata organization has lost few hundreds of their young engineers and professionals, who left en masse to join elsewhere.

Some organizations, on the contrary, do not review the progress of the new employees, who get permanent automatically after completion of their probationary tenure, despite the reason that they are unproductive or less than optimally efficient.

Thus, a good induction and placement program needs to ensure retention of employees by keeping their motivation high, while at the same time, getting rid of the unproductive employees within the organizations.

Recruitment Metrics

Efficient recruitment function benefits the organization to gain sustainable competitive advantages through competent human resources. For measuring recruitment efficiency, organizations make use of several metrics as under:

- **Recruiting Cost ratio** (RCR) includes manpower hiring costs and the new employees' salaries for the period of induction. Also, it considers the cost of underperformance of new employees for the initial period of three to six months, depending on the nature of work assigned. It is calculated using the following formula:

RCR = (Total hiring costs/Total Compensation cost up to the period of induction + cost of underperformance during the initial period of three to six months) × 100

- **Recruiting efficiency** is measured in terms of attracting more talented people for the vacancies. Talent attraction is understood considering the ratio of people finally selected from the interview.
- **New hire performance** is measured in terms of performance results of newly recruited people even after the initial period of induction and training.
- **Recruitment manager's satisfaction** can be understood in terms of the degree of satisfaction on the percentage of good performers among the new recruits, percentage of new recruits who are continuing for more than a year, i.e., beyond transition phase and so on.
- **Employee starts** is measured in terms of the difference between the date of offer and the actual start or joining date.
- Likewise, organizations develop several recruitment metrics, depending on their requirements.

Key Points

- Recruitment, selection, induction and placement are important tools for hiring manpower from external sources.
- Human Resources Planning (HRP) helps the management to identify manpower requirements keeping pace with corporate objectives and strategies.

- After assessment of manpower requirement, it is important to identify how these requirements can be met from internal sources by restructuring and redeployment. Additional manpower requirements, if any, have to be met through external hiring.
- The recruitment process includes preliminary screening, psychological testing, interview, selection, placement and induction. At all these stages, certain norms are required to be followed to ensure proper selection and placement.
- Different formulae for recruitment metrics help in assessing the efficiency of the organization's recruitment process.

Important Terms

Follow-up orientation: This orientation is conducted after the initial induction of an employee, preferably within a period of six months or so. The purpose of such an orientation is to give guidance to and counsel the employees to ensure that they are reasonably satisfied and gradually settling with the organization.

Internal recruitment: This is the process of hiring from within the organizations. In some cases, organizations also try to staff higher managerial vacancies from their existing employees. In such cases, they need to develop their existing manpower adopting suitable training and development functions.

Metamorphosis stage: This is the final stage of socialisation. At this stage, employees understand the organizations and identify themselves with the organizations. They develop a sense of belongingness and become a contributor to achieving organizational goals and objectives.

Non-directive interview: This type of interview is meant for helping the candidates to feel relaxed and free to talk. Interviewers become listeners and allow the candidates to reveal their personality, in-depth knowledge in a free and relaxed atmosphere.

Patterned interview: This is also known as structured or standardised interview. It is intended to assess the candidate's emotional strength and stability, industry, ability to get along well with others, self-reliance, willingness to accept responsibility, motivation etc.

Stress interview: This interview assesses the candidates' emotional balance under a situation of tension and stress. Such tension is, therefore, deliberately created by interruptions, provocations, silence and criticism or even by firing questions. Interviewers in such a situation deliberately become more unfriendly and even, at time, hostile. For selection of executives, who are required to work under stress, such method is often adopted.

Self-assessment Questions

1. Define recruitment. What are the important recruitment functions? Why are such functions important for an organization?
2. What is internal recruitment? Why is it important for an organization? Do you think it is necessary to have a recruitment policy for an organization?
3. What are the different recruitment processes? Briefly state their merits and demerits.
4. Briefly discuss the importance of selection process and mention the steps involved in the process.
5. You have been retained by an organization to select a few management trainees. State the process you would consider and why.
6. What is the objective of an induction program? What important areas need to be considered for an effective induction program?
7. What are the different steps involved in an induction program? In what way have induction and placement now become important for Indian organizations?
8. Define attitude. Why is the study of attitude necessary for the HRD profession?
9. What are the different tools for attitudinal measurement? From an organizational point of view discuss in detail at least two measurement tools with due emphasis on their relative merits or demerits.
10. You have been retained by a company to study the attitude of their 50 employees on the recently introduced pension scheme. Develop at least 5 structured close-ended questionnaire, using Likert's Item Analysis Scale and interview the employees. Analyse all the responses using Factorial Method and measure the attitude of the employees.
11. Write short notes on the following:
    - i. Differential placement
    - ii. Job rotation
    - iii. Probationary period
    - iv. Follow-up orientation
    - v. Stress interview
    - vi. Application blank
    - vii. Deputation
    - viii. Successive hurdles
    - ix. Equal Appearing Intervals Scale
    - x. Cumulative Scale
    - xi. Summated Rating Scale
    - xii. Employee empowerment and attitudinal change

Sample Application Blank

Name of the Post
Advertisement No.

Personal Data

Full Name: **Ms/Mr**	**Applicant's Photograph**
Date of Birth, State, Marital Status	
Nationally, Whether SC/ST	
Height:……………..cm. Weight:……………kgs.	Vision : Normal/Corrected Spectacle Lens Nos.
Address to which we should write: Telephone No.	Permanent Address Telephone No.
Father's/Husband's Name and Occupation:	
If you have any relative employed in/or on the Board of our company, please give details.	
Details of previous employment in this company or its sister concerns, with reasons for leaving.	
Details of previous employment elsewhere, with reasons for leaving	

Languages: Mother Tongue	Speak	Read	Write

Education

Examinations	**School/ College**	**Year From**	**Attend To**	**Major Subjects**	**Class, % Of Marks And Ranks**
Scholastic Achievements					

TRAINING					
Name of the Firm/Institution		From	To	Details of Training	Stipend, if any
WORK EXPERIENCE					
Employer		From	To	Position held and nature of work	Salary p.m. Basic Total

EXTRA-CURRICULAR ACTIVITIES

Types of activities	**At School**	**At College**	**Elsewhere**
Official Position held :			
Sports			
Participation			
Positions held			
- Captain, Secretary/ Manager			
Have you ever been convicted? It so, give full details			
Have you had any major illness, operations or accidents?			
Any other information that you would like to furnish:			
Name and addresses of three persons other than relatives to whom we may write for reference :			
Name	Address		
Minimum Salary Expected:			
We appreciate your time and effort your have spent in completing this application. Would you please check your application to ensure that you have completely and accurately answered each and every question?			

I declared that the particulars given above, are to the best of my knowledge, correct and complete and undertake to advise the company immediately of changes, if any, in respect of my particulars given above. I confirm that there is no legal bar in my applying for an accepting the above mentioned employment.	
Date	Signature of the applicant
I have verified the certificates and testimonials where necessary	
Date	Officer-in-Charge

Selected Bibliography

1. Bhattacharyya DK (2012). *Human Resource Management*, 3rd edition. New Delhi: Excel Books.
2. Bhattacharyya DK (2012). *Human Resource Planning*, 3rd edition. New Delhi: Excel Books.
3. Bhattacharyya DK (2007). *Human Resource Research Methods*. New Delhi: Oxford University Press.
4. Bhattacharyya DK (2012). *Principles of Management*. New Delhi: Pearson.

12 Psychological Testing

Learning Objectives

After reading this chapter you will be able to:

- Understand psychological testing and its application in recruitment
- Outline the tests of personality for recruitment
- List the various theories of personality
- Appreciate the test of intelligence quotient and emotion
- Understand the use of NLP
- Discuss the ethical issues of psychological testing

Overview

Individual work abilities of persons extend across cognitive abilities, acquired expertise, personality styles, motivation and physical attributes. It is our conventional belief that personality affects our behaviour, more particularly our work-related behaviour. Hence, understanding personality before recruitment through some personality test measures have now almost become a normal practice for organizations.

The process of testing for selection of employees started from the late 19th century, and it is now used throughout the world. Right from the beginning of employee selection testing, personality test has been in existence. In fact, it was the industrial psychologists who had shaped and defined the role of testing in scientific selection of employees. Over the years, industrial psychologists put in their best efforts in developing valid and reliable methods and standards of recruitment testing. Their efforts have now made testing more scientific and helped in making the selection process fair. Also, over the years, application of personality testing during recruitment has become more prominent.

At the beginning of the 20th century, psychologists in general emphasised on the use of scientific methods to improve performance, selection, motivation, and training, separating it from engineering management. Psychologists developed the assessment tools to ensure proper development of workers and optimum utilisation of human resources. The purpose of all psychological testing during the process of recruitment was to predict the behavioural propensities of prospective employees, and the degrees of its future replication in real-life work environment.

Test of Personality for Recruitment

The word personality is derived from the Latin word *persona*. It denotes a mask, and hence personality is often said to be our superficial social image. It is said that personality is the reflection of the most dominant characteristics of our behaviour.

Personality is the study of the person, that is, the complete human individual. In recruitment and selection, individual personality is important because personality of individual employees consists of their dynamic mental structures and coordinated processes of the mind, which determine their emotional and behavioural adjustments to the organization. Personality is dynamic because mental structures of individual employees continuously develop over their lifetime. Personality and individual behavioural pattern of employees become an important construct to adjust and succeed in work situations. Particularly in a changing business environment, to get the right fit, employers make use of personality tests in selection and recruitment decisions. This apart, personality assessment is also important for cultural transformation in an organization. With the understanding of cognitive and emotional bases of human behaviour, personality assessment has gained further importance.

Theories of Personality

Theories of personality can be understood in the context of pioneering contributions of some eminent psychologists. Some of them are listed below.

Sigmund Freud (1856–1939): He defined the classification of the states of mind as conscious and unconscious. Our conscious mind is present in perceptions, memories, thoughts, fantasies and feelings. In an organization, employees exhibit their conscious mind. However, Freud said that the conscious mind cannot show the real reflection. It is the unconscious mind which drives, restricts, or motivates behaviour, even though it is not apparent. According to Freud, id, ego and superego state of mind influence and shape personality. The id state of mind translates our needs into motivational forces, i.e., instincts or drives. This state of mind elevates to ego state and develops our personality and problem-solving abilities. This is what we call the secondary process of the mind. With id state of mind (primary state) when we face problems to achieve our goals, we gain the experience, which gradually matures into the superego state.

Personality disorders take place in employees when they fail to keep record of such experiences and frame strategies to avoid the same. They become a problem for the organization. After Freud, Anna Freud (1895–1982), his daughter, extended his work further.

Erik Erickson (1902–1994): He was a Freudian ego psychologist, focused more on society and culture-related issues. Erickson stated that we develop our personalities through certain stages. Each stage involves certain developmental tasks that are psychosocial in nature and also each stage has certain virtues or psychosocial strengths, which helps us through the rest of the stages, and in this process we develop our personalities.

Carl Jung (1875–1961): Another Freudian, he used the theory of collective unconsciousness of humanity. Jung's theory divides the psyche into three parts: the ego (conscious mind), personal unconscious (not presently conscious but can be) and collective unconscious (psychic inheritance). Collective unconscious is the reservoir of our experiences and it influences our behaviour, especially our emotions.

Alfred Adler (1870–1937): He postulated a single 'drive' or motivating force behind all our behaviour and experience. It is our common desire to fulfill our potential and come closer to our ideals.

These apart, there have been other theorists of personality like Albert Ellis, Aaron Beck, Erich Fromm, BF Skinner, Hans Eysenck and so on.

William Sheldon (1898–1977): His work is based on that of Ernst Kretschmer (1930). He developed a model of matching physical types with psychology or personality of people. Table 12.1 shows his grouping of personality types according to physical characteristics.

The connection between the three physical types and their respective personality types helps us to a great extent to shortlist the prospective candidates for a job.

Reviewing all the above theories, it is, therefore, evident that personality testing in recruitment is our attempt to capture or summarise an individual's 'essence'. Personality is the science of describing and understanding persons. Clearly, personality is a core area of study for psychology. Individual intelligence also influences different aspects of personality in

Table 12.1 Personality constructs with matching physical type

Physical type	Physical features	Psychology type	Psychological characteristics
Ectomorphs	Slender, often tall, people, with long arms and legs and fine features	Cerebrotonics	Nervous types, relatively shy, often intellectual
Mesomorphs	Stockier people, with broad shoulders and good musculature	Somatotonics	Active types, physically fit and energetic
Endomorphs	Chubby people, tending to be 'pear-shaped'	Viscerotonics	Sociable types, lovers of food and physical comforts

many different ways. In fact, intelligence is sometimes considered to be a part of personality. The study of personality can be from different perspectives as listed below:

- Trait perspective
- Biological perspective
- Psychoanalytic perspective
- Learning perspective
- Phenomenological perspective
- Cognitive perspective

Measurement of Personality Traits

Many psychologists have tried to reduce the many traits to a few essential ones. Among the best known essential trait approaches that we follow in measuring personality traits are:

- Murray 1938 (20+ 'needs')
- Cattell (16 traits): 16 personality factors questionnaire
- Eysenck (3 traits): Eysenck Personality Questionnaire (EPQ)—Extraversion, Neuroticism and Psychoticism
- Costa and McCrae (5 traits): NEO—Neuroticism, Extraversion, and Openness to Experience, Agreeableness and Conscientiousness

Murray's theory observes that our behaviour is driven by an internal state of disequilibrium. In other words, we lack something and this drives us, or we are dissatisfied and we desire for something. According Murray, our personality is driven by our secondary needs: achievement, dominance, affiliation, and nurturance.

Cattell (1905–1998) viewed language as a useful source of information about personality. He had identified 16 personality factors (16 PF) as under:

- Reserved versus warm
- Concrete reasoning versus abstract reasoning
- Reactive versus emotionally stable
- Deferential versus dominant
- Serious versus lively
- Expedient versus rule-conscious
- Shy versus socially bold
- Utilitarian versus sensitive
- Trusting versus vigilant
- Practical versus imaginative

- Forthright versus private
- Self-assured versus apprehensive
- Traditional versus open-to-change
- Group-oriented versus self-reliant
- Tolerates disorder versus perfectionist
- Relaxed versus tense

Eysenck (1916–1997) designed the Eysenck Personality Questionnaire (EPQ). He believed that people could be described in terms of two supertraits, which he believed had a biological basis:

- Introversion–extraversion (continuum of sociability, dominance, liveliness etc)
- Emotionality–stability (neuroticism) (continuum of upset and distress)
- Psychoticism was added later. But this aspect is less researched. This was a predisposition towards becoming either psychotic or sociopathic (psychologically unattached to other people). It also indicated a tendency to be hostile, manipulative and impulsive.

Other studies on primary personality traits are: Mayers–Briggs Type Indicator (MBTI) and the Big Five Model. MBTI is essentially a 100-question personality test to understand people's feelings and actions in a given situation. The responses are then classified into four major types, such as extroverted versus introverted, sensing versus intuitive, thinking versus feeling and judging versus perceiving. These were then combined into 16 personality types—ESTJ, INFP, ESFP, INTJ, ESFJ, INTP, ENFP, ISTJ, ESTP, INFJ, ENFJ, ISTP, ENTJ, ISFP, ENTP and ISFJ.

Attributes of some of the types are as under:

- **ESTJ**—Practical and organised on a logical basis
- **INFP**—More focused on their inner world and driven by thoughts and emotion
- **ESFP**—Derive their energy from the external sources and not within the organization
- **INTJ**—Are driven by their inner world and they are more emotion driven.
- **ESFJ**—Believe on facts and take decisions based on their personal values
- **INTP**—Take decisions on the basis of logic.

The big five model

This model is often considered as the better alternative to MBTI. The five big personality factors are:

- Extroversion
- Agreeableness

- Conscientiousness
- Emotional stability
- Openness to stability

The Five-factor model is commonly measured by NEO (Neuroticism, Extraversion, Openness) given by McCrae and Costa (2003) to categorise personality as under:

- Neuroticism (Emotional stability)
- Extraversion (Introversion)
- Openness to experience (Closeness to experiences)
- Agreeableness (Disagreeableness)
- Conscientiousness (Lack of conscientiousness)

Personality and Employment Testing

Use of personality testing for selection decisions has historical roots. Initially, industrial psychologists were against the use of personality testing. They used to discard this as unreliable and invalid. In fact, human resource management professionals initially emphasised on the use of personality scores for selection.

Personality testing became more prominent when disciplines like psychology, engineering and management eventually merged to solve the organizational problems. Initially the use of cognitive ability tests in recruitment received wide acceptance, as it was construed as a more valid predictor for acquisition of job skills, and to some extent, even job performance. However, in case of personality tests, because of poor validity and eventual possibility of easy faking, it was not so easy to gain acceptance.

Moreover, personality as a predictor of performance did not get acceptance, as numerous studies could not establish this. But there exists more or less common agreement that managers possess some set of personality traits. Some of the research studies in modern times, however, could show results about the role of personality testing in employee selection.

Validity of the selection tests

Psychological tests need to be valid. The degree of validity of a test measure widely varies with respect to circumstances, use of specific tools and its application. Primarily, the validity of a selection test depends on how the characteristics of the measurements relate to the selection test for the given job requirements. We consider selection test scores as valid, when there is a link between the test score and job performance.

The degree of validity is understood in terms of employment selection tests, when results of one test can predict job performance behaviour related by others.

Types of validity

For selecting employees, we use validity on three counts: criterion-related, content and construct. Criterion validity shows the correlation or other statistical relationships between the selection test score (predictor) and job performance (criterion). With high test score, if one performs high, we call it high criterion validity. Content validity indicates content of the test reflects some important job-related behaviour and the measurement of knowledge and skill for the said job-related behaviour. Construct validity measures constructs or abstract job characteristics, which are crucial for the performance of the job.

In most of the psychological tests used for selection, criterion-related validity is considered.

Validity of selection tests is essential for any organization using psychological tools. Those organizations that use criterion-related validity basically use two core strategies: (i) concurrent validation study that collects predictor test scores from the current job performance measures and (ii predictive validation study in which predictor test scores are obtained from job applicants while hiring. However, job performance measures are obtained only when new employees get sufficient time to learn the job, and there is a correlation between the predictor test and job performance scores.

Another aspect of validity study is that the specific job for which the test is done is similar to the job for which the test was originally developed. Such similarity can only be ensured when the organization systematically undertakes job analysis to identify the tasks, duties, responsibilities and work condition of the job and knowledge, skills and abilities that are essential for the successful performance of the job.

Further, to understand validity of psychological tests for recruitment, we determine the **validity correlation coefficient**, which is the correlation coefficient between an employee's selection test score and one or more relevant measures of job performance. With higher validity coefficient, we get more valid test score. Predictive validity is the most important property of employee selection. Such validity has the ability to predict job performance, learning, and success.

Differences in the characteristics of samples create problems for validity study. It is known to us that different demographic groups of people tend to perform differently, while taking the same tests.

Validity and reliability

Validity and reliability are the two important constructs for any psychological test. Through validity and reliability, we get precision in our measurement of test scores. Validity represents how well our measurement variable measurement is related to what we are actually supposed to get. Reliability, on the other hand, tells us to what extent our test measure is reproducible, when we conduct a retest.

To minimise threats to validity, we focus on designing the psychological test measure scientifically. We do it to arrive at the desired logic. Also we focus on cross-verification of our results through measurement or observation. Similarly, analysis, preventive action etc can also help in minimising errors in validity.

Validity, therefore, helps us to approximate the truth of propositions, inferences or conclusions. External validity means the truth of psychological measures in the form of generalisations. Therefore, threats to external validity mean a lesser degree of generalisability of our test measures. The problem of generalisability may be due to people, places, or times. Construct validity, on the other hand, refers to the degree to which inferences can be legitimately related to the operationalisation of our test results to the theoretical constructs. Construct validity, thus, relates to generalising about people, places or times. These apart, we have translation validity, face validity, content validity, criterion-related validity, predictive validity, concurrent validity, convergent validity and discriminant validity.

In translation validity, we focus on whether the operationalisation is a good reflection of the construct. In criterion-related validity, we examine whether the operationalisation behaves the way it is given in our theory of the construct, i.e., the operationalisation should be predictable based on our theory of the construct. In face validity, we look at the operationalisation, i.e., translation of the construct. Content validity essentially checks the operationalisation against the relevant content domain for the construct. Criterion-related validity checks the performance of our operationalisation against some criterion. Predictive validity, on the other hand, assesses the ability of operationalisation to make a prediction. Concurrent validity assesses the ability of operationalisation to distinguish between groups. In convergent validity, we examine the degree to which the operationalisation is similar to other operationalisation. Discriminant validity examines the degree to which the operationalisation is not similar to (diverges from) other operationalisation.

For the industrial psychologists, these validity issues may not be relevant, but depending on the nature of the research issue, it is necessary to understand what type of validity need to be examined for accuracy and precision of the psychological test measures.

Test of Intelligence as Employability Test

Intelligence is mental capacity that, among other things, involves the ability to reason, plan, solve problems, think abstractly, comprehend complex ideas, learn quickly and learn from experience. Intelligence is not merely book learning or a narrow academic skill. It reflects a broader and deeper capability for comprehending our surroundings.

A popular theory of intelligence is based on psychometric testing, i.e., intelligence quotient (IQ) test. However, as some researchers were dissatisfied with traditional IQ tests, they developed alternative theories of intelligence suggesting that intelligence results from independent capabilities that uniquely contribute to human intellectual performance. Measuring the IQ of a large population, we can arrive at a normal distribution. The approach to understand intelligence over a long period of time is based on psychometric testing. Such intelligence quotient (IQ) tests define general intelligence.

Based on the results of a series of studies, Spearman (1927) concluded that there was a common function (or group of functions) across intellectual activities including what he called intelligence which helps us in sensory discrimination. This common function became known as 'g' or general intelligence.

To objectively determine and measure general intelligence, Spearman invented the 's' factor using mathematical proof. This led to the development of the two-factory theory of intelligence. According to this theory, every test can be divided into g factor and an s factor. The former measures the 'general' factor or common function among ability tests. The s-factor measures the 'specific' factor unique to a particular ability test.

Some of the widely accepted IQ tests measures are: Stanford–Binet, Raven's Progressive Matrices, the Wechsler Adult Intelligence Scale and the Kaufman Assessment Battery for Children.

Intelligence tests are widely used in educational, business and military settings due to their efficacy in predicting behaviour. The g is highly correlated with many important social outcomes—individuals with low IQs are more likely to be poor performers.

To measure IQ, we conduct verbal intelligence test. A verbal intelligence test measures the following:

- **Information**— A persons level of general knowledge
- **Comprehension**—How well he can understand questions and grasp concepts
- **Arithmetic**—A person's mathematical abilities
- **Similarities**— Measures abstract thought
- **Digit Span**— Measures attention span
- **Vocabulary**—Familiarity with meanings of words

Performance intelligence test

After conducting IQ tests, we can obtain two separate IQ scores for a person. These are: verbal IQ and performance IQ with individual scores for each subset within the verbal and performance categories.

- **Digit symbol:** Mental flexibility with random symbols
- **Picture completion:** Ability to notice differences between two pictures
- **Block design:** Mentally construct printed designs in your head
- **Picture arrangement:** Arrange pictures in a logical order
- **Object assembly:** Place the correct part in relationship to a whole

Both of these scores (verbal + performance) can then be combined to give an overall IQ score.

Classification of people based on IQ: It is the measurement of a person's intelligence that is calculated on the basis of special tests. The average IQ is by definition 100. Above 100 indicates a higher than average IQ and scores below 100 indicate otherwise. Scores can range between less than or more than 100, but it should not fall below 50 or above 150. Based on IQ scores, we can classify people as under:

- Less than 70: considered mentally challenged
- 70–80: borderline retardation
- 80–90: below average
- 90–110: average
- 110–120: above average
- 120–130: superior
- Above 130: very superior

Emotional Intelligence (EI)

Emotional dimensions of behaviour of people are still not considered by many organizations, as we still believe only in verbal and cognitive intelligence. We, however, develop our thought process through interaction. Gradually it has been recognised that our emotions carry some sensible meanings, and it requires understanding. It was Daniel Goleman (1995) who had institutionalised the adoption of emotional intelligence measures in organizations, particularly during recruitment. Goleman's approach could help us in understanding the relation between reason and emotion. In organizations, we integrate emotional intelligence, personality, and intelligence quotient for achieving excellence in employees' performance. To recruit the right fit also, we make use of such an integrated approach.

Goleman (1995) defined emotional intelligence as the 'capacity for reorganising our own feelings and those of others, for motivating ourselves, for managing emotions well in ourselves and in our relationships'. Thus, Goleman's basic argument is that our rational thinking alone cannot predict success. Even with high intelligence quotient (IQ), people may fail. Obviously for this reason, organizations always endeavour to develop leadership skills and competencies among employees for enhancing their emotional intelligence.

Two aspects of EI

To be successful we require the effective awareness, control, and management of one's own emotions, and those of other people. This is the essential premise of Emotional Quotient (EQ). Thus, EQ embraces two aspects of intelligence:

- Understanding self, goals, intentions, responses, behaviour and
- Understanding others and their feelings

The five domains of EQ

Goleman identified the five 'domains' of EI as follows:

- Knowing your emotions
- Managing your emotions
- Motivating yourself
- Recognising and understanding other people's emotions
- Managing relationships, that is, managing the emotions of others

Emotional Intelligence has relationship with other behavioural studies like Neuro-Linguistic Programming (NLP), Transactional Analysis and empathy. By developing our Emotional Intelligence in these areas and the five EQ domains, we can become more productive and successful at what we do and also help others to be more productive and successful.

Neuro-Linguistic Programming (NLP)

Neuro-Linguistic Programming (NLP) is an interpersonal communication model to establish the relationship between desired behavioural patterns and the pattern of our thought process, and thus help us to increase the self-awareness among people thereby transforming them to an emotionally matured person. Richard Bandler and John Grinder, the founders of NLP, through their studies believed that there exists a connection between neurological processes ('neuro'), language ('linguistic') and behavioural patterns. Hence, through programming we can organise the same to achieve specific goals of life.

NLP was originally promoted by its co-founders in the 1970s as an effective and rapid form of psychological therapy capable of addressing the full range of problems which psychologists are likely to encounter, such as phobias, depression, habit disorder, psychosomatic illnesses and learning disorders. It also espoused the potential for self-determination through overcoming learned limitations and emphasised well-being and healthy functioning.

Ethical Guidelines for Psychological Testing

Ethical guidelines on the use of psychological testing mandate to provide feedback to the persons who participate in such assessment in terms of general assessment/issues, reliability and validity, norm groups, feedback to the applicant etc.

To apply psychological testing in job interviews, it is important to consider following issues:

- Process of identification of constructs for a particular job
- Process of reporting the test results
- Previewing of test information before administration
- Process of integrating psychological test scores and interview results
- Norms for providing hiring recommendation

Psychometric Tools

Some reliable and valid psychometric tools are discussed here.

Change management survey

A typical change management survey is designed as shown here.

Think about the change that is affecting you at work and tick the answer that is typical of your reaction.

		Yes	No
1.	I think the changes that are happening are for the best		
2.	I need to make the best of change		
3.	I am obstructive to the changes that are taking place		
4.	I feel angry about the changes		
5.	I would prefer to stay as we were before the change		
6.	I am prepared to help others to accept change		
7.	There may be benefits to be gained from change		
8.	I withhold my support for change		
9.	I am anxious about change		
10.	I don't want to know about change		
11.	My workplace will be better as a result of change		
12.	I am willing to find out more about change and how it will affect me		
13.	I blame the management		
14.	I feel frustrated that I have no control over change		
15.	If I ignore change, it may not affect me		
16.	I feel committed to change		
17.	Change is not as bad I originally thought		
18.	I openly resist change		
19.	I am upset at the need to change		
20.	I can't believe that change is for the good		
21.	I can see the benefits of change		
22.	I accept the need to change		
23.	I make my complaints known about change		
24.	I feel sad at the loss of the status quo		
25.	I would rather get on with what I am doing than be involved in change		
26.	We will benefit positively from the change that is happening		
27.	I have started to explore what change means for me		
28.	I am looking for other work possibilities that are not affected by change		
29.	I feel emotional about losing our old ways of working		
30.	Change won't affect me		

Scoring method for the survey results: The change management survey is based on the transition curve developed by Rosabeth Moss Kanter (1999). It helps us to understand the following reactions to change:

C	=	Commitment
A	=	Acceptance
R	=	Resistance
E	=	Emotion
D	=	Denial

The score is obtained as follows. Put a tick mark by each statement where you scored 'yes'. Then, total the number of ticks in each column as shown in the table here. Look at the highest score in a category (there may be cases of similar scores in several categories). This indicates where you are on the change curve.

1	2	3	4	5
6	7	8	9	10
11	12	13	14	15
16	17	18	19	20
21	22	23	24	25
26	27	28	29	30
Total C=	*Total A =*	*Total R =*	*Total E =*	*Total D =*

Denial: A typical reaction in the early stages of change is to deny that it will take place or that it will affect you. Your reaction can manifest itself in disbelief, burying your head in the sand, or behaving as if nothing had happened or will happen.

Emotion: At this stage pent up emotions are evident. There is grieving for the loss of status quo. Your emotion can vary from expression of anger and frustration to sadness.

Resistance: Here people outwardly show their resistance to change. Your resistance can manifest itself through outspoken dissent, unhelpful behaviour and blame. It is at this stage that people who see the change in a negative light may begin looking for alternative employment.

Acceptance: Here people begin to see that change is going ahead. Perhaps it is not all that bad and there may be ways of making the most of it.

Commitment: By this stage people support and are committed to change. They see the benefits and make positive steps to implement it.

It is possible for people to experience emotions in several of the categories. For example, they may be beginning to accept change, yet be critical on certain aspects.

Helping people through the transition

Based on your collected response, you can draw a transition curve as shown in Fig. 12.1.

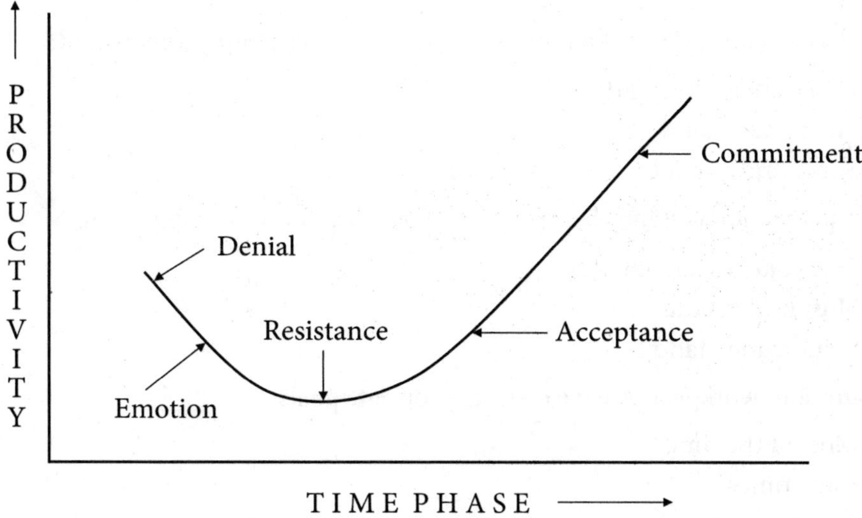

Fig. 12.1 Phases of transition

Behaviours displayed on the left side of the transition curve should not be ignored:

- Identify early on who will be the winners to change and who will be losers, what will help the change and what will hinder.
- Let people know as much as possible about the changes taking place and when and how the changes will affect them.
- Give people opportunities to express their concern.
- Consult and involve people in the changes.
- Hold regular feedback and communication sessions. Allow negative views to be aired in a supportive way.
- Allow adequate time for change to take place—do not expect it to happen overnight.
- Celebrate success.

Team-building quiz

Change is the constant in today's fast-paced world. Companies require appropriate strategies, people, culture and capabilities to survive and thrive. A sample quiz for the team-building propensity of the organization is shown here.

Sample quiz: Read the quiz below and answer the following questions to assess your organization's need to spur innovation, open communication, build teamwork and strengthen trust.

1. We have a clear vision of a preferred future that our people understand:

   A. Everyone understands

   B. Most understand

   C. Some understand

2. Our people understand their roles and contribution to the bottomline:

   A. Everyone understands

   B. Most understand

   C. Some understand

3. Teams and workgroups have clear, appropriate goals:

   A. Most of the time

   B. Some times

   C. Rarely

4. We have free and open communication:

   A. Most of the time

   B. Some times

   C. Rarely

5. We conduct business according to a clear set of values:

   A. Most of the time

   B. Some times

   C. Values are not articulated

6. Innovation is encouraged:

   A. Most of the time

   B. Some times

   C. Rarely

7. Employees have freedom to perform without micromanagement:

   A. Most of the time

   B. Some times

   C. Rarely

8. We tend to rush to action without taking time to plan:

   A. Rarely

   B. Some times

   C. Most of the time

9. A few people tend to dominate meetings:

   A. Rarely

   B. Some times

   C. Most of the time

10. Managers help employees develop their full potential:

    A. Most of the time

    B. Some times

    C. Rarely

11. We can handle honest, straightforward confrontation:

    A. Most of the time

    B. Some times

    C. Rarely

12. We have the right mix of people and skills to achieve top performance:

    A. Most of the time

    B. Some times

    C. Rarely

13. Our people look forward to coming to work:

    A. Most of the times

    B. Some times

    C. Rarely

14. Our turnover rate is:

    A. Among the lowest in our industry

    B. About average

    C. Higher than most

15. We measure performance results:

    A. Most of the time

    B. Some times

    C. Rarely

16. Mutual respect and trust is:

A. High
B. Moderate
C. Low

Team-building results: Score 3 points for each A answer, 1 point for each B answer, and subtract 2 points for each C answer.

A score of 35 or better indicates a high-performing organization. Reward your team and take them to another level on a high ropes challenge course. A score of 21 to 34 indicates a competitive organization. Strengthen your team performance with training focused on those areas with the greatest leverage. A score 20 or less indicates that there are serious competitive weaknesses. Consider going back to the drawing board to review mission, vision, values and strategy.

Key Points

- Industrial psychologists make extensive use of various psychological tests before finalising the selection of a prospective candidate for the job. The importance of psychological testing is understood from the fact that employees' ability to work extends beyond cognitive abilities and acquired knowledge and skill and includes personality and work behaviour.
- Industrial psychologists help in employee selection by helping organizations to assess the employees' potential capabilities in job assignment. They also help in personality assessment to ensure that employees become the right-fit for the job.
- More rigorous understanding of the holistic person requires industrial psychologists to make use of testing of IQ, EI etc. More advanced tools like NLP can also help in more accurate understanding of the likely behavioural pattern of employees.
- Use of psychological tools and techniques alone cannot serve the purpose. Industrial psychologists need to ensure their reliability and validity. Also complying with the ethical norms is considered extremely important.

Important Terms

Cattell's 16 PF: Developed by Cattell it views language as a useful source of information about personality covering 16 personality factors.

Denial phase of change: A typical reaction in the early stages of change is to deny that it will take place or that it will affect us.

Emotional processing: It is the process of absorbing emotional disturbances. It focuses on the ability to process emotional information, more particularly the ability to recognise their meanings and relationships, without manipulating the emotions.

Mayers–Briggs Type Indicator (MBTI): MBTI is essentially a 100-question personality test to understand from people their feelings and actions in a given situation.

Personality: It is the reflection of the most dominant characteristics of our behaviour.

Personality disorders: It takes place in employees when they fail to keep a record of their untoward experiences and frame strategies to avoid the same.

Self-assessment Questions

1. Explain the importance of psychological testing for recruitment.
2. What is personality? Why personality assessment is done for recruitment?
3. Define reliability and validity. Why reliability and validity are important for psychological tests?
4. Define intelligent quotient. How is it measured?
5. Why is IQ measurement necessary for employees' selection?
6. Explain how emotional intelligence of a person influences his/her workplace.
7. Explain the concept of NLP. Discuss how NLP relates to emotional intelligence.
8. What are the ethical issues in psychological testing?
9. Write short notes on the following:
   i. Emotional Quotient
   ii. 'g' and 's' factors of intelligence
   iii. Content validity
   iv. Reliability
   v. Big Five Model

Selected Bibliography

1. Arthur WJ, D Woehr and W Graziano (2001). Personality testing in employment settings: Problems and issues in the application of typical selection practices, *Personnel Review*, 30, 657–76.
2. Dunnette MD (ed.) (1976). *Handbook of Industrial and Organizational Psychology*. Chicago: Rand McNally.
3. Goleman D (1998). *Working With Emotional Intelligence*. New York: Bantam Books.
4. Guion RM (1965). *Personnel Testing*. New York: McGraw-Hill.
5. Guion RM and RF Gottier (1966). Validity of personality measures in personnel selection, *Personnel Psychology*, 18, 135–64.
6. Gatewood RD and HS Field (1998). *Human Resource Selection*, 4th edition. Fort Worth: Dryden Press.
7. Heneman HG III, TA Judge and RL Heneman (2000). Staffing Organizations, 3rd edition. Burr Ridge: McGraw-Hill.
8. Hunter JE and RF Hunter (1984). Validity and utility of alternative predictors of job performance, *Psychological Bulletin*, 96(1), 72–98.
9. Mayer JD and P Salovey (1995).Emotional intelligence and the construction and regulation of feelings, *Applied and Preventive Psychology*, 4(3), 197–208.
10. McClelland DC (1973).Testing for competence rather than intelligence, *American Psychologist*, 28(1), 1–14.
11. Murray H A (1938). *Explorations in Personality*. New York: Oxford University press.
12. Schmidt FL and JE Hunter (1998). The validity and utility of selection methods in personnel psychology practical and theoretical implications of 85 years of research findings, *Psychological Bulletin*, 124(2), 262–74.
13. Singh S (2002). *Emotional Intelligence for High Performance Organizations*. New Delhi: New Age Publications.
14. Spearman CE (1927). *The Abilities of Man*. London: Macmillan.

13 Performance Management

Learning Objectives

After reading this chapter, you will be able to:

- **Understand the concept of performance management (PM)**
- **List the performance objectives and standards**
- **Outline the process of performance management**
- **Appreciate the role of appraisals**
- **Discuss the types and methods of performance appraisal**

Overview

For achieving the business goals of an organization, it is necessary to manage performance of the employees effectively. Industrial psychologists need to support organizations in designing effective performance management systems. Performance management (PM) is an integrated process. It starts with the setting of goals and objectives for the organization as a whole, and then cascades such goals and objectives to divisional or departmental goals and finally to employee-level goals in the form of key result areas (KRA). Also the integrated performance system needs to appraise performance at periodic intervals, and accordingly decide the development al needs of the employees. It also helps in decisions on compensation design.

Performance Management

PM is an ongoing process, involving employees and the managers. it consists of the following tasks:

- Identification and description of essential job functions and relating the same to the mission and goals of the organization
- Developing realistic and appropriate performance standards
- Giving and receiving feedback about performance
- Writing and communicating constructive performance appraisals
- Planning education and development opportunities to sustain employee improvement and building their performance capabilities

It is clear from above that performance management is an excellent method of helping organizations achieve sustainable development. Performance management is effective in organizations, when people employed with them can understand what they are expected to do, how they should do the same and demonstrate a high degree of responsibility for what they achieve.

Among others, performance management emphasises managing, supporting and developing human resources at all levels within the organization. An integral part of performance management is systematic monitoring of individual and team performance, rewarding the people who deliver their best and take corrective or remedial action for those who lack in their performance.

Evolution of Performance Management

The evolution of the concept of performance management is relatively new. In human resource management practices, performance appraisal systems were found all along, focusing more on negative HR decisions, like demotion, dismissal, wage cut etc. However, with the development focus, the concept has changed and now we call it performance management, and consider this function strategically important. With such shift in focus from command-and-control, today we have embraced a facilitation model of managing people, recognising the importance of employees. Thus, performance management systems are aligned with the mission and strategies of the organizations, as organizational goals and objectives are mission-based, and achieving such goals and objectives leads to organizational success.

As a process, performance management systems provide opportunity to the employees and the managers to discuss developmental goals and jointly create a plan for achieving those goals. Development plans contribute to organizational goals and the professional growth of the employee.

However, with the increased focus on teamwork and the emergence of networked organizations, there is a need to shift the decision-making responsibility to the work execution or operational level. This among others has increased the importance of team performance, i.e., shifting the individual goals to team goals.

Benefits of Performance Management

An effective performance management system provides multiple benefits for the organizations, which ultimately cascades to improved top line and bottomline.

- It focuses on key objectives and priorities for the organization, aligning with the management by objectives and the organisational strategy as a whole. Obviously, people in the organization derive clarity and shared vision. This also ensures optimal utilisation of resources by unifying the efforts in the right direction.
- It acts as a motivating force for the employees as they get a clear picture about what they contribute to the organization and how their contributions relate to organizational success.

Organizations also provide the required support to the employees, helping them to achieve the results.

- It enables organizations to monitor how they function as a whole, as it emphasises as a whole on the achievement of targets assigned to the individuals. The monitoring process helps in identifying the gaps in performance and thus acts as an important control device for intervention and improvement.
- It helps the organizations to align their important HR decisions like promotion, increment, transfer, training, manpower planning etc.
- Based on the performance track of employees, organizations can also draw up their plans and frame strategies to stay ahead of the competitors.
- It helps organizations also to fulfil their commitment to different stakeholders, as all people working with them try to meet their assigned tasks and responsibilities.

Process of Performance Management

To develop an effective process of performance management, organizations requires an ongoing 'dialogue' with their employees. It requires sustained efforts to develop the right organizational attitude to manage the performance, so that it improves the overall functions of the organization. Important processes, therefore, can be listed as under:

- Make sure that employees understand the objectives and priorities of the organization.
- Help people to focus on their efforts, rather than acting on hunches.
- Justify the benefits (to people) so that they can manage and improve their performance.
- Help the people to deliver the results through extending appropriate support.
- Align the organizational reward systems with the performance management.

Setting of performance objectives: Setting appropriate performance objectives is critical for effective performance management. Such objectives can be higher profits, shareholder value, customer satisfaction etc. The objectives must be:

- be focused on the result and not on the activity
- be consistent
- be specific
- be measurable
- be related to time
- be attainable

We call them SMART objectives. Setting up of SMART objectives needs consideration of factors, like assessment of the strengths, weaknesses, opportunities and threats for the organizations.

Performance domains

Performance domains are based on the focus of organization on performance measures. Based on the type of measurement or measurement criteria, we have four performance domains: (i) Mission (ii) Process (iii) Critical performance subsystems (iv) Individual

Mission domain: It identifies the purpose of the organization, based on the changing business focus and customers' expectations. Mission provides overall direction and performance targets for achieving the cherished goals and objectives of the organization. Depending on the changing business focus, organizations redefine their mission and accordingly requirements about performance of the employees also change.

Process domain: Process consists of a series of steps required to produce a product or service. For example, quality control or management focuses on the process performance domain. A defined process cuts across various subsystems. Market research, new product development, product design, customer service, financial planning and management, each follows a process. Designing performance management, based on the process requirements, helps the organization to achieve results in each process and its subprocesses.

Critical performance subsystems: This domain defines internal performance subsystems that always directly connect to the internal environment and frequently with the external one. The mission domain always interacts with the external environment. These subsystems differ from the process domain by cutting across multiple performance subsystems. Examples include:

- Programs for implementing new policies and procedures to ensure a safe workplace or for a non-profit, ongoing delivery of services to a community
- Products or services to internal or external customers
- Projects like automating the billing process, moving to a new building etc
- Teams or groups organized to accomplish a result

Individual domain: It focuses on individual performance management to achieve results and goals with some performance standard. These results and goals are recorded and referenced during a performance appraisal process. Ongoing training and development is provided as needed. Ideally, the supervisor and employee exchange ongoing feedback during the appraisal period to enhance the individual's performance.

Performance Management System

Performance Management System (PMS) is a set of techniques and procedures for improving organizational performance. To sustain competitive advantage, organizations not only need to recruit the best people but also focus on their continuous development through an effective PMS. While development of people is possible through ongoing training and development and skill and knowledge renewal, it must precede PMS, as PMS, *inter alia*, establishes the basis for identifying training and development needs. Watson and Wyatt, eminent management consultants, recently observed in one of their surveys that only 30% of workers feel that their company's PMS actually helps improve performance. The survey also found that many organizations lack in setting clear performance goals, generating honest feedback and using proper technology to streamline their performance management systems. In many cases, managers often felt reluctant to provide candid feedback. They merely count on the actual work done.

Requirements of PMS

To implement performance management systems in organizations and to gain advantage out of it, every organization needs to consider following aspects:

- Establishment of specific job assignments
- Writing of job descriptions, assigning responsibility for strategic initiatives, develop and apply performance standards
- Discussion on job performance with the employee and provide feedback on strengths and improvements needed
- Conducting the annual performance evaluation plan for improved performance and employee development goals

Main Features of PMS

Bevan and Thompson (1992) outlined the main features of PMS as follows:

Focus on setting objectives: PMS helps to percolate the organizational objectives to employees and translating them to individual targets.

Develop systems for ongoing review of objectives: PMS tracks the achievement of objectives. Such a review largely depends on the type of PM techniques used by an organization. It may be MBO or 360° or the more recent technique like the balanced score card.

Develop personal improvement plans: PMS helps in developing the personal improvement plans for the employees. A particular employee may lack in performance or he/she may exceed the targets given.

Alignment with training and development: It focuses on managing and developing employees' performance by aligning them with organizational objectives and strategies.

Formal appraisal with feedback: With a proper performance appraisal tool, PMS helps in giving feedback to employees. Both negative and positive feedback sensitises employees and helps them to objectively analyse their shortfalls and positive aspects.

Pay review: PMS helps in introducing the performance-based compensation system.

Organizational capability based on competencies: PMS helps in improving organizational capability through improvement in competencies. It also helps in appropriate organizational change keeping pace with the competition. It also helps in human resource planning.

Any performance management system has the following dimensions: (i) Output or result dimension (ii) Input dimension (iii) Time dimension (iv) Focus dimension (v) Quality dimension (vi) Cost dimension.

Standards of Performance

Standards of performance are written statements describing how well a job should be performed. Performance standards are developed collaboratively with employees, whenever possible, and explained to new employees during their induction programs , and annually for the existing employees. The standards can also be developed following the directive approach. Here managers write the performance standards, in consultation with management representatives, and then share the same with the concerned employees. The performance standard provides a benchmark against which we evaluate work performance. With the job description, we describe the essential functions and the tasks to be done. The performance standard defines how well each function or task must be performed in order to meet or exceed expectations.

In the process of developing performance standards both the managers and employees must know each others' expectations, as well as the performance of essential functions and related tasks. Such consensus eases the process of ongoing feedback and performance counselling.

Whether it is a directive approach or a collaborative approach to develop the performance standards, organizations need to ensure access to the following documents to the employees.

- Up-to-date copy of the job description
- Copy of the departmental goals and missions
- The structured performance appraisal form

Performance standards must be written in clear language, describing the specific behavioural requirements and actions to meet or exceed the expectations.

Guidelines for performance standards

While writing the performance standards, we must follow some important guidelines as under:

- It must be related to the employee's assigned work and job requirements.
- Performance reporting systems must be adequate to report quantitative data.

- As quantifiable measures may not be generated in all cases, we must develop the same as specific as possible to ensure that qualitative information is verifiable.
- While developing performance standards, it is also necessary to align the same to organizational objectives, like cost control, higher rate of productivity, customer satisfaction, on-time completion of projects etc.

Checklists for effective performance standards: The following checklists can help us to judge the effectiveness of performance standards.

- Are the standards realistic?
- Are they specific?
- Are they measurable and verifiable?
- Are they integrated with the organizational goals?
- Are they challenging?
- Are they clear and understandable?
- Are they dynamic?

Performance metrics: The use of performance metrics is now becoming popular in organizations. Many organizations develop function-specific performance metrics to judge the performance of employees. Profit performance, return on investment, earnings per share etc are certain traditional types of performance metrics. But now-a-days, we have many customer-focused metrics. With performance metrics it is also possible to use the Balanced Score Card, for holistic management of employees' performance. The balanced score card has four specific perspectives: (i) Customer perspective (ii) Finance perspective (iii) Internal business process perspective and (iv) Learning and development perspective. Every employee, irrespective of his or her functional area, contributes to these perspectives, which can be measured through function-specific performance metrics. Using the balanced score card, organizations can make the performance management system more scientific.

Performance Appraisal

Performance means the degree or extent to which an employee applies his skill, knowledge and efforts to a job assigned to him and the result of that application. Performance appraisal means analysis, review or evaluation of performance or behaviour analysis of an employee. It may be formal or informal, oral or documented, open or confidential. However, in organizations we find formal appraisal systems in documented form. It is, therefore, a formal process to evaluate the performance of the employees in terms of achieving organizational objectives.

Performance Appraisal is the most crucial area of PM activities. After allocating targets to employees, team members and the departments or divisions, performance appraisal is carried out periodic intervals using various tools. Such tools are different for appraising individual and collective performance. Effectiveness of performance appraisal can be understood in terms of its potential to identify the knowledge and skill gap and develop the training and development programs. Thus, performance appraisal can reinforce the training activities and ensure proper allocation of activities to the employees.

Importance of performance appraisal

For every HRM-related decision like transfer and promotion, remuneration, reward, training and development, besides long-term manpower planning and organizational development, performance appraisal is necessary. A well-documented performance appraisal system helps in understanding the attributes and behaviours of employees. It is also necessary for motivation, communication, strengthening superior–subordinate relationship, fixing KPAs and KRAs, work planning and for improving the overall performance of the organization.

Functions of performance appraisal

The primary functions and objectives of performance appraisal are given below.

- To identify and define the specific job criteria; many organizations set KPAs and KRAs at the beginning of the year for employees based on mutual discussions
- To measure and compare the performance in terms of the defined job criteria; KRAs and KPAs are also designed in such a way that they can help in measuring job performance in quantitative or qualitative terms
- To develop and justify reward system, relating rewards to the employees' performance
- To identify the strengths and weaknesses of employees and to decide on proper placement and promotion
- To develop suitable training and development programs for enriching performance of the employees
- To plan for long-term manpower requirements and to decide upon the need for organizational development programs, duly identifying the change areas for overall improvement of the organization
- To identify motivational reinforcers, to develop communication systems and also to strengthen superior subordinate relationships

Objectives of performance appraisal

The main objectives of performance appraisal are listed here.

- It serves various purposes like remediation, development, innovation and motivation.
- It meets developmental objectives to stimulate growth of the employees both in their present and future jobs.
- It identifies training and development needs, ensures placement and promotion etc.
- It discovers ways to deal with a new job and also to identify and develop better ways for existing jobs.
- It motivates through performance-linked rewards, facilitates communication and ensures better interpersonal relations.

Biases in Performance Appraisal

Despite developing structured and scientific performance appraisal systems, organizations often encounter the problem of errors or biases in the appraisal process. Such errors or biases primarily occur due to the raters, as they are often unable to carry out objective appraisals. There are many such errors and biases in performance appraisal. We have discussed the following common errors and biases in this section.

- Halo and horn effect
- Leniency error (Loose rater)
- Error of strictness (Tight rater)
- Central tendency error
- Recency effect
- Contrast error
- Similarity (similar-to-me) effect

Halo and horn effect: The halo effect is the outcome of the rater's general impression about the person whom he/she is rating. In such cases, the rater gives a high rating despite poor performance. Thus, due to better interpersonal relationships, halo effect occurs even when the employee has performed below par. . The horn effect is the opposite of halo effect. Raters influence with horn effect, by giving a poor rating, even when the employee has performed well. Many organizations try to solve such rating biases through sustained training for the appraisers.

Leniency error: This type of error is also seen widely in organizations. Some appraisers feel that poor rating to the employees may damage their morale, and adversely affect their future performance. Hence, they overrate the employees. These raters are also known as 'loose raters'.

Error of strictness: This error is just the opposite of the leniency error. These raters always underrate the subordinates, even when they perform well. Such raters are also called 'tight raters'. This type of raters suffer from the syndrome of insecurity, as they fear successful subordinates may rise to their position and replace them.

Central tendency error: Such raters either give extreme poor or extreme good grades, resulting in an average performance score for all rated employees. Often this lackadaisical attitude is attributed to their disrespect to the performance appraisal systems.

Recency effect: Such raters take stock of the latest information pertaining to the employees' performance when appraisal time approaches, and based on such information rate the employees. As a result with good performance in the recent past, employees get better rating, despite their poor performance in the beginning or middle of the performance cycle.

Contrast error: This error is the raters' tendency to rate employees relative to the performance of other employees, rather than their individual performance. Thus, the appraisal grade of the employee might be affected by the grades of others.

Similarity effect: Such raters always try to personify themselves with the ratees. Hence, when they find some similarities with the latter, they give a high rating.

Most of the organizations focus on eliminating the rating errors by training.

Role of appraisals in PM

PM is a continuous process, and more holistic in nature. Performance appraisals, on the other hand, are periodic activities. Therefore, while PM is dynamic, performance appraisal is static. Performance appraisals are a part, or subset of performance management. Without performance appraisal systems, PM becomes meaningless. Thus, appraisal plays the crucial role in performance management systems, as it reduces the annual performance into a number, equating one with another, and in the process facilitates objective assessment of performance, and allows decisions to be made based on the performance. Performance appraisal, therefore, makes the performance management process more effective and productive. With the appraisal results, managers can improve performance and build competency, wherever required.

Methods of Performance Appraisal

Effective design of an appraisal process requires consideration of several factors. Some of the processes and methods followed by the organizations to make the appraisal effective are as follows:

- Determining the job criteria and appraisal standard, i.e., the decision on measurement parameters

- Timing of appraisal, i.e., the decision on the frequency of appraisal
- Selection and shortlisting of appraisers
- Providing objective feedback to employees to help them to understand their strengths and weaknesses

Different organizations follow different types of performance appraisals. Selection of a particular type of appraisal method depends on the objectives of the organization, and the specific expertise of the assessors. Some appraisal techniques are quantitative, and require the assessors to possess specific knowledge on quantitative techniques. Lack of such expertise, often compels the organizations to select some traditional methods of appraisal. In this section, we have discussed both the traditional and modern methods of performance appraisal.

Traditional methods

Some common traditional methods of performance appraisal are straight ranking method, paired comparison techniques, man-to-man comparison, grading method, linear rating scale and so on. These and some others are discussed in this section.

Straight ranking method: This is one of the oldest and simplest methods of performance appraisal. Under this method, employees are appraised in order of merit with some numerical rank and accordingly they are placed or grouped. Such grouping separates employees according to their efficiency level, varying from 'most efficient' to 'least efficient'. It is a blunt quantification of performance without considering the behavioural parameters and only considers an individual employee's level of efficiency in relation to others. For such obvious deficiency, this system does not provide a scientific basis for performance appraisal of employees.

Paired comparison techniques: This method is considered to be relatively better as each employee is compared with others in pairs at a time. For each performance trait, individual performance is tallied with the other in the pair and then the rank order is decided. As it is a tedious process, it is time-consuming and difficult to administer when there are a large number of employees. In Table 13.1, one such comparison on trait reliability is shown.

Table 13.1 Trait reliability of a rated employee

As compared to	A	B	C	D	E
A	X	–	–	–	–
B	X	+	–	+	–
C	+	–	X	–	–
D	+	–	+	X	–
E	+	+	–	+	X

Man-to-man comparison: As per this method, some factors like leadership, initiative, interpersonal relationship etc are selected. The rater uses a scale for each factor to analyse the performance scores. The aggregate of an individual's performance is compared with another. This method is more like a factor comparison method and is extensively used in job evaluation. However, the method suffers from the problem of maintaining uniformity in the rating scale and is not preferred by the organizations for its obvious complication.

Grading method: As per this method, some features to measure the performance of employees are identified. Some of these features are leadership, communication power, analytical ability, job knowledge etc. The raters mark/rate such features according to a scale and match and employees' performance to the standard definition of the grade. For example A, B, C, D, E types of grade definitions for each feature may be developed by a rater to indicate, A = very significant, B = Significant, C = Moderate, D = Average, E = Poor. Such types of grading are of much use for selection of an employee or grading them in written examinations.

Graphic or linear rating scale: This is a continuous scale which normally enables a rater to mark somewhere along a continuum. Usually, a printed form is given to a rater along with the factors to be rated, giving a continuous scale against each such factor. This method, therefore, enables quantification of performance scores and to analyse its significance using statistical techniques. Since making a rating cluster is difficult for obvious differences in individual characteristics of each job, this system may not always ensure objective appraisal.

Forced choice description method: This method combines the objective and subjective assessment an employee's performance against each rating element. Positive and negative phrases are given asking the rater to indicate applicability of such phrases as objectives in describing the employee whose performance is rated. For its obvious complexity, this system is not used much.

Forced distribution method: It is a method to evaluate performance according to a predetermined distribution scale. For example, the rater is asked to distribute 5% of the total employees on top of the scale, indicating their superior performance and promotability, 10% may be put immediately below this level, indicating their good performance and future promotability. This system is easy to understand and can be applied to organizations without much hassles.

Checklist method: It is a mere process of reporting employees' performance by compiling yes/no responses. Final rating is done by the personnel vis-à-vis HR department based on such reports. It is not an objective method of appraisal.

Free easy method: It is an open-ended qualitative appraisal of performance, giving an opportunity to the rater to put down his impression in subjective form on important job factors. Since it is descriptive and essay type, it is likely to be biased and judgmental errors may crop in.

Critical incident method: This method measures performance in terms of certain 'events' or 'critical incidents' instrumental for success or failure on the job. Such critical incidents are identified by the rater after in-depth study of the working style of the employees. As negative incidents get more focus and incidents have to be recorded with utmost care, it is not free from defects.

Group appraisal method: It is an evaluation of an employee by multiple judges. The immediate supervisor of the employee and a few others discuss the performance standards and then evaluate the performance of the employee. The greatest advantage of this method is that it is relatively free from bias even though it is time-consuming.

Field review method: The review is conducted by the HR department by interviewing the supervisor of an employee to understand the subordinate's performance. Normally for such type of appraisal, the appraiser gets equipped with certain questions and more in the form of an informal interview, asks those questions about the employees, whose performances are to be reviewed, to their respective supervisors. Since this process of appraisal is an indirect method of appraising the performance, it may not always reflect the true performance level of the subordinate employees. Such an interview always has a sensitising effect on the interviewee, whose responses may be somewhat coloured by opinion. Moreover, this method keeps the key managerial personnel always busy for appraisal. Despite such defects, the process being simple to administer, centralising the performance appraisal function, most of the organizations prefer to have this type of appraisal for lower level employees.

Modern methods

The traditional methods of performance appraisal suffer from the major limitation for their obvious emphasis on assessing individual performance or task, considering it as an isolated factor. To eliminate such narrow and partial approach, the modern techniques of performance appraisal have been developed and are widely practised by the organizations, particularly for managerial and supervisory employees. Some of these techniques are discussed in this section.

Management By Objectives (MBO): It is a comprehensive management approach which is adopted for performance appraisal as also for organizational development. When MBO is used for appraisal only, its primary focus is on developing objective criteria for evaluating the performance of the individuals. Identification of common goals is jointly done by the superior and subordinate managers of an organization. After such identification, each individual's major area of responsibilities is defined. Such defined responsibility becomes the basis for evaluating the performance of the individual employee.

Most of the organizations emphasise on developing KRAs through the MBO exercise, as this approach necessitates joint meeting of the supervisor and the employee to define, establish and set goals or objectives, which the individual employees would achieve, within a prescribed time limit. Such an exercise also establishes ways and methods to measure performance. Goals are mostly work-related and career-oriented and are integrated with overall organizational objectives. Periodic evaluation of employees' performances is done in terms of goals and if required, these goals may be revised. MBO also calls for superior–subordinate interaction and supportive role of the supervisor, including counselling and coaching.

However, the MBO system lays more stress on tangible goals and hence intangible goals like morale, good interpersonal relations, commitment to the job etc are often ignored. Moreover, it is time-consuming and expensive.

Assessment centre method: This method tests employees in a social situation by a number of assessors, using a variety of criteria which may include paper–pencil test, interviews, in-basket exercise, business game, role play or a leaderless discussion. The assessors or evaluators are drawn from experienced executives working at different managerial levels. Under this method, performance of employees is evaluated both individually and collectively. This method is useful in measuring interpersonal skills, organising and planning ability, creativity, resistance to stress, work motivation, decision-making power etc. This approach iis used extensively for selection and development for more than 30 years (Thornton, 1992). The basic format of the assessment centres is to evaluate employee behaviour, relating the same to several performance dimensions through the use of assessment exercises, especially work simulations. Along with such evaluation, dimensional ratings are also done, and then the validity is examined. For assessment centres, validity is important as it involves in-basket exercises. Content validity of assessment centres can be done through job analysis. Criterion-related validity is done through job performance, managerial success and training efficiency. Construct validity is examined through traits and exercises methods.

Human asset accounting method: This method attaches money estimates in the value of manpower of an organization. The process is somewhat like estimating the value of goodwill and can be appraised by developing a procedure for periodic measurement of certain variables. Such variables are either key variables or intervening variables. The former are policies and decisions of an organization, its leadership strategies, skills and behaviour of an employee etc. The latter include loyalties, attitudes, motivations, interpersonal relations, communication and decision-making. Measuring such variables over several years and quantification of human assets are difficult for the obvious problem in developing the accounting procedure. It is not a very popular method of performance appraisal. However, this system is more appropriately used for evaluating the collective performance of an organization, rather than individual appraisal of an employee. This method is useful for organizational development, as it helps in identifying the changed areas more scientifically than any other method.

Behaviourally Anchored Rating Scales (BARS): This method helps in measuring and improving job performance more accurately. For each performance area, some standard statements are provided. These are then put on the scales in BARS. While developing such BARS, group discussions are conducted to identify significant job dimensions that need to be evaluated. BARS may be of different types for different job dimensions. Normally, they are presented vertically with scale points ranging from five to nine. Because of its behavioural orientation, it is considered as the most useful technique of performance appraisal. Moreover, this system provides opportunity to both appraisee and appraiser to interact and participate in developing standards for each performance area. Despite its several advantages, this system is not preferred because it is time-consuming.

360°appraisals: This appraisal method is now widely used around the world. It requires performance feedback from all important stakeholders of the organization like the ratee, his/her superiors, peers, other team members, customers and suppliers. Apart from its effectiveness in reporting performance, this method also ensures total employee involvement (TEI) and employee empowerment. This method also reduces subjective evaluation system in an organization.

However 360°appraisal can be considered in an organization only when following aspects about an organization hold true:

- The organization is not able to meet challenges that come its way because of increased competition or global expansion.
- People in the organization feel the need to change their behaviour to combat increasing competition and to progress in their careers but are unsure about what and how to change.
- There is no formal system in place through which people receive information on what others think about their behaviour.
- 360° feedback is not a package, which can be delivered by a given date. It is a process that needs to be implemented in steps. Before implementation of 360° feedback, it should be designed to support a corporate strategy or goal.
- Every employee should understand what it is and how it works.
- Employee development should be high on the agenda of the organization, and employees must be convinced about the support of the feedback processes.
- Sufficient resources should be available to ensure that the integrity level of the process is high.
- The employees should be trained in the process.
- Employees must trust that the information would be used for developmental purposes and should be willing to receive and give feedback.

For better results, organizations implement 360° feedback in stages. In addition to effective performance appraisal, it also helps in bringing cultural change in the organization and leads to organizational development.

Potential appraisal: This process helps the management to identify the hidden talents, skills, or knowledge of employees. It is future-oriented, and is usually done, integrating the same with the performance appraisal process, to identify the potential employees for higher positions with increased job responsibilities. Some of the techniques used for potential appraisal are self-appraisals, peer appraisals, superior appraisals, MBO, psychological and psychometric tests, management games, role play and leadership exercises. Some the purposes of potential appraisal are:

- Advising employees on their overall career development and future prospects
- Helping the organization to chalk out succession plans
- Motivating the employees to further develop their skills and competencies
- Identifying the training needs

Thus, potential appraisal is a holistic approach for studying wholesome qualities of an employee with a given intellect, personality and character.

Steps in Performance Appraisal

Irrespective of the methods applied for performance appraisal, the steps are usually in a set pattern as listed below.

- Establishing the performance standards; it is done mostly while developing the job description
- Communication of standards to the employees
- Measurement of performance
- Comparison of performance with the job standards
- Discussing the appraisal results with the employees
- Initiating the corrective action, where necessary

Performance Counselling

It is a process of advising an employee, listening to his problems and enabling him to find a satisfactory solution on his own. Performance counselling is a process to help subordinates analyse their performance objectively. It helps in identifying training and development needs and also ensures improvement in the future performance of an employee.

Basically, performance counselling attempts to help an employee in the following ways.

- It helps an employee to understand his own strengths and weaknesses. More effective counselling sessions can even enable employees to make their independent SWOT analysis, i.e., strength, weakness, opportunities and threats in achieving their independent performance.
- Since good performance counselling believes in giving feedback about employees' behaviour as also their performance, it helps in improving professional and interpersonal competence of employees.
- It helps in setting goals and formulating the action plan for further improvement of employees.
- It helps the employees to identify different alternatives for dealing with problems.
- A good performance counselling session is supportive and being empathetic, employees feel encouraged to openly discuss their aspirations, conflicts and problems.

Effective performance counselling

The conditions for effective performance counselling are listed below:

- A climate of mutual trust, confidence and openness needs to be ensured at the outset.
- The subordinates should feel free to participate in the review process and also in giving the correct feedback. This is important as counselling is not merely a one-way process of communication.
- The focus of performance counselling is on development of the employee. This should not be considered isolated from other issues such as remuneration and rewards, promotion, motivation etc.

Phases of Performance Counselling

The different phases of performance counselling are described here.

- **Building rapport**: This is the first phase of performance counselling in which a climate of acceptance, support and openness is sought to be established. During this phase, subordinates should be assured that their superiors are keenly interested in their development. This phase is said to be successful if it generates confidence in the employees and let them share their perceptions, problems and feelings without inhibitions.
- **Exploration**: In this phase, apart from visiting the employees and creating a climate of openness, the counsellors help them understand their strengths, weaknesses, opportunities and threats. The success of this phase lies in making the employees discover all these on their own and at the same time initiate remedial measures independently.

- **Action planning**: Specific plans and actions for the development of employees are identified at this phase. The counsellor helps the employees to implement such action plans for effective results. For making such action plans acceptable, some counsellors prefer to develop the plans by brainstorming with the employees. This process enables the employees to develop the action plans independently.

Features of performance counselling

The performance counsellor should be a good listener and pay attention to the ideas, feelings and sentiments of the person being counseled. This enables the counsellor to understand and analyse the subordinate's concerns. The effectiveness of the performance counselling session, therefore, depends on the efficiency in asking questions. The questions should be framed in such a way that they get constructive suggestions from the subordinate, should be open-ended and empathetic. The questions should not be critical or should not appear as if the intention of the counsellor is to test or evaluate the subordinate person.

The performance counselling process should ensure communication of feedback to the subordinates in such a manner so as to evoke constructive response from them. Since, giving negative feedback is embarrassing, feedback should always be descriptive and non-evaluative. It should be focused on the behavioural attributes rather than on the subordinate himself. Feedback should be made more data-based and suggestive. It should be continuous and verifiable.

The counselling interview

Before beginning the counselling session, the counsellor needs to study the subordinate's job responsibilities, his/her education, training and experience, job performance and his past jobs. He/she should make adequate planning of the discussion, the issues involved and determine the development need to be discussed with the employee.

The interview should be sincere, informal and friendly. The counsellor should explain the purpose of the discussion to the interviewee and also emphasise on the issue that the interview is essentially a two-way communication. The subordinates should be encouraged to appraise themselves and discuss their thoughts or opinions. The counsellor should focus on the strong points and encourage the subordinates to suggest ways to improve themselves. It is essential for the counsellor to reach an agreement on the development plans and also to summarise the points discussed in the session at the end of the interview. He should make a record of the plans mutually agreed upon during the interview.

Performance Management Scale

Here we have defined a five-point scale with rating points.

5 = Almost always performs as described by the role model standards

4 = Sometimes performs as described by the 'role model' standards and sometimes performs as described by the 'meets expectations' standards.

3 = Almost always performs as described by the 'meets expectations' standards

2 = Sometimes performs as described by the 'meets expectations' standards and sometimes performs as described by the 'below expectations' standards.

1 = Almost always performs as described by the 'below expectations' standards

Sample Performance Rating Form

Name of the employee______________________________

Level: Entry-level employee

Manager's name ______________________________

Key work responsibilities:	Results/goals to be achieved
1. ____________________	1. ____________________
2. ____________________	2. ____________________
3. ____________________	3. ____________________
4. ____________________	4. ____________________

Four Pillars of Managing Performance

An effective performance management system is one that integrates both the individual's and group's performance with the organizational goals, objectives, strategies, i.e., the overall business plans. Keeping this aspect in view, we observe four pillars of performance management as under:

- Define and agree on what performance the organization needs.
- Guide the development of individuals so that they can have the skills and knowledge needed to perform effectively.

- Motivate individuals to perform effectively.
- Provide data about the condition of the organization's human capital.

With these four pillars firmly in place, managers can successfully manage performance, and ultimately help the organization to achieve success.

Key Points

- ☛ Industrial psychologists extend support to organizations for developing effective performance management systems, as employees' performance, among others also involves behavioural variables.
- ☛ Performance management systems (PMS) are holistic and integrate organizations' goals and mission with the performance of the employees.
- ☛ Performance management (PM) helps in identifying gaps in the knowledge and skills of employees and accordingly helps the organizations in identifying their training and development needs.
- ☛ Performance appraisal is a subset of performance management systems. Through effective performance appraisal, we can accurately ascertain employee development needs.
- ☛ Performance appraisal results also help in important human resource management decisions, like compensation design, promotion, lateral transfer, job rotation, job enrichment needs of the employees, and even the need for counselling the employees to help them to excel in future performance.
- ☛ Results of performance appraisal also update the organizations to prepare their skill inventories, based on which organizations can take the effective strategic decisions in future.

Important Terms

Counselling interview: It is a friendly, informal and sincere two-way communication process. Although it is a formal process of performance review, the informal environment encourages subordinates to open up and they feel encouraged to discuss their own appraisals and about themselves.

Group appraisal method: It is an evaluation of an employee by multiple judges. The immediate supervisor of the employee and a few others discuss the performance standards and then evaluate the performance of the employee. The greatest advantage of this method is that it is relatively free from bias even though it is time-consuming.

Mission performance domain: It identifies the purpose of the organization, based on the changing business focus and expectations of customers.

Performance goals: Organizations set the performance goals through the job description and structure the same through mutual discussion and acceptance both by the managers and the employees.

Self-assessment Questions

1. Define Performance Management (PM).
2. What are the important objectives of Performance Management? Develop SMART objectives for a HR Manager.
3. Define performance standards. How are such standards developed?
4. Develop tentative performance standards for various levels of employees.
5. Explain the term performance metrics. How is it developed? For designing a customer-focused metrics, what are the factors need to be considered?
6. Define performance appraisal. Briefly state its importance and objectives. What are the steps you would like to follow for appraising the performance of a managerial employee?
7. What are the different performance appraisal systems followed in an organization? Select at least five methods and briefly discuss their strengths and weaknesses.
8. Traditional performance appraisal system emphasises on assessing the individual performance as an isolated factor. Briefly discuss the newer techniques of performance appraisal, critically reviewing the shortcomings of the traditional system.
9. Discuss the effectiveness of MBO and BARS in performance appraisal. Develop KRAs for a HR Manager of an organization and identify five important performance criteria for assessing the performance on a six-point BARS.
10. Develop a standard performance appraisal form for supervisors in an organization, selecting at least ten factors for review. Recommend your proposed development plans for such supervisors based on your review.
11. Briefly state the importance and objectives of performance counselling. What are the conditions for effectiveness of performance counseling?

12. Write short notes on the following
    i. Counselling interview
    ii. Assessment centre method
    iii. Field review
    iv. Critical incident method
    v. Key Performance Areas (KPAs)
    vi. Collaborative performance standards
    vii. SMART

Selected Bibliography

1. Bhattacharyya DK (2011). *Performance Management Systems and Strategies.* New Delhi: Pearson.
2. Bernardin HJ and RW Beatty (1984). *Performance Appraisal: Assessing Human Behaviour at Work.* Boston: Kent Publishing.
3. Cardy RL and GH Dobbins (1994). *Performance Appraisal: Alternative Perspectives.* Cincinnati: Southwestern Publishing Co.
4. Cederblom D (1982). The performance appraisal interview: A review, implications and suggestions. *Academy of Management Review*, 7, 219–27.
5. Grote D (1996). *The Complete Guide to Performance Appraisal.* New York: American Management Association.
6. Locke EA and GP Latham (1990). *A Theory of Goal-setting and Task Performance.* Englewood Cliffs: Prentice-Hall.
7. Murphy KR and JN Cleveland (1995). Understanding Performance Appraisal: Social, Organizational and Goal-based Perspectives. Thousand Oaks: Sage.

Annexure I Checklist of Observable Behaviour

Please go through each of the items listed below. Whenever the item description distinctly tallies with the observable behaviour in the rate, tick in the column marked YES. If it is not so, please tick in the column marked NO. This checklist is not an assessment of performance. It is to be used for developmental purposes.

Sl No	Description	YES	NO
1.	Pay attention to documentation. Is systematic in record keeping for future references.		
2.	Is clear and concise in written communication.		
3.	Has the capacity for self-analysis and correction of his weaknesses.		
4.	Has the aptitude for systematic and methodical work. Is patient with minute details.		
5.	Makes positive attempts to update himself in his professional field and learn new things.		
6.	Does not accept sub-standard work.		
7.	Does not lose heart in spite of failures or setbacks.		
8.	Has a sense of humour.		
9.	Promotes healthy industrial relations in his department or workplace.		
10.	Is skilled in organising complex activities.		
11.	Is trustworthy. Does not let down colleagues for personal gain.		
12.	Has the courage of his convictions. Expresses dissent where he is convinced of a different approach to the task or problems.		
13.	Respectful of elders and superiors. Polite. Does not hurt colleagues or subordinates.		
14.	Finds it very easy to get to know people and get along with them.		
15.	Clear in his verbal communication. Is seldom misunderstood. Can convey his thoughts precisely and clearly.		

Annexure II Specimen of Confidential Rating of Overall Performance

Please initial in any one of the following	
The individual has achieved an exceptionally high standard of performance. In significant areas of responsibility, he has exceeded expected standards. Performance is consistently excellent.	Outstanding
The standard of performance has been consistently above average and in several areas, responsibilities were discharged so as to merit favourable comment rather than mere satisfaction.	Superior
The individual has performed well by and large and to the satisfaction of his superior,	Satisfactory
Not up to the minimum requirements of the position	Unsatisfactory

This employee has worked under my supervision

From ____________

to____________

Signature of the rater

Date:__________

Designation

Department

Signature of the reviewing authority

Date:__________

Designation

Department

Annexure III Strengths and Weaknesses of Different Performance Appraisal Methods

Method	Strengths	Weaknesses
Appraisal by objectives (MBO)	• Provides a quantitative measurement of performance, which is verifiable. • Weak performance areas can be quickly identified and thus provides a meaningful basis for improving the performance.	• Appraisal being result-oriented, it is not suitable for determining the potential. • Individual performance areas being different, it does not facilitate peer comparison.
Graphic rating	• Simple and popular method • Facilitates peer comparison and provides an objective basis for decision on remuneration, rewards and promotion • Certain common criteria may be provided for improving the quality of comparison	• Highly subjective and weighting of factors may be necessary for improving the quality of analysis • Unreliable • Does not provide facility for feedback and development of the employee
Essay type	Its proper use can provide quality information which can help in taking meaningful decisions for placement, promotion and development	• Requires good writing ability • Appraisers should have the maturity for proper assessment. • Being subjective, inter-employee comparison is difficult.
Critical incidents method	• Highly objective, it provides factual data on performance and behaviour • Usually helps in improving the communication and development of employees • Useful as a supportive evaluation	• Since performance is analysed on incidents, it tends to be fragmented • Not an an independent method of evaluation • Does not provide any basis for comparison

Forced distribution	• Free from any bias and is uniform in standards	• Also not an independent method of appraisal; better used as a control instrument • Not suitable for communication and employee development.
Straight ranking method	• Simple and helps in taking decisions on salary progression and promotion	• Does not provide feedback and also cannot be used for large groups and interdepartmental comparison

14 Training and Development

Learning Objectives

After reading this chapter, you will be able to:

- **Understand the importance of training and development**
- **Outline the characteristics of training programs**
- **List the types of training programs**
- **Outline the steps for designing training programs**
- **Appreciate the importance of training policy and needs analysis**

Overview

Employee development is a management function with a high priority. Like their involvement in performance management and other important HRM functions, industrial psychologists also play an important role in training and development by designing training programs to meet the behavioural deficiencies of employees.

Thus, training and development is an important employee development activity. Apart from the need for internal staffing, training enhances job-related skills and also facilitates acquiring of new skills required for averting skill obsolescence in an organization. Employee development or human resource development is a macro concept and it consists of organised services of learning activities within a given time limit for achieving desired behavioural changes in the employees. From the organizational point of view, human resource development (HRD) is a process and it helps employees improve their functional capabilities for present and future roles. It also develops their general capabilities, harnesses their inner potential and thereby facilitates for self and organizational development.

There are a lot of misconceptions about training, education and development functions vis-à-vis HRD. Training concerns people already employed with the organization and whose jobs are so defined that we are able to identify the desired job behaviours. Training enables employees to perform better in their present job position. Education is a future-oriented behaviour for identifiable job positions. Development, on the other hand, is to conduct learning experiences for a future undefined job. Despite such differences, we consider them together as they all contribute to employee development.

Purposes of Training

Training is defined as systematised, tailor-made program to suit the needs of a particular organization for developing certain attitudes, actions, skills and abilities in employees, irrespective of their functional levels. Training, therefore, serves the following important purposes for an organization.

- To increase the performance level of an employee and to develop him/her in such a manner that he/she can rise to the position of higher responsibility
- To constantly develop manpower to meet the current as well as future needs of the organization
- To ensure effective utilisation of human resources
- To integrate individual goals with those of the organization by creating a climate so that an individual employee can best achieve his/her goals by striving for the goals of the organization.
- To let employees identify with the organization

Need for training

Most of the organizations prefer internal manning of position than external hiring for obvious motivational benefits and cost effectiveness. Even though training, prima facie, emphasises on increasing the performance level of an employee, a continuous training function enables the organization to develop employees for future responsibilities in the organization itself.

The needs for employees' training in an organization may be categorised as follows.

Updating knowledge: Technological advancement, business environmental changes and new management philosophies have now made it imperative for the organizations to renew and update the knowledge and skills of the employees. This ensures people do not become redundant for obvious functional incompetence. Therefore, the first and foremost need for employees' training is to sustain their effective performance and also to develop them for future managerial positions.

Avoiding obsolescence: Recent economic liberalisation by the Government of India has necessitated organizational restructuring, which inter alia, calls for training of the employees, irrespective of their functional level, for their redeployment in restructured jobs. Therefore, the second important need for training is to avert functional obsolescence.

Improving performance: Continuous training is required to renew and update knowledge and skills of employees to make them functionally effective.

Developing human skills: Apart from emphasising on technical and conceptual skills, new training programs also emphasise on developing human skills of employees. Such skills are necessary for effective interpersonal relations and sustaining a healthy work environment.

Imparting trade-specific skills: In industrial employment, the convention is to recruit workers and employees through compulsory apprenticeship training. It enables an organization to impart industry- and trade-specific skills to workers.

Stabilising the workforce: Training helps in stabilising the workforce, avoiding the problem of manpower obsolescence by developing their capabilities, so that they can withstand the technological change and make the organization dynamic in this changed process.

Classification of Training Programs

Depending on the functional level and occupational categories of employees, an organization can classify training programs as shown in Table 14.1.

Apart from the above routine training programs, organizations also focus on continuous development of employees on the latest management practices like total quality management, lean management, six sigma techniques etc. These training programs help in enhancing the capabilities of employees to manage the organizations even in this era of business uncertainty.

Table 14.1 Types of training

Level of the workers	Types of training
Workers	Introduction Job training Craft training Special purpose training
Supervisors	Induction Foremanship/shop floor supervision Manpower management
Staff members	Introduction Professional Technical Human relations
Managers and executives	Induction Executive training Training in executive development

Induction and orientation

These terms are interchangeably used to give a friendly welcome to the new employees as members of the organization so also to introduce the new employees with the available installations (plant and machineries, systems), work norms, organizational objectives and the job positions of the employees. Some organizations make available programmed instruction materials to new employees to help them get acquainted with the departmental rules and regulations, their entitlement for leave, pay, overtime, retirement benefits and other miscellaneous privileges which affect their whole service. Tata Iron and Steel Company circulates a brief booklet titled 'Write your future in Tata Steel' to all their new employees, to illustrate their career prospects. However, such documented materials cannot be made available by all organizations. They try to supplement it through a brief induction program.

Supervisory training program

Supervisors monitor the work of other workers and are the arms of the management. They must have adequate skill, experience, ability and leadership. A supervisor is required to do the job in five broad areas, i.e., knowledge of the work, awareness of responsibilities, capacity to instruct, skill in improving methods and ability to work with people. Tentative content of a Supervisor Training Program may be drawn based on content prescribed by Earl Planty and William Mocorx as shown in Table 14.2.

Table 14.2 Sample three-day training program on managerial role in the new millennium

	ACTIVITY	PURPOSE (for participants)	PURPOSE (for organization)
Day-1	Customer Relationship Management (CRM)—What is it and why is it important?	To help participant to know in details about CRM and how by developing CRM skills they can achieve excellence in their day to day function.	To develop CRM competencies and achieve increased business results by retention of customers. This will lead to increase in the market share for the organization and propel the pace of growth

	CRM practices and how they help in turning around an organization	To understand the CRM practices and how organizations worldwide benefit from adoption of CRM practices including cases of those who could turn around by practising CRM	To benchmark the CRM practices with other leading organizations worldwide and emulate their examples for better business results
	Personal Effectiveness —seven habits and how to develop and practice those	To understand the seven habits of Stephen Covey and how to develop and practise those for achieving excellence in dealing with people and feel individually enriched	To get the advantage of excellent practices of employees which will-reduce the customer response time and enhance customer satisfaction
	Essentials of Quality Management with details of cost and quality relationship and how it enhances competitive strength of an organization	To understand different quality management practices and save cost through quality enhancement	To get the benefit of multiskill and better results from employees to achieve business growth in globally competitive market
	Quizzes and Case Studies to test the lessons learnt	To put learnt lessons in action and achieve gradual perfection to deliver results	To measure training effectiveness and consider for its continuance for developing different sections of employees
Day-2	Creativity and innovation in managing customers with exercises and quizzes	To develop creative/lateral thinking and translate the same into action through innovation in dealing with customers and offering services to customers	To get the benefit of increased result for creativity, translating the creative thinking into action; creativity will enhance competitive strength for the organization

Essentials of team management and team management practices with exercises and quizzes	To learn how teams can be formed and managed and get the benefit of synergy through team-building; also how team formation can reduce the dissonance in day-to-day action and how customers can benefit from effective teams	To multiply gains for the benefit of synergy, which will enhance performance due to collective efforts and reduce customer response time and increase customer satisfaction
Managing conflict with exercises and quizzes	To manage conflict and translate conflict into better performance	To reduce dysfunctional conflict and translate conflict into creativity for better organizational results
Understanding the change imperative—Why do we need to change?	To understand the degree of change in the individual's day-to-day activities for their own survival and organizational stability and growth	To reap the benefit of positive attitudinal change of employees and remain competitive with active support and cooperation from all cross-section of employees
Understanding model of excellence	Integrating the organizational practice of excellence with individual excellence.	To get the benefit of excellence by developing a proactive employee role
Quizzes and Case Studies to test the learnt lessons	To put into practice learned lessons and measure their individual effectiveness	To measure effectiveness in training and put into use the learnt lessons

Day-3	Introduction to HR with focus on motivation, leadership, compensation designing, competency mapping in three-sessions	To understand how HR can help an organization to get strategic advantage	To derive benefit from proactive HR practices
	Six Sigma and HR	To develop the Six Sigma culture and feel committed to the organization	Develop an enabling organization culture to truly convert it into a good performing one; also consider for future continuation of such training programs for overall growth of the organization

Training for top and middle management

Training for the top and middle management consists of the following eight areas:

- **Planning**: This covers the policy, general programs and plans of the organization and also methods for effective action.
- **Control**: To check current performance against predetermined standards (as mentioned in the plans) to ensure progress and also to record experience from the working of plans to serve as guide to possible future operations
- **Co-ordination**: To balance the team efforts ensuring proper allocation of activities among different members of the group
- **Motivation**: This covers employees' morale and given by proper leadership. The art of self-motivation has to be included in the top managers and executives training program.
- **Inspiration**: Top managers and executives should be able to inspire the employees in general. This requires mastering the art of inspiring others. Inspirational leadership style works wonders in persuading people to deliver the results.

- **Communication**: This skill is an essential prerequisite for top level managers and executives. This is because at that level effective communication brings the desired results. Therefore, adequate thrust on systematic communication training is most important for top and middle level managers.
- **Decision**: Top and middle level managers by virtue of their position need to take decisions frequently. Decision-making is both a science and an art. Effective decision-making requires broad-based knowledge on various decision alternatives. Systematic training on decision-making helps the managers to develop their skills to achieve results.
- **Integration**: Integration helps in conceptualising the holistic situation. Managers can quickly relate the information and data and can truly interpret the outcome. Training can also facilitate developing the knowledge and skill of integration.

Training Needs Analysis

Training Needs Analysis (TNA) is a prerequisite for developing needs-and-competency-based training curriculum and courses to promote quality and demand-driven training programs. In all organizations, to reap the benefit from training and development, programs are designed based on the TNA results. The TNA survey is reinforced by research on competencies in relation to achieving the strategic objectives. Analysis is further strengthened by interviews and focus group discussions (FGDs). Appropriate training interventions then selected from different methods e.g., self-study, workshops, conferences, seminar, coaching, mentoring, action learning, involvement in cross-departmental projects and exchange programs among others. The TNA is used in different data gathering techniques such as survey, interview, FGDs, document search and direct observation. The TNA survey instrument is divided into four sections: (a) personal profile of the respondent (b) respondent's assessment of his/her organization; (c) self-assessment of training needs and (d) preferences of training service providers and training arrangements. The objective of the self-assessment of training needs is three-fold: to identify the knowledge and skills areas that the respondents perceived to be important to their work, to gauge the respondents' proficiency level in those areas, and to determine what are considered to be training priority. This self-assessment is meant to determine the knowledge and skills areas that would be responsive to the needs of the individuals in terms of increasing their capacity and enabling them to perform better in their job.

Training needs assessment methods

Some of the commonly used HRD needs assessment methods are explained below:

- **Context analysis**: It is based on the business needs of the organization. Through this analysis, organizations try to identify type of training to be conducted, analyse how such identified HRD program help in solving the business problem, and finally what was their past experience with such programs.
- **User analysis**: This analysis is done from the stakeholders' perspectives, i.e., the potential recipients of the HRD programs and the managers, instructors and faculty members involved in such process. Through this analysis, organizations try to answer questions like who will receive the training and what are their level of existing knowledge on the subject, what their learning style is and who will conduct the training.
- **Work analysis**: Organizations analyse the tasks studying the job and the task requirements for performing the job. This is also known as a task analysis or job analysis and this analysis seeks to specify the main duties and skill level required. This helps ensure that the training, which is developed, will include relevant alignment to the job content.
- **Content analysis**: This pertains to analysis of documents, laws and procedures used on the job. Therefore, it answers the questions about knowledge or information used in the job. All these information are obtained from the job manuals, documents or regulations. Content of the training should not conflict or contradict the documented job requirements. Content analysis can be best performed leveraging the experience of a worker who performs the job and also the domain knowledge of the subject matter expert.
- **Training suitability analysis**: Through this, we analyse whether training is the desired solution for HRD. We have to appreciate that training is one of the several solutions to performance problems. It may not always be the best solution. Thus, it is important to determine whether training will be effective or not.
- **Cost-benefit analysis**: This is done through analysis of the return on investment (ROI) of training. Effective training results in a return of value to the organization that is greater than the initial investment to produce or administer the training.

Several basic TNA techniques include: (i) direct observation (ii) questionnaires (iii) consultation with persons in key positions, and/or with specific knowledge (iv) review of relevant literature (v) interviews (vi) focus groups (vii) tests (viii) records and report studies (ix) work samples.

Training needs analysis survey

This is a sample questionnaire to identify TNA. However, organizations may develop their own survey questionnaire, depending on their own priorities.

For trainees

Please fill in the following details:

1. Name of respondent
2. Number of years in service
3. Job title and Code
4. Grade
5. Number of years in the present grade

0–12 months ☐	2–5 yrs ☐
1–2 yrs ☐	over 5 yrs ☐

6. Number of years in the present post

0–12 months	☐	2–5 yrs	☐
1–2 yrs	☐	over 5 yrs	☐

7. Number of people directly reporting to you

8. Did you attend any training programs in the last one year, if yes give details

Yes/ No

9. Please give your brief career history, including details of any management experience, qualifications and number of people managed.

10.

1. Specific skill requirements

(Here list out the skill sets as identified for the job)

2. Strategic awareness

(Here also organization has to decide the nature of strategic awareness required for the specific job. However, some sample generic strategic issues are listed for reference).

Application of risk management

Application of benefits analysis/business cases

Formulation of functional strategies

Working with cross-functional teams

Application of strategic management principles

3. General skill requirements

A. Markets

Application of:

Market knowledge

Product knowledge Commercial awareness B. **Processes** (This again depends on the specific job)
Any other issues not identified above (please specify)

For answering question number 10, following scales may be used:

Level of importance	**Degree of difficulty**
A. Crucial	**1.** A great deal
B. Very important	**2.** Quite a lot
C. Fairly important	**3.** A little
D. Minor	**4.** None

Steps for Designing the Training Program

Identification of training needs

Traditionally, identification of training needs is left to the HRD department. In trying to keep pace with organizational requirements, the department would identify series of training modules for different categories of employees and publish such training calendars to circulate among other departments to depute their employees for such training courses. Depending on the facilities available, some of these training courses are also offered utilising in-house training faculty, while for others (where expertise is not available) such training may either be offered by retaining professional trainers or by deputing employees to attend some training courses externally.

However, to ensure better utilisation of employees' acquired knowledge and skill, identification of training needs are now being left with the respective departmental heads, who because of their proximity with the employees concerned can better suggest the training and development needs. Hence, right at the beginning of the year, HRD department circulates the format for suggesting training requirements of different departments, which after necessary processing, they develop as training calendars. Head of the department through performance appraisal, job evaluation and keeping in mind future requirements (due to change of technology etc), may identify such training requirements and also study the cost–benefit aspect closely monitoring employees' post-training performance.

Incidentally, it has now also become one important corporate practice in line with the requirements for ISO certification. The following steps are involved in designing the training program.

Selecting strategies: The first step is to choose a strategy or strategies for training methods. Strategies prioritise training objectives and also help in selecting training areas which may be skill formation, developing conceptual understanding etc.

Breaking objectives: The second step is to break the general training objectives into different parts like, knowledge, understanding and skills. Each constituent part of the training objective is matched with appropriate training events.

Choosing methods: This step helps to use specifications for different training methods, to decide on the time required and to identify the facilities required for the program as a whole.

Deciding on packages: The fourth step is to decide different packages in which programs could be offered. An organization at this stage considers different training packages, keeping in view the time and cost aspects.

Designing the program: This is the final step followed by any organization, to design their training programs.

Sequence of a training program

Any training program should follow the order of sequence of action, as under, to make if effective.

- Designing the program matching with the learning process
- Matching the program to the organization's expectations
- Developing the training group
- Identifying the themes of training
- Achieving consistency in training

Designing the training program

Training requires more than just information-giving or skills development. It requires the trainer to have a thorough understanding of the training process and the role and value of proper and systematic planning and evaluation of the program. Thus, importance of preparing a well-designed training program requires proper planning. Proper designing of the training programs is an essential prerequisite for success of the training programs.

Designing is right at the planning phase and it largely depends on what training intends to achieve and how best it can be achieved. However, program designing is just not limited to listing the items to be covered in training delivery. It is much broader and holistically it covers every aspect of the training. The following steps are important in designing relevant and effective training programs.

Assessment of training needs: Assessment of needs is the primary step in any training process. It is the step that provides baseline information upon which the training program is designed and developed. Operationally, it can be achieved by answering who, what and whom. While who clarifies the categories of people who have the training needs, what unearths the kind of needs of participants in the training program and whom helps in identifying proper trainers (in-house or external).

During the preparation stage of the training design, it is necessary to conduct some sort of discussion with potential trainees and possibly their supervisors. This might be done through conducting a survey, preparing a questionnaire or simply listening to workers and their supervisors.

Specifying training objectives: In this second step, needs are turned into objectives. Once the training needs have been identified, it is important to translate those needs as realistic objectives. Remember that the training objectives are the changes that the trainers set out to accomplish through the training. The objectives should help to develop and conduct the training and provide the trainees with the knowledge and the skills they require. The objectives set also provide trainees with a clear understanding of what they will be expected to do as a result of the training. This should help both the trainers and the trainees to evaluate the learning that has taken place through the training.

Preparing a work plan: A work plan is a plan of operations. It helps to establish what is needed. Example of a work plan is given below:

- Training staff—how many, to do what, when?
- Training—who requires it, when, where, how long?
- Media communications—what is required, where will it be obtained?
- Equipment—what we need and where?
- Stationery and materials—what and where?
- Transport required—where, when?
- Administration—are there secretaries and support staff needed and are they available?
- Finance—who controls funds? Are adequate funds available?

Organising training content: The content of a training program should be derived from the training objectives. Trainers develop a framework that draws out the content of the training. A good way to develop this framework is to list the objectives and prepare an outline using the said format.

Select training methods and techniques: Outlining the training content should ensure that the trainees learn something. The training content should have learning activities that help the trainees accomplish the training objectives. To help them understand the material, it is necessary to use training methods that allow reviewing the key points communicated, using relevant and realistic examples, and restating new ideas in different ways using familiar words and analogies. It is especially important when communicating to the trainees that there is consistency in the definitions and units of analysis used. Different methods of training can be used to develop the skills of trainees, to ensure better understanding of the material and influence attitudes and behaviour.

Identify the training resources needed: At this point it is necessary to identify the resources needed to conduct the training. We need to determine what facilities, equipment and materials are required, in addition to identifying necessary administrative and personnel support.

Assemble and package lesson plans: At this point the training objectives, training content, training methods, and the training resources should be pulled together into a plan that can be used for conducting the training. The plan should serve as a written record on how the training is conducted.

Develop media for training: The materials prepared for the training need to be practical and relevant to the day-to-day work of the trainees. It is hoped that the material included in the training manual provides an adequate base of information to address the needs of the trainers.

Pre-test the training program: A test run of the training program would ensure that everything—the training objectives, media used for supporting the training program, teaching methods etc. work as intended. It is during this phase we identify unexpected problems so that changes and corrections can be made in time.

Implement and manage the training: It involves the following steps:

- **Preparation:** Knowing the objectives of the training, and being clear on the strategy to apply and the content of the training
- **Setting:** Ensuring a cheerful and relaxed environment that promotes learning
- **Handling participants:** This is a delicate process that requires patience and politeness. The trainees should be allowed and encouraged to participate.
- **Climate-setting:** Setting the right atmosphere to relax and welcome participants
- **Present the objectives:** Letting the trainees know why they are gathered, the objectives of the units and sessions and what is expected to take place
- **Breaking the ice and openers:** Introducing warm-up activities and ways for the participants to get to know each other
- **Initiate the learning experience:** This is the core of the training. Ensure that the participants are handled in a way that promotes participation and allows them to express their ideas by asking questions. The training discussions also need to be kept on track. Motivation needs to be maintained throughout the training by relating the material to real life situations that the trainees experience and keeping the interest alive.
- **Conduct a refresher training session:** The training should finish with a session which reviews the course content providing trainees with an opportunity to ask questions.

Evaluate the training: Evaluation, is generally, considered as the final part of the training process. However, it is best undertaken as an ongoing process conducted throughout the training and on completion of the individual modules. During the program, evaluation enables adjustments to be made to the training as it proceeds. The training program should be kept flexible and if the evaluation shows that certain aspects of the program are not working, then the original plan should be amended and modified accordingly. A final evaluation should be conducted at the end of the training enabling the entire program to be assessed. This will provide a basis for reporting on the training whilst giving guidance for future training of its kind. An example of the evaluation format that could be used is given in the Appendix.

Need for a Training Policy

To ensure consistency in the Training and Development (T and D) function, the HR department of each organization develops a suitable training policy, defining the scope, objective, philosophy and techniques. Such a training Policy, *inter alia*, serves the following purposes.

- It defines what the organization intends to accomplish through training.
- It indicates the type of persons to be responsible for training functions.
- It identifies the formal and informal nature of training.
- It spells out the duration, time and place of training.
- It indicates the need for engaging outside institutions for training.
- It embraces and includes training in relation to labour policies of the organization.

Structure of a training policy

The training policy is specific to an organization. However, a more generic training policy may be drawn in line with the following guidelines: (i) Outline the mission statement (ii) Develop objectives (iii) Outline of the training department's roles

A tentative mission statement for training function of an organization can be as follows:

Our mission is to provide training and development to all cross-sections of employees of the organization, ensuring measurable and demonstrable benefits keeping pace with organizational as well as individual needs.

Some of the tentative objectives of training functions can be as under:

- To provide training in product updates to all employees within the next six months
- To support the company's objectives in reaching its goals

- To develop and implement a management training program for all middle level managers within the next 12 months
- To provide customer service skills training to all new help desk employees no more than two months after being hired

Every organization tries to relate their training policy with their mission and objectives. Training policies must be clearly written and widely communicated.

Checklist for an effective training policy

For assessing the effectiveness of a training policy, a checklist may be drawn as under:

- Evaluation of training programs
- Selection of employees
- Availability of training
- Location of training sessions
- Programs to be established
- Length of training (number of days)
- Training design standards
- Training fee plans
- Outside services and programs
- Policy revision
- Link from training to performance appraisals

Introducing the training policy

Under this head of a training policy, general information is drawn up to introduce the policy to the employees and various other stakeholders. A tentative general information template is reproduced below:

> *'Human Resources and Employee Services department provides training for a variety of computer applications, skill upgradation, management subjects, supervisory development etc for all staff members, supervisors, executives and managerial level employees. Minimum six man-days training is compulsory for all. All such training programs are designed and delivered primarily using in-house faculty strength. But wherever necessary, the company may invite outside experts. In all training programs, books and other instruction materials will be provided to the participants. In each training program the number of participants is limited to only ten and departmental heads need to ensure registration of participants in advance. No training program would be conducted if number of participants falls short of ten'.*

Training Methods

In this section we will discuss some important training methods used by organizations.

On-the-job training: Under this technique, an employee is put on-the-job and is trained to perform the said job thereby helping the employee to acquire the skills for performing the said job in future. Most of the organizations utilise the services of senior workers to impart such training. Apprenticeship, creation of assistants to positions, job rotation and special assignments are different nature and forms of such training programs.

Job instruction training: It follows step-by-step learning. Usually steps necessary for a job are identified in order of sequence and an employee is exposed to the different steps of a job by an experienced trainer.

Vestibule training: This method duplicates on-the-job situation away from actual worksite with machinery and equipment similar to those used in actual production or operation and is used to help employees to acquire a new skill. Usually, training is given away from the production centre.

Training centre: Such site trainings are given in the form of lectures, conferences, case studies, role play and discussions.

Simulation: It also duplicates the actual condition encountered on a job. The vestibule training method or the business-game methods are the examples of business simulation.

Apprenticeship: Such training is given for a longer duration to help the employees to acquire skills in specific trade(s). A major part of this training is given on the job.

Off-the-job methods

These methods consist of the following: (i) Lectures (ii) Conferences (iii) Group Discussion (iv) Case analysis (v) Role play (vi) Program instruction (vii) T-group training

Lectures: Through lectures, participants are motivated to learn. Lectures focus on understanding rather than enriching knowledge and skills through reading assignments and experience. However, empirical studies on the effectiveness of training through lecture methods indicate that this is not effective for obvious inability of participants to retain the information and failure of trainers to make such sessions more interesting relating to on-the job experience.

Conference method: It is a participative group centred method through which participants develop knowledge and understanding by small group discussions and active participation.

Group discussions: This is also a very useful method of training and is usually based on papers prepared by trainees on a given subject. The trainees read their papers which are usually followed by critical discussions. It may, however be a follow-up discussion on some statement or on a paper presented by an expert.

Case study: This method helps trainees to learn on their own by independent thinking. A set of data or some descriptive materials are given to the participants asking them to analyse, identify the problems and also to recommend solutions for the same.

Role playing: This training method particularly helps in learning human relations skills through practice and imbibing an insight into one's own behaviour. Trainees of such programme are informed of a situation and asked to play their roles in an imaginary situation before the rest of the class. This, therefore, helps in the enriching of interaction skills of the employees.

Programmed instruction: This method is a pre-arranged desired course of proceeding to the learning or acquisition of specific skills or knowledge. Information in such programs is conveniently broken down into different units, to allow the trainees to learn at their convenient pace.

T-group training: This method is a form of sensitivity training. It takes place under laboratory condition and trainees are mostly instructed in informal kind of training. The trainer in such a training program is a catalyst. He helps the individual participants to understand how others perceive his behaviour, how he responds to others and how and when a group acts either in a negative or in a positive way.

E-learning: Training programs delivered via intranet have now been thought of as the most cost-effective route. It is not only cost-effective but also caters to the real-time information needs of employees. However, it involves convergence of several technologies like hardware, software, web designing and authoring, instructional design, multimedia design, telecommunications and finally internet and intranet network management. Organizations can outsource e-learning training modules at a relatively cheaper rate. Even though training through e-learning is globally increasing, we do not have adequate empirical evidence to justify this.

Changing Pattern of Training and Development in India

The Government of India has now gone in for major economic restructuring with a view to consolidating its position in the world market and achieving internal economic balance and growth. Liberalisation in terms of major changes in the industrial policy, as a part of the economic restructuring, has brought in a lot of competition for the over-protected Indian industrial organizations in general. Allowing free flow of foreign capital and direct participation of multinational organizations in the corporate sector have made the Indian industrial organizations exposed to intense competition.

The effect of such liberalisation in the domestic front on the Indian industrial organizations has again been multiplied by certain developments internationally which are more in the form of global trade restrictions. Certification as per the quality system standards (developed by the International Organization for Standardisation) of the products of the Indian industrial organizations is now almost essential for going global. Total Quality Management (TQM) is now a widely discussed issue in the corporate world.

Major economic restructuring at the macro level and the global changes taken together have prompted the Government of Indian to start a National Renewal Fund (NRF) in order to give effect to the exit policy on the one hand and to upgrade the skills of the employees retained through intensive training on the other. Organizations, in order to trim their workforce, will henceforth have to implement Voluntary Retirement Schemes (VRS) by making extra payments by way of compensation (exit incentive) in addition to the normal statutory payments. The remaining employees (who do not opt for VRS) will now have to be trained vigorously in order to adapt them to the changed job requirements, vis-à-vis upgradation of technology, modernisation and restructuring of jobs.

Training the employees on TQM strategy at a time when the Indian economy has gone in for major restructuring has assumed much importance primarily because today a corporate organization in India cannot expect to survive merely by developing a strategic plan based only on extrapolation of production and profit figures. It has to survive in a highly competitive environment both at the domestic and global fronts. Thus, restructuring of the production process, based on technological dynamism in an organization, has become imperative. Economic restructuring at the macro level has an inevitable impact on the production process in an organization at the micro level. Restructuring of a production process, as a natural consequence of economic restructuring, necessitates restructuring of manpower in an organization. Since trimming of surplus employees in an organization by offering them golden handshake under the VRS is restricted only to those who opt for the offer, the only other effective way open is to redeploy the surplus employees after intensive need-based training.

Keeping in mind the important performance areas in TQM Strategy in the corporate sector, training programs are arranged for all categories of employees. Such training programs are usually on:

- Total Quality Management
- Product familiarisation
- Process familiarisation
- Multiple skills development
- Simple problem-solving techniques

- Statistical Process Control,
- Quality Circle concept and
- Total productive maintenance

The duration of each training program varies from one week to two weeks depending on the participant's level and power of understanding.
For managers and executives, TQM techniques call for appreciating these issues.

- Formal education and age are not really the factors that determine the effectiveness or otherwise of learning TQM techniques. These techniques essentially have their roots in basic humanism. The conceptual and technical aspects of TQM can only be appreciated at a deeper level, if training programs on TQM genuinely have the humanistic tone.
- Attitudinal changes at the top are important to operationalise TQM in an organization. Unless the top level personnel change their attitudes, e.g. accepting a flatter organization structure, following an egalitarian approach, becoming receptive to change on a continuous basis, encouraging participative management and supporting group performance, it is not really possible to inculcate TQM culture in an organization.

These apart, Indian organizations are focusing on training on six sigma techniques, lean management practices, supply chain management etc. Six sigma techniques require the employees to be more innovative in recreating the process, so that defects never arise. It is an attempt to achieve organizational excellence through zero-defects manufacturing, i.e., the highest level of quality. Lean management practice requires the organization to be flexible enough in optimising the resources in a changing business scenario. Supply chain management helps in value-added customer services with resource optimisation.

Training Evaluation Models

Evaluation is an integral part of training. Evaluation tools help to determine the effectiveness of training interventions. Despite its importance, many organizations do not give adequate focus on training evaluation. Evaluation goals involve multiple purposes including evaluation of learning, evaluation of instructional materials, transfer of training, return on investment and so on. The six general approaches to training evaluation are as follows: (i) Goal-based evaluation (ii) Goal-free evaluation (iii) Responsive evaluation (iv) Systems evaluation (v) Professional review (vi) Quasi-legal

Goal-based and systems-based approaches are predominantly used in the evaluation of training (Philips, 1991). The goal-based model is most influential, and its framework was suggested by Kirkpatrick. Under the systems based model approach to training evaluation, we consider context, input, process, product etc. Some of the widely used models are discussed here.

Kirkpatrick four-level approach

This conceptual model helps in determining the types of data to collect and answer following four important questions.

- **Reaction**—were the participants pleased with the program?
- **Learning**—what did the participants learn in the program?
- **Behaviour**— did the participants change their behaviour based on what was learnt?
- **Results**—did the changed behaviour affect the organization?

The model can be explained using the framework shown in Fig. 14.1.

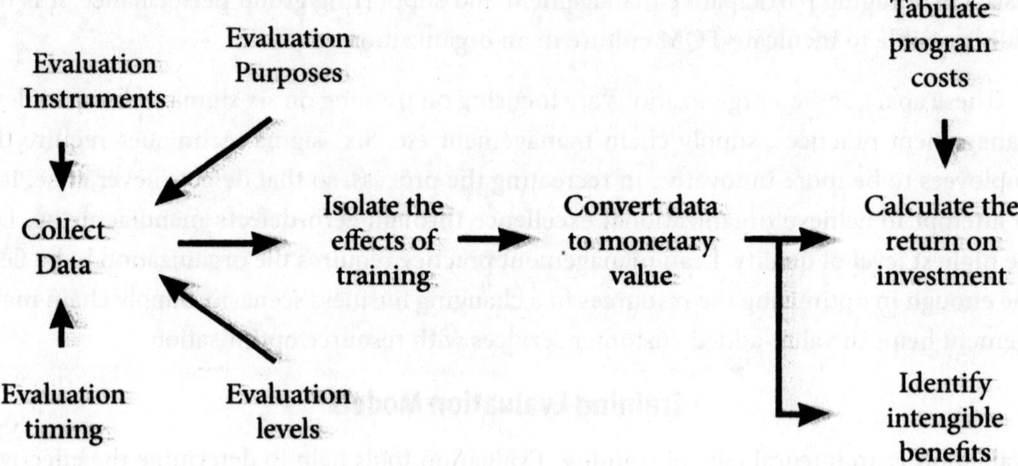

Fig. 14.1 Kirkpatrick's model for training evaluation

Hassett's training investment analysis approach

This model focuses on the following four important areas and then measures the training effectiveness:(i) Needs analysis (ii) Information gathering (iii) Analysis (iv) Dissemination

Context, Input, Process, Product (CIPP) model

This model was formulated by Worthen and Sanders (1987). It is similar to the CIRO model. It emphasises on context, input, process and product.

Kaufman's five levels for evaluation

This model extends the scope of evaluation of training impact beyond the organization. It includes how training benefits the society and the surrounding environment of the organization. Table 14.3 lists the levels of evaluation and major evaluation areas under this model.

CIRO approach

The approach derives its name from the following evaluation categories: (i) Content evaluation (ii) Input evaluation (iii) Reaction evaluation (iv) Outcome evaluation. Under these four heads, evaluation categories are developed depending on the organizational requirements.

Table 14.3 Kaufman's model for evaluation of training impact

Level	Evaluation areas
a. Enabling	Quality input availability like human, financial and physical resources
b. Reaction	Methods, means and process acceptability and efficiency
Acquisition	Individual and small group mastery and competency
Application	Individual and small group utilisation within the organization
Organizational output	Payoff to the organization
Societal outcomes	Payoff to the society

Table 14.4 Philip's model for training evaluation

Level	Brief description
Reaction and planned action	Measures participants' reaction to the program and outlines specific plans for implementation
Learning	Measures skills, knowledge or attitude categories
Job Applications	Measures change in behaviour on the job and specific application of the training material
Business Results	Measures business impact of the program
Return on Investment	Measures the monetary value of the results and costs for the program, usually expressed as a percentage

Philip's five-level ROI

This model extends Kirkpatrick's framework making the process of evaluation more specific. Table 14.4 lists the major points of evaluation under this approach.

These apart there are also some commonly used models like Training Validation System (TVS) Approach (Fitz–Enz, 1994) and Input, Process, Output, Outcome (IPO) Model (Bushnell, 1990).

A comparison of several system-based models (CIPP, IPO and TVS) with a goal-based model (Kirkpatrick's) is presented in Table 14.5.

Financial utility model

This model requires measurement of any given intervention or effect of a training program. This model was used by Godkewitsch (1987) to calculate the financial utility to a company for implementing a training program. The model is described by the following equation.

$$F = N\,[(E \times M)] - C$$

where F = financial utility

N = number of people in the training program

E = effect or outcome of the training program

M = financial value of the effect or outcome

C = financial cost per person of implementing the training program

Table 14.5 Comparative features of training evaluation models

Kirkpatrick (1959)	CIPP model (1987)	IPO model (1990)	TVS model (1994)
Reaction: to collect data on participants' reactions	**Context**: to obtain information about the educational needs to establish program objectives	**Input**: to evaluate performance indicators like trainee qualifications, availability of materials, appropriateness of training etc	**Situation**: to collect pre-training data on current performance levels and to define a desirable level of future performance
Learning: to evaluate how far the learning objectives have been met	**Input**: to identify training strategies to achieve the desired result	**Process**: to plan, design, develop and deliver the training programs	**Intervention**: to identify the reason for the gap between the present and desirable performance and assess how training can solve the problem
Behaviour: to assess change in job performance as a result of training	**Process**: to assess the implementation of educational program	**Output**: to gather data from the training interventions	**Impact**: to evaluate the difference between the pre- and post-training data
Results: to assess costs versus benefits of training	**Product**: to gather information on the results of the training intervention and interpret its worth and merit	**Outcomes**: to measure long-term results in profitability, competitiveness etc	**Value**: to measure differences in quality, productivity, service or sales.

Net present value method

Net Present Value (NPV) compares the value of money now with the value of money in the future, taking into account all the associated costs. We can use the NPV to determine ROI in training. To illustrate income foregone during the training period, costs of courses, learning materials and other related expenses are to be considered as costs. Then, we require quantifying the future benefits that are likely to accrue as a result of training. To assess the future benefits, we can extrapolate the current performance changes (after training) using learning curve formula.

To calculate the NPV we can use the following formula:

$$NPV = I_0 + I_1 / (1+r) = I_2 / (1+r)^2 + \ldots\ldots + I_n / (1+r)^n$$

(I = income amounts for each year, the subscripts are the year numbers, starting with 0. The discount rate is r. The number of years of the duration of the investment is n.)

Evaluation through behavioural assessment

W Leslie Rae (2004) has advocated this model of training evaluation. The main features of this model are listed in Table 14.6.

Table 14.6 Behavioural assessment of training impact

Behavioural Issues	A (pre-trained ability—assess before training)	B (post-trained ability—assess after training)	C (revised pre-trained ability—assess after training)	A to B (change compared with initial pre-trained ability (B minus A)	C to B (change compared with revised pre-trained ability (B minus C)
Being aware of my own behaviour					
Being aware of the behaviour of others					
Being aware of the reactions of others to my behaviour					
Being aware of my reaction to the behaviour of others					
Being aware of how much I talk					
Being brief and concise					

Being aware of how much I support others					
Always explaining my disagreements					
Being aware of how much I build on the ideas of others					
Sensing the feelings of others					
Being aware of how much I interrupt others					
Being aware of how much I really listen to others					
Telling others what my feelings are					
Being aware of what behaviour modification I need to do					
Knowing how to modify my behaviour					
Being aware of how much I bring out the views of others					
Being positive					
The general level of my interpersonal skills					
Totals and Total movements					

This test is known as three-test behavioural assessment. Using the above behavioural points we first assess trainees before training (A). After the training course or program, assess new ability of trainees (B), and revise pre-trained ability assessment (C). For each question, we score out of ten: 0 = lowest and 10 = highest. The C to B movement best indicates the change after training. The final column—the C to B movement, is the improvement from the revised or validated pre-trained ability to the post-trained ability. Movement from A to C could be for different reasons—it reflects a person's new informed view of how they used to be—discussion can be useful. If there is little difference between A, B and C scores it is important to investigate why the persons appears not to have altered their view of themselves nor derived any apparent learning benefit from the training.

Approaches to Training and Development

Approaches to training and development depend on organization-specific practices. Some organizations value knowledge as their basis of competitive advantage. Such organizations emphasise on learning, and accordingly they nurture new ways of thinking, exposing their people through continuous learning. Training, per se, is the process of enhancing job-specific skill, while learning is a process of knowledge creation. Some organizations adopt a more formalised approach to training and development, i.e., understanding of skill and competency gaps of employees through scientific performance management systems, design the training and development programs, and deliver the same to identified participants either through in-house trainers or hiring the services of training experts. Again there are some companies, whose approaches to training are specific to their areas of core competencies, where they feel the need for capability development of people. These are usually focused on leadership, business skills, operational effectiveness etc. All their training programs centre on such core issues.

While offering the training and development programs, approaches of the companies also differ. Some may prefer classroom training, web-based training, e-learning, on-the job training etc. Another approach to training and development is to value the personal development of employees, so that they can rise through the career ladder.

Aims and objectives of T and D

Companies focus on designing or developing training programs, based on identification of training needs. While designing the training programs, it is necessary to identify its aims and objectives. Aims and objectives of training and development, therefore are program-specific, and vary between organizations. Here we list some of the aims and objectives of training and development.

- To familiarise people on the process and products/services of the company
- To improve the skills and knowledge of people related to their jobs
- To build capabilities of people to perform better in their jobs
- To gradually make people competent to assume higher managerial roles in the organization
- To transform attitude of employees to make them more positive and proactive in their jobs

Differences between training and development

Although the terms training and development are interchangeably used, theoretically they are different. Some of the differences can be listed as under:

- Training focuses on systematic programming of behaviour to improve the performance of employees in their current job. Development, on the other hand improves job performance along with the improvement of personality. Development therefore is more a process of maturing employees building their potential to assume responsible future roles.
- Training is more short-term, as it is job-specific and mostly conducted for non-executive employees. Development, on the other hand is for the longer term, and conducted for executive and managerial employees.
- In terms of purposes, training aims on improving productivity, quality and personal growth of employees. Development aims at increasing the managerial effectiveness to meet the future needs of the organization.
- Training frequency is relatively less, while development is an ongoing process.
- Training is considered as an event, while development is a process.
- Training results are measurable, while the results of development can be understood only in terms of organizational growth.

Management development techniques

Management development is an effectively planned human resource development activity for grooming the future managers of the organization. Future managers are identified through a process of succession planning. Unlike training and development programs, management development programs are more elaborate in scope. It may extend beyond the organization, i.e., deputing potential managers to undergo some programs in educational or professional bodies, job rotation, job enrichment etc.

A formal technique of management development program may make use of classroom training, seminars, passing of some examinations etc. In terms of focus, management development programs emphasise more on those aspects, which are generic, like leadership development, communication, negotiation, conflict management, strategy formation, business simulation etc. Taking the potential managers through formal management education programs, as part of management development is also very common in many organizations. Such organizations emphasise on sponsoring their future managers to undergo such programs. To develop team-building skills, often such potential managers are exposed to outbound training, more in the form of adventure. Again training on developing emotional intelligence is very common in management development programs. Some organizations also make use of coaching and mentoring as a technique for management development.

Key Points

- Training and development is an important employee development function through which the organization gains sustainable competitive strength. It has become important particularly in this era of business uncertainty.
- Industrial psychologists facilitate designing of need-based and efficient training programs through the process of identification of behavioural inputs required for the employees. Effective design of the training and development programs requires at the outset understanding of various training issues through training needs identification exercises and also developing of effective training evaluation models.
- Technological change, increased global competition and consequent problem of manpower obsolescence, imply that training and development function is more and more important. On the one hand, this helps the organization to reduce the problem of manpower obsolescence, and on the other hand, it provides opportunity for the organization to sustain in competition, developing the capabilities of people.

Important Terms

CIRO approach: This method is based on the following evaluation categories, i.e., content evaluation, input evaluation, reaction evaluation and outcome evaluation.

Cost–benefit analysis: It helps an organization to measure the cost vis-à-vis benefit of training, keeping in view the long-term perspectives.

Hassett's training investment analysis: This model focuses on four important areas like needs analysis, information gathering, analysis and dissemination to measures the training effectiveness.

Kirkpatrick model: This conceptual model helps in determining the types of data to collect and answer four important questions, like reaction, learning, behaviour and results.

Kaufman model: This model extends the scope of training impact evaluation beyond the organization. It includes how training benefits the society and the surrounding environment of the organization.

Self-assessment Questions

1. Identify the need for manpower training in an organization. What are the important purposes served by training?
2. List out training programs for different levels of employees and elaborate at least two such types of training programs for workers.
3. What are the steps involved in designing a training program? What sequence of actions does a training programusually follow?
4. Do you think there is need for a training policy in an organization? Briefly outline some of the areas which need to be focused in such a policy.
5. Develop at least three sample training modules for supervisors, duly pointing out their objectives, course contents, eligibility of participants, duration and so on.
6. What are the different training methods available for an organization? Which are the methods you recommend for white-collared and blue-collared employees respectively?

7. Do you think the recent economic liberalisation policy of the Government of India has made training function more important for an organization? Elaborate your answer duly listing out important training areas in the context of the changing environment.
8. Write short notes on the following:
   i. T-group training
   ii. Role playing
   iii. Vestibule training
   iv. Simulation
   v. Orientation program
   vi. Craft training
   vii. Human skills

Selected Bibliography

1. Bhattacharyya DK (2006). *Human Resource Management*, 2nd edition. New Delhi: Excel Books.
2. Bhattacharyya DK (2006). *Human Resource Planning*, 2nd edition. New Delhi: Excel Books.
3. Bhattacharyya DK (2007). *Human Resource Research Methods*. New Delhi: Oxford University Press.
4. Castle JA (1996). An integrated model in quality management, position TQM, BPR and ISO 9000, *The TQM Magazine*, Vol. 8(5): 7–13.
5. Daft RL (1995). *Understanding Management*. Orlando: Harcourt Brace and Co.
6. Dessler G (1998). *Human Resource Management*, 7th edition. New Delhi:, Prentice Hall.
7. French WL (1990). *Human Resource Management*, 4th edition. Boston: Houghton Miffin.

Appendix Model Feedback Form: Training Program on Strategic Human Resource Development

1. What was your expectation in joining the program? (Indicate your choice in order of preference, if any).

   - To get some insights to the new concept
   - To understand the relevance of the content in present day business situation
   - To apply the learned skill in my present organization
   - To have a break and no utilise time for a meaningful cause
   - All the above
   - None of the above

2. Do you think, your expectations have been fulfilled, (please tick your answer)

   - Very significantly
   - Significantly
   - Partially
   - Not at all

3. In columns 'b' and 'c' below, select a number that represents your opinion using the five-point scale (from low to high); also indicate your view on 'd' and 'e'

A	B	C	D			E	
Topic	Gained new information	Presentation	Time allotted			This was difficult	
			More	Less	Right	Yes	No
Topic 1	1 2 3 4 5	1 2 3 4 5	☐	☐	☐		
Topic 2	1 2 3 4 5	1 2 3 4 5	☐	☐	☐		
Topic 3	1 2 3 4 5	1 2 3 4 5	☐	☐	☐		
Case Study	1 2 3 4 5	1 2 3 4 5	☐	☐	☐		
HR games	1 2 3 4 5	1 2 3 4 5	☐	☐	☐		

4. Indicate three changes you would like to make to the course
5. Which aspects of the process helped you to learn?
6. Which aspects of the process were not liked by you?
7. How do you overall rate the training program?
   - Excellent
   - Good
   - Moderate
   - Average
   - Poor
8. Any general suggestions?

Name : Signature with date

INDEX

M

N

O

P